Language, Sexualities and Desires

# Language, Sexualities and Desires

## Cross-Cultural Perspectives

Edited by

Helen Sauntson
*University of Birmingham*

and

Sakis Kyratzis
*Kingston University*

First published 2007 by
PALGRAVE MACMILLAN
Houndmills, Basingstoke, Hampshire RG21 6XS and
175 Fifth Avenue, New York, N.Y. 10010
Companies and representatives throughout the world

PALGRAVE MACMILLAN is the global academic imprint of the Palgrave
Macmillan division of St. Martin's Press, LLC and of Palgrave Macmillan Ltd.
Macmillan® is a registered trademark in the United States, United Kingdom
and other countries. Palgrave is a registered trademark in the European
Union and other countries.

ISBN-13: 978–1–4039–3327–0 hardback
ISBN-10: 1–4039–3327–8 hardback

This book is printed on paper suitable for recycling and made from fully
managed and sustained forest sources.

A catalogue record for this book is available from the British Library.

Library of Congress Cataloging-in-Publication Data
Language, sexualities, and desires : cross-cultural perspectives / edited
    by Helen Sauntson and Sakis Kyratzis.
        p.   cm.
    Includes bibliographical references and index.
    ISBN 1–4039–3327–8 (cloth)
    1. Language and sex.   2. Language and culture.   3. Communication—
    Sex differences.   4. Language and languages—Sex differences.
    I. Sauntson, Helen, 1972–   II. Kyratzis, Sakis, 1969–
    P120.S48L363 2007
    306.44—dc22                                                     2006048539

10   9   8   7   6   5   4   3   2   1
16   15   14   13   12   11   10   09   08   07

Printed and bound in Great Britain by
Antony Rowe Ltd, Chippenham and Eastbourne

# Contents

# List of Figures

# List of Tables

# Acknowledgements

Helen Sauntson (Ch. 6) would like to express her gratitude to David Ralphs for permitting her to use the website www.comingoutstories.com for research purposes and to Lexie Don and Liz Morrish for commenting on earlier drafts of her chapter.

Stephan Grosse (Ch. 7) wishes to thank his reviewers, Dr Margaret Rogers, University of Surrey, Guildford, and Dr Rosa M. Rodriguez Magda of the Fundaciön Valencia Tercer Milenio for their helpful suggestions and comments.

Every effort has been made to contact copyright holders. In the event that any copyright holder has been inadvertently overlooked, the publisher and author will make amends at the earliest opportunity.

# Notes on Contributors

**Deborah A. Chirrey** is a Lecturer in English Language at Edge Hill College of Higher Education in Lancashire, UK. Initially her main research interest was in the phonetics of Scottish English accents but, more recently, she has refocused her work on language and sexual identity. She has published in both of these areas. Currently, she is investigating the role of published advice literature and of the Internet in providing language scripts for individuals who are intending to come out.

**Jennifer Coates** is Professor of English Language and Linguistics at Roehampton University, UK. Her published work includes *Women, Men and Language* (originally published 1986, 3rd edn 2004); *Women Talk: Conversation between Women Friends* (1996), *Language and Gender: a Reader* (1998) and *Men Talk: Stories in the Making of Masculinities* (2003). She recently finished editing a book on narrative with Joanna Thornborrow (*The Sociolinguistics of Narrative*, 2005). She has given lectures at universities all over the world and has held Visiting Professorships in Australia, New Zealand, the USA, Germany, Switzerland, Spain and Italy. She was made a Fellow of the English Association in 2002. She is currently investigating the role of humour in informal talk.

**Yvonne Dröschel** is a Research and Teaching Assistant in English linguistics at the University of Fribourg, Switzerland. She has studied at the University of Lausanne, Switzerland, and at the University of East Anglia, UK. Under the supervision of Professor Peter Trudgill, she is currently working on her PhD thesis on the use of English as a contact language in multilingual Switzerland. Her main field of interests are sociolinguistics, languages in contact and linguistics and gender.

**Stephan A. Grosse** is a multilingual researcher and language professional specialising in intercultural communication and foreign language pedagogy. His particular interest lies in qualitative research with a focus on applied linguistics, sociology, linguistic anthropology and gender theory. He is the recipient of several competitive awards and honours including a teaching assistantship from Kent State University, Ohio, USA, and a postgraduate research scholarship from the University of Surrey, England. He is also a licensed translator and conference interpreter with extensive skills in cross-cultural mediation and is currently also engaged in tour management and operations for educational and performing arts tours.

**Michael Hoey** is Baines Professor of English Language at the University of Liverpool, UK. He is an Academician of the Academy for Social Sciences and chief advisor to Macmillan Publishers on dictionaries. He co-edits (with Tony McEnery) a series of corpus linguistics monographs for Routledge. His single-authored monographs include *On the Surface of Discourse* (1983), *Patterns of Lexis in Text* (1991), *Textual Interaction* (2001) and *Lexical Priming: a New Theory of Words and Language* (2005). He has also written over 60 articles. He has lectured by invitation at universities or conferences in 40 countries.

**Sakis Kyratzis** is a Senior Lecturer in English Language and Communication at Kingston University, UK. His main research interests lie in the cross-section between semantics and pragmatics. His published work relates to functions of metaphors in political discourse and in everyday interaction.

**William Leap** is Professor and Chair of the Department of Anthropology, American University (Washington, DC), USA, where he teaches courses in linguistics, public anthropology and gender/sexuality studies. His publications include *Word's Out: Gay Men's English*, the edited collections, *Beyond the Lavender Lexicon, Public Sex/Gay Space*, and (with Tom Boellstorff) *Speaking in Queer Tongues*, and (with Ellen Lewin) *Out in the Field* and *Out in Theory*, as well as numerous articles on gay/same-sex identified men's language use in daily life. His discussion of language, sexual subjectivity and space in this volume builds on his ongoing studies of language, (homo)sexual geographies and citizenship in Washington, DC and Cape Town, South Africa. Related work examines frictions between sexual dissidence and urban restructuring in these locations, as described in personal narratives and public media.

**Lia Litosseliti** is Lecturer in Linguistics at City University, London, UK. Her research interests range from critical linguistics, discourse analysis, and gender and language, to education (particularly the role of collaborative argumentation) and research methodologies. She is the author of *Gender and Language: Theory and Practice* (2006), a book focusing on current theorisations of gender and language, and *Using Focus Groups in Research* (2003), a step-by-step guide to using focus group methodology in the social sciences. She is also co-editor/co-author of *Discourse Analysis and Gender Identity* (2002), and of a forthcoming collection on theoretical and methodological approaches to gender and language study.

**Liz Morrish** is Subject Leader of Linguistics at Nottingham Trent University, UK. Her research interests lie in the area of language and sexual identity. She is primarily interested in the ways in which individuals manage the construction and performance of their sexual identities through language. She is on the organising committee of the annual Lavender Languages and Linguistics series of conferences which take place at American University, Washington, DC. She is currently co-authoring *Language and Sexual Identity* with Helen Sauntson of the University of Birmingham, UK.

**Pia Pichler** is a Lecturer in Linguistics at Goldsmiths College, University of London, UK. Her research originates in language and gender studies and her PhD work explored the discursive construction of adolescent femininities in the spontaneous talk of British girls from different social and ethnic/cultural backgrounds. Her publications include 'The construction of bicultural femininities in the talk of British Bangladeshi girls' (in Janet Cotterill and Anne Ife (eds), 2001) and she has recently been working on a book manuscript entitled 'Talking young femininities'.

**Helen Sauntson** is a Lecturer in English Language at the University of Birmingham, UK. Her main teaching and research interests are in the areas of discourse analysis, language, gender and sexuality and language in education. She has published work on classroom discourse and language and sexual identity.

# Introduction: Language, Sexualities and Desires

*Helen Sauntson and Sakis Kyratzis*

## Introduction

Recent work on language and sexuality has called for a greater focus upon examining how sexualities are enacted in situated and localised contexts of interaction (Bucholtz and Hall, 2004; Leap and Boellstorff, 2004). In attempting to answer these calls, this book looks at how sexualities are grounded in particular sociocultural contexts, and examines some aspects of the interplay between sexuality and cultural knowledge and experience. Rather than approaching the subject from a sociological or psychoanalytic point of view, as previous research has done, this collection, instead, looks at language first and tries to investigate how sexuality is represented in different cultures by examining how different people speak and write about sexuality. The chapters address a number of issues concerning the relationships between language, culture and sexuality. These include: how people use various linguistic features (e.g. lexis, metaphor, conversational features) to construct their sexual identities and relationships, and how this varies from culture to culture; how people express love and desire through language; what people's linguistic behaviour reveals about different conceptualisations of love, desire and sexuality within different cultural settings; how membership of specific social groups, based on sexuality and lifestyle choices, may be signalled through language; and how social and political discourses of love, desire and sexuality may be identified and constructed through language.

The chapters all contain new and original data collected from a variety of cultural settings and historical, social and political contexts. Data are interpreted through a careful consideration of the cultural context in which they were produced and received. The chapters consider a

1

range of sexual identities and forms of desire and their analysis is predominantly grounded in applied linguistic approaches. Although much existing work provides valuable insight into various aspects of language and sexuality, it is hoped that this collection will enhance our understanding and offer some new ways of exploring the topic. We believe the originality of this book lies firstly in its explicit and critical examination of cross-cultural perspectives on language and sexuality. Secondly, we aim to present empirical data which lend themselves to exploring a range of different sexualities. We do not, for example, focus exclusively on heterosexuality or homosexuality. Finally, this collection provides analyses of language and sexuality using primarily linguistic theoretical and applied frameworks, rather than situating itself centrally within queer or feminist theory, although clearly relevant aspects of these theories will be drawn upon. Overall, it is hoped that through its close analysis of original situated data this book will provide not only a range of empirical evidence to illustrate aspects of the relationship between language, culture and sexuality, but also a contribution to current theoretical debates in the area of language, desire and sexual identity.

The main purpose of this introduction is to present a brief and selective overview of some current trends and theories in relation to language, culture and sexuality and, in doing so, we aim to contextualise the chapters presented throughout the rest of the collection.

## Language and sexuality

Research which examines the relationship between language and sexuality has been in existence for more than 50 years, although most work has centred upon homosexuality. Early work focused primarily upon the expression of sexuality through specific lexical items (e.g. Legman, 1941; Cory, 1951; Rodgers, 1972). From the 1980s, there was a shift from looking at the ways in which sexuality is reflected in language towards an examination of how sexualities are discursively constructed through language (e.g. Hall and Bucholtz, 1995; Leap, 1995, 1996). More recently, language and sexuality research has been informed by aspects of queer theory and feminist theory (e.g. Livia and Hall, 1997). Bucholtz and Hall (2004) note how these theories have provided useful approaches for studying power relations surrounding sexuality and gender respectively. We argue that power is an integral part of culture and culture, itself, is organised around power relations. These organising principles are often encoded in the linguistic practices of that culture's speakers.

Bucholtz and Hall also note how queer linguistics is centred around analyses of the regulation of sexuality by dominant heterosexuality. Again, these processes of regulation are culture-specific and the chapters in this collection provide some illumination of these processes.

Butler's (1990) work on gender performativity has been particularly influential in recent years. Livia and Hall (1997) take Butler's theories of gender performativity back to their linguistic roots by citing Austin's (1962) work on speech acts. In an Austinian definition of a speech act, to say something is to do something, so that we literally perform actions by producing utterances. This notion has informed much current theorising of language, gender and sexuality – we speak our gender and sexuality into existence. One of the potential problems with performativity is that Austin's speech acts are socioculturally located and their meanings shift across contexts and cultures. The speech act is actually unstable – the act itself does not carry meaning, but, instead, meaning is located in the interaction between the act (text) and context. So, gender and sexuality are not simply brought into being by speaking or doing, but via a process of interaction between the speech act and the grounded sociocultural and situational context in which it is produced and received. This is precisely one of the reasons why researchers such as Bucholtz and Hall (2004) and Leap and Boellstorff (2004) have called for greater attention to be paid to localised contexts of interaction in the study of language, discourse and sexuality. Work which sets out to explore the discursive construction of sexuality must focus upon linguistic performances which occur within grounded contexts and situations.

Cameron and Kulick (2003) have documented the development of language and sexuality research in greater detail than we have space for here. One point we would like to emphasise is that language and sexuality research has developed from a range of disciplines, not just linguistics. Work which examines various aspects of the relationship between language and sexuality has occurred, and continues to develop, in fields such as gender studies, queer studies, social theory, sociology, anthropology and media and cultural studies. Although we acknowledge that the interdisciplinarity of language and sexuality is extremely valuable (in providing different perspectives and enabling us to focus upon a range of aspects), the chapters in this collection are quite firmly rooted in the discipline of linguistics. We feel that the close and systematic data analysis enabled by applied linguistic approaches provides a valuable contribution to our overall understanding of the relationship between language and sexuality. The work presented in the chapters uses a range of types of linguistic analysis including spoken discourse analysis, metaphor analysis, lexical analysis, written narrative analysis, appraisal analysis and critical discourse analysis.

## Desires and sexualities – addressing some current issues

We have included the terms 'desires' and 'sexualities' in the title as a reflection of the book's breadth and scope. The two are contested terms, but we are using 'desires' here to refer to sexual desires, practices and activities. 'Sexualities' is a broader term referring to forms of social identity which are performed and produced in contexts of interaction. Sexual identities refer to the groups we identify with and the kinds of social practices surrounding sexuality that we engage in. The two are linked so that desire and sexual identity are constituent components of sexuality. It is necessary to include both terms in the title as some chapters foreground an examination of linguistic expressions and enactments of forms of sexual desire and/or practice (e.g. Hoey (Ch. 8)), while others foreground analyses of the ways in which sexuality is linguistically construed as a form of social identity with little or no reference to desire or sexual activity (e.g. Morrish and Leap (Ch. 1); Sauntson (Ch. 6)). Some chapters usefully illustrate quite explicitly how desire and sexual identity are interrelated and how this is reflected and enacted linguistically (e.g. Grosse (Ch. 7)). 'Desires' and 'sexualities' are pluralised in the title to reflect the plurality of types of desires and sexual identities that are considered throughout this volume. These types are variegated along sociocultural as well as sexual lines – sexuality does not simply differ along a homo-heterosexual continuum, but also simultaneously varies across and within cultures along racialised, classed and gendered lines. It is hoped that the essays in this collection capture some interesting and fruitful illustrations of these variations.

We acknowledge that it is important not to inaccurately polarise desire and sexual identity as mutually exclusive components of sexuality and argue that there is a place for considering both, although not necessarily simultaneously, within the study of language and sexuality. In the context of linguistic interaction, the different components of sexuality may be highlighted or suppressed to greater or lesser degrees so that, at times, issues surrounding sexual desire seem to require being at the forefront of investigation, while at other times, the relationship between language and sexual identity would appear to demand closer scrutiny. In focusing only on language and desire, we do not wish, in the words of Bucholtz and Hall (2004: 485) to 'marginalize issues of gender, power and agency'. Likewise, in focusing only on issues of sexual identity, we do not wish to ignore completely the roles that sexual desire, activity and practice play in the sociocultural linguistic construction of sexualities. What is important to emphasise is that the study of one seems to entail at least some consideration of the other. We agree wholeheartedly with Bucholtz and Hall (2004: 486), who argue that sexual desire cannot be studied in isolation, but must be considered alongside issues of identity which inevitably emerge when the social phenomenon of language forms the central object of inquiry:

> Desire cannot be separated from power and agency, and in any event the social meanings of sexuality are not just restricted to desire. These meanings can be uncovered only with reference to the ideologies, practices, and identities that produce them, phenomena that are embedded within racialized, classed, and gendered relations of power.

This is an important argument which we believe is supported and illustrated through the range of sociolinguistic analyses presented in this volume. Discussions which begin with a primary focus upon language and desire inevitably end up discussing, even if only in passing, the social and cultural ideologies of sexuality which are construed in each set of language practices under scrutiny. These practices and ideologies are always imbued with power relations. This happens precisely because desire does not exist outside of its sociocultural and political contexts. For example, Hoey's examination (Ch. 8) of linguistic expressions of erotic desire in poems and narratives leads to an important consideration of the social system of gender and the way in which it interacts with desire in US and Brazilian sociocultural contexts. Similarly, Grosse's discussions (Ch. 7) of the gay male sexual desires represented in the diary accounts he analyses are context and culture-specific – they accrue meaning and are understood within the sets of sociocultural practices and settings in which the texts are produced and received. In spoken discourse, Pichler's conversational data (Ch. 3) shows clearly that the adolescent girls' explicit talk about sexual activity and desire functions to enable them to construct certain kinds of sexual identities for themselves and others. The way that talk about desire interacts with other dimensions of cultural practice results in a diverse range of (hetero)sexual identities among the girls. Sexuality, then, is not just psychological or physical, but is also social and cultural. It is not something which is experienced in a social or cultural vacuum, rather, our sociocultural experiences shape and influence our perceptions and constructions of sexuality.

This book is intended to be more empirical than theoretical in its primary emphasis and for this reason we have not included an extensive theoretical overview of work in the field of language and sexuality in this introduction. For a more detailed coverage of current theoretical issues and debates, see Kulick (2000), Cameron and Kulick (2003), Campbell-Kibler *et al.* (2002), Bucholtz and Hall (2004) and Morrish and Sauntson (forthcoming). In following Bucholtz and Hall's (2004) and Leap and Boellstorff's (2004) calls for the study of language and sexuality to involve greater examination of language use in localised contexts, the chapters presented here are intended to provide illustrations of the importance of sociocultural settings in the linguistic construction of desires and sexualities. We would like this book to stand primarily as empirical support to the approaches towards language and sexuality proposed by Bucholtz and Hall (2004). However, each chapter does contain a theoretical orientation to contextualise the data analysis and this should give the reader an adequate feel for what the most salient issues and debates currently are. Through its emphasis upon analyses of new empirical data, it is hoped that this book can ultimately be used to further both theoretical and empirical lines of enquiry in language and sexuality scholarship.

## Language and culture

Definitions of 'culture' vary to reflect different theoretical paradigms and perspectives. Although we do not extensively set out to engage with definitional debates or struggles over the various interpretations of culture, it is perhaps useful to outline some understandings of culture which inform the rest of the chapters. Firstly, Goodenough (1957: 167) offers the following general and frequently cited description: 'A society's culture consists of whatever it is one has to know or believe in order to operate in a manner acceptable to its members.' Goodenough emphasises that the knowledges and beliefs which constitute culture are learned rather than biologically inherited. Geertz (1993: 89) offers another classic definition which more obviously draws attention to the role that language plays in culture: '[Culture] denotes an historically transmitted pattern of meanings embodied in symbols, a system of inherited conceptions expressed in symbolic form by means of which men communicate, perpetuate, and develop their knowledge about and attitudes toward life.'

Language is one of these 'symbolic forms'. Burke *et al.* (2000) draw on Saussure's groundbreaking work in semiology to explain the symbolic nature of culture. The symbolic meanings that are shared by a society are arbitrary, but it is these meanings on which culture is based. As the meanings are arbitrary, they have to be learnt. These meanings are inscribed in and enacted through language which, in Saussure's terms, is a system of signs. These systems differ across cultures so, as Geertz (1993: 12–13) argues, when we come into contact with the actions or behaviours of people from a culture other than our own, we are experiencing 'lack of familiarity with the imaginative universe within which their acts are signs'. Within this paradigm, a system of linguistic acts constitutes a system of linguistic signs. If the acts themselves are specific to a particular culture, so then are the signs, including the linguistic signs that make up the language of the members of the culture. We therefore agree with Kramsch (1998: 3) that language *expresses, embodies* and *symbolises* cultural reality. Many of the chapters in this collection focus upon an analysis of how linguistic acts and signs operate within particular discourse contexts and how people employ them to inscribe, create and construct cultural symbolic meanings concerning sexuality.

This interrelationship between language and culture is a well-documented phenomenon (so much so that Agar, 1994, talks of 'langa-culture' in order to emphasise the strong link between the two). Our world view is a combination of shared cultural meanings and models that are encoded in language (Bonvillain, 1993: 52). As Sapir (1921: 207) claims: 'Language does not exist apart from culture, that is, from the socially inherited assemblage of practices and beliefs that determines the textures of our lives.' Language is a central component of the practices, values and beliefs that make up any type of 'culture' and cannot be separated from it. A language's vocabulary and grammar, according to Sapir (1949: 90–1), is not a mere collection of meanings and structures, but a 'complex inventory' of whatever is culturally significant to a community. Concepts that are important to a culture are visible in various aspects of its language, some of which are focused upon in this collection (e.g. metaphor, lexis, discourse structure). Therefore, in order to understand a culture we should look at language first.

Bucholtz and Hall (2004: 492) highlight the importance of language and culture in producing identities:

Language is the mediating level between structures of power and human agency [ . . . ] Language is a primary vehicle by which cultural ideologies circulate, it is a central site of social practice, and it is a crucial means for producing sociocultural identities. Thus, any sociocultural analysis of language is incomplete unless it acknowledges the relationship between the systems of power and the ways that they are negotiated by social subjects in local contexts. Sociolinguistic research has demonstrated that ideologies are not only imposed from above but are also built on the ground, in sociocultural and interactional practice.

This foregrounds the need not only for culturally grounded and localised research, but also for research which has sociocultural linguistic analysis at its heart in order to enhance our understanding of the precise means by which language operates at the 'mediating level' they describe. This is precisely what the chapters in this volume set out to do: to examine the ways in which language mediates the sociocultural production of sexual identities and desires in situated contexts of use in which sets of linguistic and cultural practices circulate and are deployed.

## Cross-cultural perspectives

We would emphasise that culture does not only operate at a national level and it is naïve to simply equate 'culture' with 'nation'. We agree with Goodenough (1994: 266–7, in Cole, 1998: 295) who argues:

> The cultural makeup of a society should not be seen as a monolithic entity determining the behaviour of its members, but as a melange of understandings and expectations regarding a variety of activities that serve as guides to their conduct and interpretation.

In other words, cultures can exist within national boundaries. While some of the chapters in this collection examine aspects of sexuality in relation to some kind of 'national culture' (e.g. Coates's examination of narrative performances of British male heterosexuality (Ch. 2)), others consider more localised and situated cultures which produce cultural heterogeneity within national boundaries (e.g. Pichler's exploration of the conversation of white British and British Bangladeshi girls in school settings (Ch. 3), Morrish and Leap's narrative analysis of the experiences of gay men in Cape Town (Ch. 1)). Some chapters focus only upon one specific sociocultural context (e.g. Chirrey, Litosselliti, Kyratzis (Chs 10, 9 and 4)), while others look at what happens when people shift between different cultural settings, either national or more localised (e.g. Hoey, Grosse, Sauntson (Chs 8, 7 and 6)). It is also important to point out that the notion of 'culture' does not necessarily correspond to any material conditions, such as a particular physical or geographical space or set of artefacts, although some cultures clearly do. Hoey (Ch. 8), for example, examines literature produced in two different cultural and corresponding geographical contexts (North America and Brazil). Similarly, Dröschel (Ch. 5) focuses upon analysing the forms and uses of gay slang across British and American cultural and geographical settings.

Parker and Aggleton (1999) point out that social and cultural factors shaping sexual experience in different settings have largely been ignored and call for academic attention to be increasingly focused upon the social, cultural, economic and political forces which shape sexual behaviours and identities in different sociocultural settings. Weeks (1999) argues that (homo)sexual identities and attitudes towards sexuality are culturally specific and situational. Vance (1999: 43) proposes that:

> Cultures provide widely different categories, schema, and labels for framing sexual and affective experiences. These constructions not only influence individual subjectivity and behaviour but they also organize and give meaning to collective sexual experience through, for example, the impact of sexual identities, definitions, ideologies and regulations.

Thus, the meanings, norms and values which surround sexuality differ across cultural settings and often reflect the broader cultural values of the group in question. Leap and Boellstorff (2004) explore these issues in a valuable collection which focuses upon (mainly gay male) same-sex desires, globalisation processes and linguistic practices in different regions of the world. This work reveals how, in many societies, there is often a tension between globalising gay identities and experience and the expression of more localised sexual and cultural identities. For example, in his analysis of the French and US gay press, Provencher (2004) finds that a similar rhetoric is used to discuss cultural and political phenomena – English lexical items, for instance, are used in the French press to refer to aspects of a globalised 'gay culture'. But there are still underlying ways of expressing gay French identities with references to French culture still being retained alongside more globalised, shared references to gay identity. Leap observes how new ways of talking about same-sex desires and erotic practices and emerging ways of naming same-sex related identities in South Africa often involve drawing on traditional South African discourses of sexuality and gender and on local linguistic resources of Xhosa, Afrikaans and English. However, they also draw on cultural frames of reference and related linguistic practices developed elsewhere, particularly in North America, and imported into South African settings. Thus, emerging South African discourses of gay sexual identity often entail a fusion of local and global linguistic practices related to gender and sexuality.

Our own collection, similarly, aims to investigate the varying roles that language plays in conveying cultural norms, values and meanings in relation to sexuality. However, in Leap and Boellstorff's collection, cross-cultural is bilingual, in that each cultural context examined involves a different language or the mixing of English with another language. In this book, most chapters focus upon English-speaking contexts, but across different localised cultures. In this way, we explore bidialectalism rather than bilingualism in relation to culture, defined as a set of localised norms, values and practices, which, we hope, is a valid and useful development of the work presented by Leap and Boellstorff. The chapters presented here also consider a range of gender and sexuality identities in relation to cultural experience.

## Chapter outlines

In Chapter 1 Morrish and Leap start by engaging with recent theoretical debates regarding language and sexuality, some of which have been touched upon briefly in this introduction. Morrish and Leap outline what they term 'desire-centred approaches' (e.g. Cameron and Kulick, 2003; Kulick, 2000) and 'identity-centred approaches' (e.g. Bucholtz and Hall, 2004; Morrish and Sauntson, forthcoming). Cameron and Kulick (2003) acknowledge that both desire-centred and identity-centred approaches are necessary for exploring the field of language and sexuality, although they still predominantly advocate an approach towards language and desire rather than language and sexual identity. As already indicated briefly, Bucholtz and Hall (2004) provide a persuasive and insightful discussion of desire-centred and identity-centred approaches and Morrish and Leap aim to develop this further by exploring perspectives on language, sexuality and gender which, they argue, are currently prioritised in identity-centred approaches. These include queer theory, political economy, and recent work in sociolinguistics which foregrounds the place of sexuality and gender within localised communities of practice. Rather than producing an entirely theoretical discussion, Morrish and Leap usefully move these debates forward by including new empirical data from two sociocultural contexts to support and illustrate their arguments. They firstly draw conversational extracts taken from Sauntson (2002) to explore how discursive constructions of sexuality are intricately tied up with constructions of gender, thus illustrating how the study of language and sexuality cannot focus exclusively upon sexual desire or activity in a decontextualised and depoliticised way. Data from extensive interviews with gay men in Cape Town, South Africa, are then used to exemplify and develop several of the theoretical themes outlined. In particular, this culturally grounded analysis shows how the performance and lived experience of sexuality depends upon the subject's race, geographical location in relation to 'gay city' in Cape Town, gender performance and economic resources.

The first part of the remainder of the book contains chapters which focus upon the expression of desires and culturally located constructions of sexualities through spoken discourse which predominantly takes the form of casual conversation between peers. Coates (Ch. 2) continues the theme of examining discursive constructions of social and sexual identities set up by Morrish and Leap by focusing upon exploring British masculinity as a culturally recognisable gender identity through which sexuality is simultaneously performed. Coates argues that one significant way in which hegemonic masculinity is created and maintained is through the denial of femininity and the corresponding denial of homosexuality. She draws on a database of spontaneous conversation, including all-male, all-female and mixed groups, and focuses on male friendship groups: these groups include men from all social classes and a wide range of ages, and involve dyads as well as larger groups. In most of the conversations, it is evident that male speakers are acting in ways that align them with hegemonic norms which prescribe 'acceptable' maleness. Coates's analysis of everyday talk begins to reveal dominant cultural values surrounding masculinity in contemporary British society.

In Chapter 3 Pichler explores the sex talk of three groups of 15–16-year-old British girls from different social, cultural and ethnic backgrounds – British Bangladeshi working class, white/mixed working class and white upper middle class. Pichler shows how each group of girls has a distinct approach to sex talk, which is characterised by a tension between dominant sociocultural discourses and the girls' efforts to construct deviant positions for themselves. Thus, their sex talk constitutes an important resource for the negotiation of sexual, gender, class and ethnic identities. Pichler's work is important for illustrating how sexuality interacts with other social practices and systems, and how these intersections are negotiated and enacted linguistically. It also illustrates how different cultural norms and practices surrounding sexuality can be found within the same domain and setting. In the words of Leap and Boellstorff (2004: 12), details of sexual lives and cultures 'are learned and shared, albeit unevenly, not only across divisions and boundaries within those domains but also among them through processes of intercultural articulation'. Pichler's data provide an insightful illustration of some salient aspects of this process.

Continuing the exploration of the conversational strategies deployed during talk about sex and sexuality, Kyratzis (Ch. 4) examines how metaphor is used dynamically in everyday discourse as a tool for attaining meaning and defining sexual identities. He focuses on how metaphor is exploited in casual conversations in order to define and understand the concepts of love and sexuality and, therefore, shows how the study of metaphor can provide useful insights in the area. In terms of data, this chapter concentrates on how new metaphors are introduced and developed in two conversations between young Greeks about sex. The analysis reveals how the concepts of love, sex and sexuality evolve cognitively within the conversation and provides an insight into how sexual identities are discursively created by the speakers in their particular cultural schemas.

In Chapter 5 Dröschel studies gay language that involves speaker-related issues as well as social and ideological representations within the utterances of gay men. Using questionnaires, she investigates some differences between British and American gay male slang and the attitudes of its users. This enables an examination of how the cultural values of the gay men are inscribed not only in the slang terms themselves, but also in how they are deployed in specific settings. It is suggested that social and cultural conditions are mirrored in the way gay identities and practices are lexically encoded, resulting in distinct slang forms and ways of using them. As a critical component of gay interaction, this kind of linguistic practice is revealing about the changing nature of homosexual subculture in the US and UK. One way to introduce the differences between the conceptual schemas by which male sexual relations and identities have been organised is to review the changes in the vernacular terms used by gay men to refer to themselves and to reconstruct how they have used the different terms tactically in diverse settings to negotiate their position in society.

The remaining chapters examine the expression and construction of desires and sexualities through a range of written discourse types. Sauntson in Chapter 6 begins to relate the theories outlined in this introduction and in Morrish and Leap's chapter to the empirical study of language, culture and sexuality. Focusing on lesbian sexualities, this chapter sets out to support recent proponents of identity-centred approaches to sexuality and language by illustrating how sexuality is a form of culturally situated social identity. Through an analysis of a corpus of electronic coming out narratives written by women identifying as lesbian (available at www.comingoutstories.com), this chapter explores how writers construct their lesbian identity not only in terms of sexual desire, but also in terms of culture, social interaction and context. The data are analysed using Martin's (2000) APPRAISAL system. Devised within a systemic functional framework, the APPRAISAL system enables the identification of sections of narrative in which writers interact with and evaluate the social and cultural contexts of their coming out. Sauntson's analysis of the stories suggests that coming out is a social and linguistic process of sexual identity construction. In most of the narratives, the writers' coming out involves social interaction and an indexing of a range of situated social and cultural practices.

In an ongoing study exploring the complex relationship between language, culture and sexuality, Grosse introduces key narrative resources of gay sexual identities (Ch. 7). From the world of the 'Yumas' in the 'Yara' in Havana, Cuba, to gay nude beaches and bathhouses in Europe, this study is intended to embrace issues such as risk, desire, ageism and pleasure and their impact on the enunciation of gay identities across linguistic and cultural boundaries. Using key ethnographic tools, including diary studies and extensive fieldwork conducted in gay environments in Latin America, Europe and the United States, this chapter sheds light on the negotiation and enactment of gay sexual identities across national and localised cultural settings.

Continuing with an exploration of the narrative resources used to encode and construct sexual identities, Hoey (Ch. 8) argues that there is a characteristic discourse pattern to narratives of love and desire that is similar to the Problem–Solution pattern (Hoey, 1994) found in many other narratives; this pattern has its own characteristic linguistic signalling. The Desire Arousal–Desire Fulfilment pattern (Hoey, 1997) is also used in advertisements, and indeed is the single most common pattern in this genre. Common to both love stories and advertisements is the triggering notion of Arousal of Desire. In this chapter, the linguistic features of this component of the pattern are examined in two languages and cultures (English and Portuguese) and two different genres: Mills and Boon narratives, ostensibly written by women and certainly written for them, and erotic Portuguese poetry, written by a man. The analysis begins to reveal some interesting cultural differences and Hoey illustrates how the language used has more to do with lust than with love and can be seen as perpetuating the objectification of women (and men).

Moving to media-based texts, Litosseliti in Chapter 9 examines the increasingly heightened anxiety or 'moral panic' surrounding hetero-sexual relationships, in the context of women and men's shifting roles, identities and relations in a rapidly changing, so-called 'risk' society (Beck, 1992). It focuses on the discursive construction of deviance (Goode and Ben-Yehuda, 1994), of perceived threats to a 'moral'/'normal' heterosexual life, and to the social order itself. Such threats typically include family breakdown, feminism going 'too far' and a 'crisis of masculinity'. Within a British sociocultural context, the chapter uses examples from the media and everyday interactions to illustrate how dominant, resistant and alternative heterosexual identities are constructed through language. The chapter illustrates how aspects of language use – such as moral abstractions, metaphors, melodramatic or exaggerated vocabulary, and discourses of prediction, symbolisation and prescription – construct particular repres-entations of women and men (e.g. representations of fathers), particular social identities for women and men (e.g. the construction of cohab-iting couples) and particular social relations between women and men (e.g. those between spouses).

Finally, Chirrey in Chapter 10 explores processes of coming out as they are represented and enacted through the discourses of advice literature for British lesbians. 'Coming out' is a phenomenon that has become widely recognised in Western cultures as a fundamental means by which an individual constructs a sexual identity that is not heterosexual. Never-theless, disclosing one's non-heterosexuality to other people is a process that is recognised as being potentially difficult and problematic, not only by those who come out, but also by their heterosexual allies. In an effort to assist individuals to come out, a body of advice literature has grown up in the way of pamphlets, leaflets and Internet sites. Chirrey's contribution presents an overview of such literature, discussing such aspects as its target readership and the nature of the advice offered (e.g. how to come out, where to come out and who to come out to). She then explores the extent to which individuals are influenced by such advice when they come out and assesses how heterosexual and non-heterosexual listeners receive and co-construct coming out discourses.

There are clearly limitations to the work presented in the collection. It is not possible, for example, for us to consider a wider range of cultural settings which include more of those outside of North America and Europe. This book does not proclaim to look at every culture and certainly does not aim to consider culture, or the crossing of culture, on any global level as, for example, Leap and Boellstorff do. However, future developments of this project may include considering cross-cultural perspectives on language, desires and sexualities in a more diverse range of cultural settings. Finally, it is important to stress, as Weeks (1999) warns, that we need to be careful not to use our awareness of different cultural patterns to reinforce, rather than confront, our own culture-based conceptions of sexuality and language. We have tried as far as possible to incorporate such an awareness into the analyses presented throughout this book and we would urge the reader to adopt a similar awareness when considering the findings and arguments presented in each chapter. Despite these unavoidable limitations and caveats, we hope that this collection provides a timely and worthwhile contribution to our developing understanding of the complex relationships between sexuality, language, culture and society.

## References

Agar, M. 1994. *Language Shock: Understanding the Culture of Conversation.* New York: William Morrow

Austin, J.L. 1962. *How to Do Things with Words.* Cambridge, Mass.: Harvard University Press

Beck, U. 1992. *The Risk Society: towards a New Modernity.* Cambridge: Polity Press

Bonvillain, N. 1993. *Language, Culture and Communication: the Meaning of Messages.* Englewood Cliffs: Prentice Hall

Bucholtz, M. and Hall, K. 2004. Theorizing identity in language and sexuality research. *Language in Society* 33: 469–515

Burke, L., Crowley, T. and Girvin, A. (eds) 2000. *The Routledge Language and Cultural Theory Reader.* London: Routledge

Butler, J. 1990. *Gender Trouble: Feminism and the Subversion of Identity.* London: Routledge

Cameron, D. and Kulick, D. 2003. *Language and Sexuality.* Cambridge: Cambridge University Press

Campbell-Kibler, K., Podesva, R., Roberts, S. and Wong, A. (eds) 2002. *Language and Sexuality: Contesting Meaning in Theory and Practice.* Stanford, Calif.: CSLI

Cole, M. 1998. Can cultural psychology help us think about diversity? *Mind, Culture, and Activity* 5 (4): 291–304

Cory, D. 1951. *The Homosexual in America: a Subjective Approach.* New York: Greenberg

Geertz, C. 1993. *The Interpretation of Cultures: Selected Essays.* London: Fontana Press

Goode, E. and Ben-Yehuda, N. 1994. *Moral Panics: the Social Construction of Deviance.* Oxford: Blackwell

Goodenough, W. 1957. Cultural anthropology and linguistics. *Georgetown University Monograph Series on Language and Linguistics* 9: 167–73

Hall, K. and Bucholtz, M. (eds) 1995. *Gender Articulated: Language and the Socially Constructed Self.* London: Routledge

Hoey, M. 1994. Signalling in discourse: a functional analysis of a common discourse pattern in written and spoken English. In Coulthard, R.M. (ed.) *Advances in Written Text Analysis.* London: Routledge, pp. 26–45

Hoey, M. 1997. The organisation of narratives of desire. In Harvey, K. and Shalom, C. (eds) *Language and Desire: Encoding Sex, Romance and Intimacy.* London: Routledge, pp. 85–105

Kramsch, C. 1998. *Language and Culture.* Oxford: Oxford University Press

Kulick, D. 2000. Gay and lesbian language. *Annual Review of Anthropology* **29**: 243–85

Leap, W. (ed.) 1995. *Beyond the Lavender Lexicon: Authenticity, Imagination, and Appropriation in Lesbian and Gay Languages.* Buffalo, NY: Gordon and Breach

Leap, W. 1996. *Word's Out: Gay Men's English.* Minneapolis: University of Minnesota Press

Leap, W. and Boellstorff, T. (eds) 2004. *Speaking in Queer Tongues: Globalization and Gay Language.* Urbana and Chicago: University of Illinois Press

Legman, G. 1941. The language of homosexuality: an American glossary. In Henry, G. (ed.) *Sex Variants: a Study of Homosexual Patterns,* Vol. 2. London: Paul B. Hoeber Inc., pp. 1149–79

Livia, A. and Hall, K. (eds) 1997. *Queerly Phrased: Language, Gender, and Sexuality.* Oxford: Oxford University Press

Martin, J. 2000. Beyond exchange: APPRAISAL systems in English. In Hunston, S. and Thompson, G. (eds) *Evaluation in Text: Authorial Stance and the Construction of Discourse.* Oxford: Oxford University Press, pp. 142–75

Morrish, E. and Sauntson, H. Forthcoming. *Language and Sexual Identity.* Basingstoke: Palgrave

Parker, R. and Aggleton, P. (eds) 1999. *Culture, Society and Sexuality: a Reader.* London: UCL Press

Provencher, D.M. 2004. Vague English Creole: (Gay English) cooperative discourse in the French gay press. In Leap, W. and Boellstorff, T. (eds) *Speaking in Queer Tongues: Globalization and Gay Language.* Urbana and Chicago: University of Illinois Press, pp. 23–45

Rodgers, B. 1972. *The Queen's Vernacular: a Gay Lexicon.* London: Blond and Briggs

Sapir, E. 1921. *Language: an Introduction to the Study of Speech.* New York: Harcourt Brace

Sapir, E. 1949. Language and environment. In Mandelbaum, D. (ed.) *Selected Writings of Edward Sapir.* Berkeley: University of California Press, pp. 89–103

Sauntson, H. 2002. Examining lesbian conversations as discourses of resistance. Paper presented at 9th Annual Conference on Lavender Languages and Linguistics, American University, Washington, DC

Vance, C. 1999. Anthropology rediscovers sexuality: a theoretical comment. In Parker, R. and Aggleton, P. (eds) *Culture, Society and Sexuality: a Reader.* London: UCL Press, pp. 39–54

Weeks, J. 1999. Discourse, desire and sexual deviance: some problems in a history of homosexuality. In Parker, R. and Aggleton, P. (eds) *Culture, Society and Sexuality: a Reader.* London: UCL Press, pp. 119–42

# 1
# Sex Talk: Language, Desire, Identity and Beyond

*Liz Morrish and William Leap*

## Introduction[1]

The main aim of this chapter is to propose that identity-centred studies of language and sexuality have affirmed the need for context-centred research, and to illustrate how identity-centred research allows the workings of desire to be examined within the domains of lived social and cultural experience. In the first part of the chapter, we chart the development of our main theoretical arguments by reviewing the primary critique offered by proponents of what we term 'desire-centred research' regarding identity-centred studies of language and sexuality. We will explain how the primary interest in identity-centred studies was not a simplistic documentation of language/identity bi-uniqueness.[2] The concern was much more complex: tracing how speakers' use of language 'at the site' conveys context- and culture-specific messages about sexual identity and other topics related to sexuality *within the social moment*, and thereby, demonstrating how certain linguistic practices convey messages about sexuality within that cultural setting. Important to note, audience-centred, interpolative, performative dimensions of these messages, and the linguistic practices conveying them, were acknowledged and explored in these earlier studies, and these iterative themes continue to be addressed in recent, identity-centred research, even as the scope of this work has broadened to incorporate new lines of inquiry – including connections between language and desire.

In the next section of the chapter, we consider several recent examples of such research. In the first set of examples, we consider sexual (and other) identities as forms of practice which emerge through discourse and other signalling structures acquired within a *community of practice*, that is, a nexus of social relations with fluid membership that is constantly in formation and that becomes a site of struggle as often as a site of solidarity and stability. Echoing Bucholtz's (1999: 209) claim that 'individuals engage in multiple identity practices simultaneously, and they are able to move from one identity to another', this example shows how identity joins desire as a product of iteration, but at the same time, and far from being context-free, that iteration itself is a product of speaker-centred linguistic practice.

In the next set of examples, we position identity and desire within larger relationships between language, sexuality and political economy within township settings in post-apartheid Cape Town, South Africa. In these settings, all iterations of sexuality coincide with reproduction of structures (material and ideological) that mediate access to economic and social opportunity. To consider desire (or identity, or any component of human experience, for that matter) as a context-free semiotic in such instances ignores the broader workings of political economy in terms of which all forms of speaker subjectivity are interpolated, and disguises the extent to which individual speakers claim subject positions in spite of economic and social regulation. Uniqueness of linguistic practices is not at issue here, though the significance of certain practices, as markers of place within a larger regulatory system, *are* relevant to the analysis, just as they are for the speakers and their everyday lives.

All of these examples build on an identity-centred analysis of language and sexuality, but are not limited by concerns with language/identity bi-uniqueness. Similarly, while both examples provide rich documentation for the interactions between linguistic practices, sexuality and desire, they show how much information will be excluded from that documentation, if items other than desire are not addressed on the research agenda. Such exclusions, we conclude, undermine interests in building understandings of language and sexuality relationships relevant to specific cultural settings and in cross-cultural regularities in the sense described throughout this collection.

## Revisiting 'uniqueness', exploring identity, intentionality and significance

Some recent discussions regarding language and sexuality have urged that researchers prioritise a general concern with same-sex desire over the particular interests defined and described in terms of lesbian, gay, bisexual, transgender, queer, and other types of speaker-centred sexual identities (hereafter LGBTQ). Publications articulating this point of view include Kulick (2000, 2003), Cameron and Kulick (2003a, b), and several essays in Campbell-Kibler *et al.* (2002). The recurring argument in these publications is twofold: first, studies of, for example, 'lesbian/gay language' (including Moonwomon, 1995; Leap, 1996; Livia and Hall, 1997) have failed to identify any structural or discursive features which mark the linguistic practices of lesbians and gay men distinctive from persons in any other sexually based identity category. Second, such an inquiry misses the point entirely, since the only feature that could be characteristic of LGBTQ language is its articulation of desire, not its expression of desire in terms of specific object choices or through specific linguistic formats.

There is no question that desire-centred studies of language and sexuality address research questions very different from those that guided earlier identity-centred studies of language and sexuality, and the authors of this chapter agree that the issues raised by those questions are worthy of further study. One purpose of this chapter is, therefore, to clarify some of the issues surrounding existing work on language and sexuality raised by desire-centred critiques of such work. We are not convinced that centring language and sexuality research entirely around desire is a viable alternative to current practice, if the intended focus for such research is a 'desire for recognition, for intimacy, for erotic fulfillment [ . . . ] none of [which] in itself is specific to any particular kind of person' (Kulick, 2003: 123). There is no lesbian, gay or other sexualised subject under this research agenda and, therefore, no reason to pay attention to personal, social or historical context of linguistic or desiring practices.[3]

Proponents of desire-centred studies of language and sexuality assert, quite correctly, that studies of language and sexuality have largely been synonymous with the language use of sexually minoritised groups like gays and lesbians. Further, and following the argument outlined in Kulick (2000), these scholars claim that studies of, for example, lesbian and gay languages have assumed, but failed to prove, that gays and lesbians use language in a specifically delineable, bi-unique fashion. That is, while these studies find that lesbians and gay men readily use linguistic and other symbolic resources to index identity, these resources also circulate in other contexts among diverse groups to index different identities. The argument concludes that this broader circulation should undermine the claim that markers of sexual identity can be analysable from discursive practice. It is claimed, on the other hand, that desire is much more amenable to discursive analysis – that it is intelligible because it is conveyed through semiotic practices which are iterable, and whose recursiveness makes them readily amenable to identification and analysis.

## Dispelling the smokescreen of *uniqueness*

The fact that studies of LGBTQ linguistic practices do not clearly demarcate the locations of morphological, phonological or other linguistic features that are completely **unique** to the linguistic practices of gay men and lesbians may, at first, appear to be a valid criticism. However, no researcher who studies LGBTQ-centred language has ever claimed to be searching for unique linguistic features – or has ever claimed to have found them. Indeed, when language and desire scholars raise this argument, references are cited generically (e.g. Moonwomon, 1995; Leap, 1996), rarely indicating where in the identified sources claims about uniqueness of linguistic features are to be found. In most cases, as careful reading will confirm, such claims are not part of the original argument, but have been read into it by other researchers. See the discussion of the 'Brown water pitcher' (Extract 1.1 below), as a case in point.

What researchers have sought to discover is the LGBTQ-related **signi-ficance** of linguistic features, that is, to identify those features within a speech event in terms of which participants are able to acknowledge and confirm references to sexuality as relevant to that context. Such features may include terms with explicit sexual references, but much more frequently those features are not coded for sexual meaning and such meanings must be contextually inferred. Linguistic forms that satisfy this 'performative effect' (Leap, 1996: 159–63; 1997) in one context may not do so in another. The issue here is interpreting social actors within social contexts – not meanings of sexuality (or desire!) embedded invari-ably within the linguistic sign.

LGBTQ language studies have not trawled for evidence of invariable referencing of sexuality within any one area of LGBTQ linguistic prac-tice. Quite the contrary; much work, to date, recognises the great amount of diversity within groups, contexts, cultures and material conditions which together lead to diverse articulations of sexual identity, even within individuals who purportedly share the same, or very similar, sexual orientation. Discussions of this point include Manalansan's (1994, 1995, 2003) writings on Filipino *bakla* in home and in diasporic settings, Roscoe and colleagues' (1988) discussions of Native American two-spirit people, Gaudio's (1997, 2001) discussions of *yan daudu* sexual subjectivities in northern Nigeria, Hall's (1997) studies of *hijra* and other 'third gender' categories in contemporary urban India, and

Johnson's (1998, 2003) reflections on the linguistic practices which African American gay men use to denote racial/sexual solidarity and contrast.

To assume that the object of inquiry in researching language and sexual identity is the search for specific structural features for LGBTQ language (Kulick 2000: 257) is to disregard the importance of contextually, culturally and locally negotiated meanings which have repeatedly proven to be the significant feature for LGBTQ – and all sexualised/gendered – languages. Indeed, we find that LGBTQ language is often as much a part of the linguistic repertoire of persons who do *not* identify as lesbian or gay (Podesva *et al.*, 2002 – and see also the earlier discussion of this issue in Gaudio, 1994). Morrish (2002a, b), for example, demonstrates that the codes of camp are not necessarily owned by homosexuals. Subtle signification of identity is precisely the process which underlies the media's outing of British public political figures like Peter Mandelson and Michael Portillo, and the mainstream press are adept at deploying the codes of camp in order to effect covert, pragmatic outing. And as Boellstorff's (2004) work in Indonesia makes clear, same-sex identified people can claim LGBTQ identities in some settings, then submerge those identities beneath mainstream-based assertions of national belonging in other settings. Whether applied to the speakers themselves, or by the speakers to others, assertions of LGBTQ identity certainly do not always fall within the domain of any single party – linguistic assertions, least of all.

How, therefore, can anyone claim that researchers have identified specifically LGBTQ language(s), if these researchers recognise that the linguistic practices in question are also attested in the discourse of mainstream straight speakers? The fact that those who identify as gay do not always 'talk' gay – and correspondingly, that structures that might be identified as gay on some occasions might wittingly or unwittingly be used by straight speakers – cannot be used to invoke fallacious arguments about language-and-identity bi-uniqueness. At one time, phonemic theory claimed that once a phone was assigned to a particular phonemic class, it would always belong to that phoneme. That artificial argument did not work for phonology, and it certainly does not work in the complex world of human interaction where conditions of culture, register, style, audience, performativity, materiality all pervade the context of communication.

What has happened, however, is that linguistic practices that often index LGBTQ identities (or are believed for various reasons to do so) have entered the general symbolic marketplace, both in response to the commodification of LGBTQ cultures outside of LGBTQ settings (Evans, 1993; Gluckman and Reed, 1997; Hennessy, 2000), as well as the more general flows of sexual cultures within national boundaries and across them (Altman, 2001; Berry *et al.*, 2003; Boellstorff and Leap, 2004). But while the circulation of these markers of non-normative sexuality has resulted in an enhanced visibility among broader audiences, neither condition has diminished the popularity of these linguistic practices within LGBTQ settings. Some gay-identified men continue to mark their sexual identities, publicly and strategically, in terms similar to the slightly campy, often acidic one-line retorts favoured by characters from American and British television sitcoms like *Will and Grace* and *Queer as Folk*, even if awareness of these codings and their meanings is now foregrounded in public culture. As Moonwomon (1995: 46) is careful to remind us, we should not trace the linguistic basis of social identity exclusively to distributions of linguistic features within linguistic domains, since most of the language-based indicators of identity occur at the level of discourse and are still revealed through a gradual recognition and/or negotiation of culture-specific shared linguistic knowledge.

## Engaging *intentionality*

A second, and related, criticism of identity-centred studies of language and sexuality has to do with connections between identity and intentionality. Unlike the case for discussions of uniqueness, intentionality is central to identity-based studies of language and sexuality, as well it should be; intentionality, like identity and the workings of significance, are all forms of linguistic practices through which speaking subjects affirm their presence within the linguistic moment.

Cameron and Kulick (2003a: 125) maintain that much of the work with intentionality has taken the form of efforts to impute 'what the speaker was *really* trying to say' from a close reading of the speaker's textual product. To our knowledge, no one studying language and sexuality from an identity-centred framework has advocated such a stance. What many have proposed, however, is the close reading of textual form combined with evidence about the speech event gleaned from ethnographic observation and other sources, in order to draw out as much of the ebb and flow of conversation (or narrative) as researchers are able to (re)construct. This is the approach to text analysis which orients Leap's discussion of the language use of gay-identified men in *Word's Out* and related publications (Leap 1999, 2002a, b, 2003), and it is the approach that orients Barrett's (1995, 1997) studies of African American drag queen/audience interaction, Gaudio's (1997, 2001) studies of the linguistic skills of the *yan daudu*, Kulick's (1997, 1998) exploration of *travesti* sexuality in urban Brazil, and Cameron's (1997) accounting of young men 'performing gender identity' through linguistic practice.

Whether researchers make the position explicit or not, all of these studies assume that speakers are being strategic in their use of language – or, in Halliday's (1978: 109) words: 'Text represents choice. A text is "what is meant", selected from the total set of options that constitutes what can be meant. In other words, text can be defined as actualised meaning potential.' Were such assumptions not to apply, linguistic practices would become arbitrary, haphazard, meaningless, formless activities, yielding arbitrary, haphazard, meaningless and formless linguistic products. Thus, there would be no reason to use conversation or narrative as a focus for linguistic analysis. Where linguistic analysis should turn to find a more reliable database for linguistic inquiry is not yet clear. Desire-centred approaches would benefit from their allegiance to text-centred research being qualified by their broader theoretical claims.

Indeed, it is not obvious how this apparent theoretical quandary regarding intentionality will be resolved by a shift in focus from identities and the intentions of communication to the 'culturally grounded semiotic practices that make them and their communication possible' (Cameron and Kulick, 2003a: 125). Certainly giving attention to the unconscious may enrich the inquiry by allowing studies of sexuality to extend beyond those identities which people consciously claim. But where is the concrete empirical basis in terms of which desire-centred research will explore the unconscious as it mediates the interface of language and sexuality? Even if research adopts a strict Lacanian reading of messages of desire nested within particular forms of linguistic practice and product, close reading of textual evidence is still required. To argue that the speaker speaks, but has no say in what s/he is saying calls to mind the generative grammarian's interests in the deep-structural linguistic competence of the ideal speaker-hearer. This theoretical perspective is eloquent, but real-world experiences remain at distance from the analysis.

## Identity gives studies of sexuality a concrete object for inquiry

The advantage of making identity the starting point for inquiry is that at least the object of inquiry is defined, and its range bounded. Hence, when the five college-age young men who were the focus of study in Cameron's (1997) now classic essay, 'Performing gender identity: young men's talk and the construction of heterosexual masculinity', actively disavowed homosexuality, and worked together to construct a hetero-sexual, masculine identity in opposition to it, their linguistic and social practices were neither random nor arbitrary, nor without blueprint. Their sense of homosexuality – and of heteronormative masculinity – was not created *de nouveau* within the linguistic moment, but incorporated a broad range of understandings and assumptions about sexual identity and desire. Cameron's close reading of the linguistic turn-taking (whose details resemble those termed *cooperative discourse* in Leap, 1996: 12–48, though certainly not with the gay-affirming outcomes) contains ample evidence of purposeful, intentional linguistic exchange, framed within, but not predetermined by, speakers' assumptions about sexual identity. Foregrounding notions of desire might clarify additional themes (or anxieties) embedded in the young men's remarks; erasing questions of identity from the analysis would remove from consideration the very issues that were of primary interest in their exchange.

A recent conversation in which Morrish was a co-participant provides a second example of how identity provides a defined, bounded focus – though not entirely a predetermined one, for analysis of conversations about language and sexuality. And once again, underscoring the theme of intentionality, the example reminds us that participants in such conversations find identity to be an equally valuable resource in that regard.

When white, middle-class, academic lesbians have what they might consider, in hindsight, a 'lesbian conversation', they only rarely focus around sex, desire or disclosures of attraction. This conversation took place between two lesbians who knew each other quite well, and a third woman of undeclared sexual identity whom the other two did not know well, but was thought to be a lesbian by both other parties (because of dress, hairstyle, etc.). They were all workmates, and were having an extended conversation about the relaxed dress code in the workplace which did not require them to wear dresses or be particularly smart. They talked about their comfort level in trousers and work boots, and how more conventional feminine attire would distract them from doing their jobs. The next day, the two 'out' lesbians had coffee. 'So, what's the story with Tanya?', inquired one. The other confessed she did not know, and was unwilling to make an assumption without the formality of a 'coming out'. 'But that's the kind of conversation you'd have with a dyke', said her friend, referring to the previous day.

This conversation had everything to do with gender, and everything to do with sexual identity as well. Some of the things which dykes talk about when 'being' dykes, in Butler's (1991: 18) sense of 'being' or specifically performing lesbian identity, include the constraints of gender normativity and the possibilities of resistance to it, and they frame those remarks in coded and not-so-coded formats accordingly. The point we are making here is not restricted purely to lesbian experience. As Leap (1996: 7–10, 35–9) has explained in his description of two self-identified gay men disputing the colour of a 'brown water pitcher', certain features of discursive practice widely attested in the language use of gay-identified English-speaking men (including cooperation, gender non-normative topics and indexing) have a performative effect on the participants' understandings of the sexual politics of the gendered moment and on those of the audience as well. In all such instances, these performative features may be difficult to decompose structurally, and they may not all be entirely unique to gay or lesbian cultures. But they are significant to the work of communication within those cultural domains, and speakers invoke that significance, sometimes accidentally, sometimes intentionally, as part of their conversational or narrative text-making. Understandably, documenting that context-related significance has been, and remains, the central concern in LGBTQ language studies as we know and engage in them; desire-centred linguistic inquiry can make important contributions to that project, as the examples reviewed in the following section will show.

## Studying the significance of desire: two examples

We see many shortcomings in a narrowly focused theorising of language and desire, but we wholeheartedly agree that LGBTQ language research should not neglect this component of human sexuality. Indeed, desire factors richly into the research projects with which we are each engaged – Morrish's studies of the linguistics of self-presentation and concealment (2002c), Leap's (2004 and forthcoming) studies of language, sexuality and political economy, Morrish and Sauntson's (forthcoming) studies of lesbian erotica – however, as our discussions of these projects will show, desire is not the only issue which orients linguistic inquiry in these projects.

### Language, desire and *Communities of Practice*
Much of the discussion of language and desire calls to mind a classic version of a Labovian speech community in which all individuals share

the same notion of desire and, thus, the same linguistic codes for expressing it; see, for example, Kulick (2000: 250–1). Most sociolinguists would now argue that such an idealised 'speech community' consisting of members with homogeneously detailed verbal repertoires simply does not exist. Hence, Pratt (1987: 51) points out the distance between the sometimes imagined homogeneity of linguistic community and the fractured experience of individuals positioned within them. She argues that a speech community approach does not deal with social relations between groups where 'language is seen as a nexus of social identity, but not as a site of social struggle or a producer of social relations' (Pratt, 1987: 56).

From such dissatisfaction with the limits of 'speech community', the Community of Practice (CoP henceforth) argument has emerged. It borrows heavily from work in social theory (Wenger, 1998) which asserts the following principles:

- boundaries between subcultures are fuzzy
- relations and influences between them need to be specified
- identities are fluid
- it is difficult to recognise linguistic varieties purely in structural terms.

CoP-centred research understands identities as multiple and fluid, and contends that identities emerge through practice and are not claimed in advance of it. It is, then, an approach which sits easily with the existence of heterogeneous groupings, in which, in the service of creating identity, all kinds of diverse subjects may be brought together for the purpose of mutual endeavour (Wenger, 1998: 75). Bucholtz (1999) asserts that individuals who are part of a community of practice need not all be equally immersed or oriented towards the practice in the same way or at all. As she explains, 'individuals engage in multiple identity practices simultaneously and they are able to move from one identity to another', which means that '[g]ender does not have the same meanings across space and time, but is instead a local production, realized differently by different members of a community' (Bucholtz, 1999: 209, 210). Work by Moonwomon (1995, 2000) and Livia (1995) and others has made clear that these discourse practices in the context of creating gender or sexual identity are anything but exclusively sexual or erotic.

The 'brown pitcher' exchange (Leap, 1996: 7–10 – presented here below) and other examples of 'gay men's English' in Leap's *Word's Out* show how the workings of such recognition unfold in various US-based speech settings – and, thereby, display the interplay of what Leap terms the twin processes of *cooperative discourse* and *language of risk*.

**Extract 1.1** The Brown Water Pitcher

1 A    can I get a glass of water?

2      [Moves toward sink where B is washing dishes]

3 B    there is ice water in the fridge

4 A    OK. Thanks.

5      [Opens refrigerator door, looks inside]

6 B    [Notices pause in action] In the brown pitcher.

7 A    [Continues to look; looks toward Bob] I don't see a brown pitcher in here.

8 B    Sure. It's brown, and round, and on the top shelf.

9 A    [Looks inside again] Nope.

10 B   [Stops washing dishes, dries hands, moves to fridge, removes pitcher,

11     pours water]

12 A   That pitcher is not brown, it is tan. [Pause; B remains silent] It is light tan.

13 B   It is brown to me. [Slight smile]

14 A   No, you said brown; so I looked for something dark chocolate.

(Leap, 1996: 7)

In this example, two gay men argue about the exact colour of a water pitcher. Unlike the highly competitive linguistic exchange commonly associated with heterosexual males (Goodwin, 1980; Coates, 2003), the interlocutors in this example recognise the potential for conflict which their disagreement may cause, and once evidence of tension begins to appear in the linguistic exchange (see Leap 1996: 7, lines 6–9) the two men quickly take steps *together* to back away from that undesirable goal, and begin to make fun of their own stereotyping of themselves, as gay men, disagreeing over the fine points of colour, shade and hue. Gay stereotype, applied by both speakers to themselves and to each other, figures prominently in the linguistic strategies used to redirect the exchange and, thereby, marks the shared familiarity with the stereotype and the broader meanings communicated through building a parody of it. No one would suggest that this exchange illustrates a uniquely gay linguistic strategy, and Leap certainly did not make such a claim in his analysis. That the use of the strategy had a performative effect on the conversation between these men is evidenced repeatedly, or iteratively, in the details of the linguistic exchange.

Extract 1.2, below, makes the same point about the significance of meaning in local production. The conversation is about the notion of a lesbian version of the popular British TV programme *Changing Rooms*, in which couples redecorate and remodel rooms in their friends' houses. Among this small group of white middle-class lesbians, the identities being performed and jointly negotiated emerge through the exploitation of shared cultural knowledge and jokes which invert gender norms as well as play off stereotypic expectations about lesbian tastes.

*Extract 1.2*   Changing Rooms

1   C   they're all so straight the people who go on this

2   A   yeah, I think we should all go on

3   B   yeah we could do a lesbian Changing Rooms

4   A   yeah and instead of telling the audience all about our children we could

5       tell them about our cats

6   All (laughing)
    (2 turns)

7   C   yeah we'd have to have strict guidelines before we went on like

8       no wallpaper

9   B   and no pastels

10  All (laughing)

11  A   we could paint big dyke symbols all over each other's walls

12  All (laughing)

(adapted from Sauntson, 2002)

There are no overt appeals to 'lesbian identity' in this passage, so what about the passage might prompt a listener (or a researcher) to identify this exchange as a 'lesbian conversation'? What claims are we making about the text, if we consider this an example of 'lesbian speech'? Moonwomon (1995: 46) supplies an answer to these questions in her discussion of lesbian conversations revolving around domestic and health matters – that authenticity in a lesbian conversation emerges from assumptions of shared knowledge. What Moonwomon (1995) proposes as shared lesbian knowledge is the sense that one's partner will be understanding and supportive, as well as share one's perception of oppression as a lesbian with breast cancer in the face of the medical establishment. Moonwomon-Baird (2000) examined the narrative of a lesbian whose various identities as a black woman, a lesbian, a recovering alcoholic and a political being all coalesce and are variously prioritised to 'describe how a lesbian sense of self is made complexly' (Moonwomon-Baird, 2000: 349).

In a similar vein, in the *Changing Rooms* excerpt, a collective lesbian identity emerges in opposition to norms of heterosexual femininity which are expressed in terms of child-bearing, colour choice and decor preference. Expectations of what usually occurs in such TV programmes are subverted with comedic irony. We notice a rapid flow of information and agreement (multiple occurrences of 'yeah' – lines 2, 3, 4, 7) about how to be a lesbian in that particular co-culture.

It is a lesbian conversation because it is *situated discourse*. Cats, wallpaper and pastels might all evoke different meanings in another culture or situation and with participants who were straight or male. Someone who claims to be a fully paid-up member of a lesbian CoP has inevitably undergone a process of acculturation and *learning*, and the CoP is characterised by Wenger (1998: 214) as 'a privileged location for the acquisition of knowledge'. During the formation of an identity, there is a transformation of knowledge, and symbols and behaviours become invested with meanings in context (Wenger, 1998: 214). The CoP member becomes expert at decoding these meanings, and part of that learning process is acquiring a sociolinguistic competence of making judgements about what constitutes a felicitous act of identity in others (Holmes and Meyerhoff, 1999: 174). And of course the meanings of acts will change in different cultural contexts. Understanding meanings of situated discourse is also what is going on in Leap's 'Brown water pitcher' example, and in the many examples of 'rehearsal' which he has also discussed (Leap, 1996: 125–39; 1999: 267). The men in those examples, like the women in the *Changing Rooms* example here, are able to participate in the linguistic exchange because they are playing by the same rules for decoding the conversation. As Lemke (2000) writes, 'because practices are not just performances [ ... ] one must learn not just what and how to perform, but also what the performance means, in order to function and be accepted as a full member of a CoP'.

Clearly the performance above is predicated on the assumption of shared lesbian desire, nevertheless that is not the feature of difference which is foregrounded by the participants or even directly indexed. What is on display in Extract 1.2 is the collective will to transgress hetero-norms and resist gender role conformity. The embedded understanding is the ability to decode these in a multivalent way as signifying lesbian identity and lesbian desire.

## Language, desire and valued sexual geography

Communities of Practice theory shows how understandings of desire can be co-constructed, as part of the linguistic give and take between participants in a conversation. Understandings of desire, formed through such means within the social moment, can also circulate *outside* of specific conversational settings, thereby assuming a status similar to that assigned to other commodities exchanged within the economic and social marketplace. Desire gains association with persons, places, activities and other 'things' through this process, each of which becomes not only desirable, but valuable through this means.

Place this process of association within a social system that stratifies mobility and restricts economic and social opportunity based on distinctions of skin colour, male vs female bodily differences, and strict allegiance to hetero-normative privilege, and you begin to sense the complex structures that regulate the geographies of everyday life in the black townships in post-apartheid Cape Town, South Africa. This discussion builds on Cape Town area field research reviewed in Leap (2004). The database includes life-story interviews from more than 85 women and men, distributed somewhat evenly across racial/ethnic backgrounds, age ranges, income levels and class positions. Leap conducted his interviews in English; township residents whom Leap trained to work with him on this project conducted interviews in English and Xhosa and worked with Leap to prepare translations of the Xhosa materials. Each interview began with the respondent drawing a map of Cape Town as a gay city, with the depiction of sexual geography presented in each map providing focus for the remainder of the tape-recorded interview. Data on place and location reviewed here come from these sections of the interviews.

Some Cape Town area townships were created during the apartheid era and the forced removal of persons of colour from the City Centre to the Cape Flats. Others began as labour compounds and pre-date the apartheid period. In all instances, townships were domains of enforced residence, where quality-of-life services were often available in limited supply. Since work could be found in the metropolitan area, township residence was preferable to economic conditions in the homelands. Even so, township residence was racialised residence, and the regulation of bodies was, at the same time, a regulation of place. For LGBTQ township residents, coping with the regulation is especially complex, given that the locations that they consider to be the most valued lesbian/gay sites are located in Cape Town's City Centre, at some distance (in some instances, as much as 30 miles) from their place of township residence area. The City Centre was proclaimed as white space under the apartheid period, and since then its associations with wealth and privilege have maintained its identification with whiteness. Underscoring this theme, the bars and clubs which LGBTQ township residents consider most desirable have names with distinctively British and American cultural associations: Manhattan's, Angels, Bronx, Detour, Broadway, Bar Code, Brunswick. Also underscoring this theme are the comments which township residents make, repeatedly, when they describe the difficulties they often encounter when seeking to visit these sites:

*Extract 1.3* Sobole *(male, 29 years old, who grew up in Guguletu township)*:
Bronx and Angels is a very nice club music which I like. But recently I stopped going there because I experienced humiliation and discrimination. When you go to Bronx you are searched whether you are carrying weapons or whatever. Or just let in without being questioned or whatever. And when you go to Angels, they want, they ask me one day: 'Are you gay? This is strictly a gay club.' And I said, 'I am aware of that.' And the bouncer quarrelled and quarrelled and I asked him: 'Do I have to wear high heels and a dress and a wig to make sure I am gay and get in here?'

*Extract 1.4* Brenda *(female, 23 years old, a long-time resident of Khayelitsha township)*:
On some occasions you are not allowed to go in there with the tekkies [tennis shoes]. We must wear a formal shoe. They say things like that. The other day, we were there, they looked, we were in jeans

and tekkies, so they were like, 'You can't come in, You are wearing sneakers.' Why when the other people are going in wearing sneakers?

*Extract 1.5*  Rae *(male, 24 years old, originally from one of the black townships near Port Elizabeth, and now a resident of one of the multiracial communities in the southern suburbs)*:

I've known about myself since I was in Standard Seven, [...] but I never had the guts to practise it. Until I almost committed suicide. Then I came to. They had this poster about this place. I decided to go there but they didn't allow me to come in. They said, members only [...] I actually went early, before they opened for the night. I stood at the door and they had the chairs on the tables and I think they were getting ready to open. I stood there. And the manager came running, looked at me strangely like I was some kind of thief. Maybe not a thief but somebody who had invaded some kind of territory.

*Extract 1.6*  Terry *(male, 34 years old, resident of Nyanga township, summarised the sentiments in many other respondents' statements when he observed)*:

Imagine me catching the last train from Khayelitsha at ten past nine, telling myself that I am getting away from this township situation of humiliation and harassment and all that stuff, trying to get a safe place for myself in Cape Town where I see many gay people being free and wandering about nicely and having good time. I go there and I refused to be entered. There is no train back home. The next train back home will be only at 6 in the morning. So tell me, where do I have to stay for the whole night and what do I have to do.

Given the frequency with which township residents report these experiences of *humiliation and discrimination* (Sobole, Extract 1.3) occurring in City Centre gay sites, and the frustration and anger which they evoke, it may seem curious that LGBTQ township residents assign such prominence to City Centre gay venues in their descriptions of local sexual geography. But these are Cape Town's valued lesbian/gay sites, the sites most closely associated with an authentically lesbian/gay experience – even if they are also sites of frustration and denial.

But increasing the value of the City Centre sites (and, at the same time, increasing the frustration and denial) is the very different inventory of sites subsumed within township (homo)sexual geographies, and the ensuing contrast in opportunities presented by City Centre and township as (homo)sexual terrains. Key sites within that township inventory are the *shebeens*, privately owned taverns which usually operate out of the owner's home, several of which are known to welcome homosexual as well as heterosexual clientele. But even there, township narratives make clear that 'straight' customers become intolerant or openly hostile when forced to acknowledge the presence of LGBTQ patrons. As Terry's reference to the *township situation of humiliation and harassment and all that stuff* suggests (Extract 1.6), the risk of homophobic violence is ever-present and ever real, even within same-sex friendly *shebeens*.

Township lesbian and bisexual women Leap interviewed report that they respond to the homophobic threat by sitting quietly, trying not to be too obvious about their sexual interests, and otherwise trying to 'keep your safety in your own hands' (as several respondents are fond of saying); if the likelihood of trouble becomes unavoidable, bisexual and lesbian women report that they simply leave the site and move on to another *shebeen*.

Some township LGBTQ men report responding to the homophobic threat with a different strategy: they visit a *shebeen* dressed in 'women's clothes', assume 'female role' in on-site social discourse, and openly display other signifiers associated with a township-familiar *isi tabane* sex/gender status. According to the commentaries of *isi tabane* persons, the idea here is to emphasise the subject's willingness to frame his expressions of same-sex desire in terms that are consistent with township sexual culture and sexual tradition. Their commentaries acknowledge the many contradictions subsumed under this public status (male body vs female attire and mannerisms, 'male' genitalia vs 'female'-related behaviour in erotic practice), all of which ensure that a public claim to *isi tabane* status becomes a transgressive act and renders the subject of that claim a likely recipient of violent attack. Even so, *isi tabane* is male sexual sameness read within the recognised domain of township sexual culture.[4]

Township men who publicly express their interests in other men outside of that domain (e.g. as 'gay-identified' men), without claiming the township-familiar *isi tabane* status, frame their sexuality in less familiar, and, therefore, more ambiguous terms; that renders them an even more likely target for homophobic violence.

Understandably under such conditions, township LGBTQ residents would be led to view the City Centre as Terry did (Extract 1.6): [ . . . ] *a safe place for myself where I see many gay people being free and wandering about nicely and having good time.* Homophobic violence may occur in areas of the City Centre which surround these sites, or during their travel from township to City Centre; and discrimination may occur when they seek entrance to a white-related, lesbian/gay location. But in the interim period, once they reach the City Centre and before they reach the bars and clubs, township residents find what their narratives regularly describe as *safety* and *freedom*.

*Being free* is an especially important reference in that regard. In township English, *being free* conveys decidedly post-apartheid messages, and draws contrasts with the restrictions on everyday life which were central to apartheid governmentality. Besides calling to mind a similar reference, the corresponding Xhosa phrase builds on a medio-passive construction (*in khululeku*, 'to be loosened or unbound') to suggest that one's freedom is dependent on the agency of others, and that decisions about one's spatial practices need to be constructed accordingly. Hence, when used here as a reference to *a safe place*, safety describes a location where the subject has to be mindful of the workings of external agency, and take responsibility for personal safety in the light of those external constraints.

But what are these City Centre locations of safety? As much as value as they assign to the City Centre's gay bars and clubs, township residents report finding freedom and safety within a very different type of City Centre geography, one composed of:

- the hallways (but not the shops and boutiques) of the Golden Acre Shopping Centre; some township respondents also mention the hallways of the nearby Gardens Shopping Centre, and the hallways of the Waterfront Mall, especially on Saturday mornings
- Green Market Square (the site of an outdoor 'flea market', and a great place for sitting and milling around)
- the OK Bazaar, Pickbell's Arcade and other stores on City Centre side-streets
- the benches and chairs lining the walkways of the Company Gardens ('where you can go and it is peaceful and nobody will bother you', explained one township resident; where 'Blacks are everywhere willing to rob you or worse', countered an elderly white gay man explaining why he no longer frequents the Company Gardens)
- the Purple Turtle (a cyber café), Moroka's Café Africaine (a bar and coffee shop), and other City Centre food service locations known to be friendly to black clientele, many of which are operated by persons of colour.

Some, though not all, of these sites are commercial in basis, and none of them are specifically 'lesbian/gay' in clientele or appeal. But *all* of them are locations where access is not likely to be regulated by bouncers or other gatekeepers (where they can *feel free*) and locations where township residents can pursue their own interests, quietly and without interruption (where they can 'keep their safety in their own hands'). And *none* of these sites are included in descriptions of Cape Town's (homo)sexual geography given by Cape Town area white or coloured lesbians and gay men.

One of the themes that stands out repeatedly in our review of the Cape Town data is the contributions that fantasy and imagination make to the LGBTQ township residents' understandings of City Centre sexual geography. These residents know 'where the gay bars are', but they have also internalised a series of cultural assumptions explaining why these sites are desirable, and they maintain those assumptions and the valued status they assign to the bars and clubs, even when entering these sites requires them to endure *humiliation and discrimination*, and sometimes results in denial of admission to the desired terrain.

Yes, we can explore township perspectives on Cape Town area (homo)sexual geographies as concrete expressions – commodifications – of desire, and we should! But the brief discussion of the township residents' comments presented here shows that the analysis cannot be limited to a discussion of fantasy and other imaginative processes. The expression of desire in these instances is very much informed by the social, cultural and historical context of the township setting and by the local and translocal processes that define sexual sameness in similar and competing ways for township and City Centre residents. In other words, while desire can be a topic suitable for analysis on its own terms, the workings of desire are more effectively explored, drawing on a political economy framework, in reference to the material as well as ideological realities through which the desiring subject negotiates desire and subjectivity. Context and culture-specific research focusing attention on the speaking subject and the significance of the subject's linguistics products and practices provides rich opportunities for research directed towards that goal.

## Conclusions

When studied in social, cultural and linguistic contexts like the *Changing Rooms* conversation or township residents' discussions of area sexual geographies, the intersections of language and desire cease being 'culturally grounded semiotic practices' whose details are not '[ . . . ] particular to any kind of person' (Kulick, 2003: 123), and the features relevant to the meanings of desires range far beyond the iteratibility of its coding. Granted, the linguistic practices relevant to articulation of desire include performative and other iteractive acts whose details are, in some sense, 'a-historical'. But other, distinctively contextualised linguistic practices are also evidenced in such articulations, as the examples reviewed in this chapter have shown. Studying desire out of context makes it difficult to explore such contextualised dimensions of sexual experience as attraction, enjoyment, jouissance, the complexities of emotion, the workings of conformity, privilege and power, and the allure of the transgressive and the forbidden. Doing so makes it even more difficult to trace how linguistic dimensions are relevant to those experiences, either in specific situations or cross-culturally.

Under such circumstances, it is worth asking whether studies of language and sexuality really need an autonomous theory of desire. Indeed, such proposals emerge just at the time when studies of embodiment are disclosing close connections between sexuality, the body, and notions of place and space (Grosz, 1992; Bell and Valentine, 1995; Probyn, 1995; McDowell, 1999; Rasmussen *et al.*, 2003), and when studies of sexual cultures are confronting linkages between sexuality, postcolonial nation-building, global economy, and displacement (Manderson and Jolly, 1997; Aarmo, 1999; Blackwood and Wieringa, 1999; Parker, 1999; Patton and Sanchez-Eppler, 2000; Carillo, 2002; Khoo, 2003; Leap and Boellstorff, 2004). The intent in such scholarship is to move away from positing any single explanations for the sexual, and to propose instead that we view sexuality as a complex, multivalent construction whose particulars have to be disclosed, not assumed prediscursively. We see good reason to welcome desire-centred research as an important addition to the analysis of that multivalent complex; but its strength lies in its alliances with other modes of inquiry, not in its misleading assertion of its self-serving totality.

## Notes

1. This chapter grows out of a synthesis of two papers presented in a Workshop on Language, Identity and Desire held during the two-day Seminar on Language, Love and Sexuality at Kingston University (UK), 8–9 April 2002. Our thanks to Kathleen O'Mara (SUNY Oneonta), Denis Provencher (U. Wisconsin – La Crosse), Helen Sauntson (U. Birmingham), Sakis Kyratzis

(U. Kingston) and other colleagues who have reviewed and commented on this text.

2. Bi-uniqueness was a claim advanced by structural linguists regarding the relationship between sound units (phones) and sound classes (phonemes.) Under bi-uniqueness, a phone could belong to one, and only one phonemic class, and a phoneme must consist of a specified set of phonetic variants. Variation, flexibility, 'coexistent' systems and 'exceptions' – all the features that sociolinguistic theory recognises as fundamental attributes of phonological systems – were not acknowledged.

3. There is no 'lesbian/gay linguistics' under this framework, either. Indeed, one of the outcomes of desire-centred research is the erasure of 'lesbian/gay' from academic inquiry, an especially ironic move given how long it took to get lesbian/gay studies accepted within the academy.

4. *Isi tabane* is not, by respondent report, an 'authentic' Xhosa term. Some Xhosa speakers insist that it is a Zulu word; others derive it, without further explanation, from the English word 'stamp'. *Isi tabane* is also one of the terms used to identify the younger man who partners with the older (male) mine worker in labour camp dormitories. Township usage, and the presence of this homosexual category in township sexual culture, may derive from, or coincide with, the homosocial bonding which was formed in those settings.

# References

Aarmo, M. 1999. How homosexuality became 'un-African': the case of Zimbabwe. In Blackwood E. and Wieringa, S. (eds) *Same Sex Relations and Female Desires: Transgender Practices across Cultures*. New York City: Columbia University Press, pp. 255–81

Altman, D. 2001. *Global Sex*. Chicago: University of Chicago Press

Barrett, R. 1995. Supermodels of the world unite! Political economy and the language of performance among African-American drag queens. In Leap, W. (ed.) *Beyond the Lavender Lexicon: Authenticity, Imagination and Appropriation in Lesbian and Gay Languages*. Newark, NJ: Gordon and Breach, pp. 207–26

Barrett, R. 1997. The 'homo-genius' speech community. In Livia, A. and Hall, K. (eds) *Queerly Phrased: Language Gender and Sexuality*. Oxford: Oxford University Press, pp. 181–201

Bell, D. and Valentine, G. (eds) 1995. *Mapping Desire: Geographies of Sexuality*. London: Routledge

Berry, C., Martin, F., and Yue, A. 2003. Introduction: Beep-Click-Link. In Berry, C., Martin, F. and Yue, A. (eds) *Mobile Cultures: New Media in Queer Asia*. Durham and London: Duke University Press, pp. 1–20

Blackwood, E. and Wieringa, S. (eds) 1999. *Same Sex Relations and Female Desires: Transgender Practices across Cultures*. New York City: Columbia University Press

Boellstorff, T. 2004. 'Authentic of course!': gay language in Indonesia and cultures of belonging. In Leap, W. and Boellstorff, T. (eds) *Speaking in Queer Tongues: Globalization and Gay Language*. Urbana: University of Illinois Press, pp. 181–201

Boellstorff, T. and Leap, W. 2004. Introduction: globalization and new articulations of same-sex desire. In Leap, W. and Boellstorff, T. (eds) *Speaking in Queer*

*Tongues: Globalization and Gay Language.* Urbana: University of Illinois Press, pp. 1–22

Bucholtz, M. 1999. 'Why be normal?': language and identity practices in a community of nerd girls. *Language in Society* **28** (2): 203–23

Butler, J. 1991. Imitation and gender subordination. In Fuss, D. (ed.) *Inside/Out: Lesbian Theories, Gay Theories.* New York: Routledge, pp. 13–31

Cameron, D. 1997. Performing gender identity: young men's talk and the construction of heterosexual masculinity. In Johnson, S. and Meinhof, U. (eds) *Language and Masculinity.* Oxford: Blackwell, pp. 47–64

Cameron, D. and Kulick, D. 2003a. *Language and Sexuality.* Cambridge: Cambridge University Press

Cameron, D. and Kulick, D. 2003b. Introduction: language and desire in theory and practice. *Language and Communication* **23**: 93–105

Campbell-Kibler, K., Podesva R.J., Roberts, S.J. and Wong, A. (eds) 2002. *Language and Sexuality: Contesting Meaning in Theory and Practice.* Stanford, Calif.: Center for the Study of Language and Information

Carillo, H. 2002. *The Night is Young: Sexuality in Mexico in the Time of AIDS.* Chicago: University of Chicago Press

Coates, J. 2003. *Men Talk: Stories in the Making of Masculinities.* Oxford: Blackwell

Evans, D. 1993. *Sexual Citizenship: the Material Construction of Sexualities.* London: Routledge

Gaudio, R. 1994. Sounding gay: pitch properties in the speech of straight and gay men. *American Speech* **69** (1): 30–57

Gaudio, R. 1997. Not talking straight in Hausa. In Livia, A. and Hall, K. (eds) *Queerly Phrased: Language Gender and Sexuality.* Oxford: Oxford University Press, pp. 416–29

Gaudio, R. 2001. White men do it too: racialized (homo)sexualities in postcolonial Hausaland. *Journal of Linguistic Anthropology* **11** (1): 31–45

Gluckman, A. and Reed, B. (eds) 1997. *Homo Economicus: Capitalism, Community and Lesbian and Gay Life.* New York City: Routledge

Goodwin, M.H. 1980. He-said-she-said: formal cultural procedures for the construction of a gossip dispute activity. *American Ethnologist* **7** (4): 674–95

Grosz, E. 1992. Bodies-Cities. In Colomina, B. (ed.) *Sexuality and Space.* New York: Princeton Architectural Press, pp. 241–53

Hall, K. 1997. 'Go suck your husband's sugarcane!': hijras and the use of sexual insult. In Livia, A. and Hall, K. (eds) *Queerly Phrased: Language Gender and Sexuality.* Oxford: Oxford University Press, pp. 430–60

Halliday, M. 1978. *Language as Social Semiotic: the Social Interpretation of Language and Meaning.* London: Edward Arnold

Hennessy, R. 2000. *Profit and Pleasure.* New York: Routledge

Holmes, J. and Meyerhoff, M. 1999. The Community of Practice: theories and methodologies in language and gender research. *Language in Society* **28** (2): 173–83

Johnson, E.P. 1998. Feeling the spirit in the dark: expanding notions of the sacred in the African American gay community. *Callaloo* **21** (1): 399–416

Johnson, E.P. 2003. *Appropriating Blackness: Performance and the Politics of Authenticity.* Durham: Duke University Press

Khoo, O. 2003. Sexing the city: Malaysia's new 'cyberlaws' and Cyberjaya's queer success. In Berry, C., Martin, F. and Yue, A. (eds) *Mobile Cultures: New Media in Queer Asia.* Durham and London: Duke University Press, pp. 222–44

Kulick, D. 1997. A man in the house: the boyfriends of Brazilian travesti prostitutes. *Social Text* **52–53**: 133–60

Kulick, D. 1998. *Travesti: Sex, Gender and Culture among Brazilian Transgendered Prostitutes*. Chicago: University of Chicago Press

Kulick, D. 2000. Gay and lesbian language. *Annual Review of Anthropology* **29**: 243–85

Kulick, D. 2003. Language and desire. In Holmes, J. and Meyerhoff, M. (eds) *Handbook of Language and Gender*. London: Blackwell, pp. 119–41

Leap, W. 1996. *Word's Out: Gay Men's English*. Minneapolis: University of Minnesota Press

Leap, W. 1997. Performative effect in three gay English texts. In Livia, A. and Hall, K. (eds) *Queerly Phrased: Language, Gender and Sexuality*. Oxford: Oxford University Press, pp. 310–25

Leap, W. 1999. Language, speech and silence in gay adolescence. In Bucholtz, M., Liang, A.C. and Sutton, L. (eds) *Reinventing Identities: the Gendered Self in Discourse*. New York City: Oxford University Press, pp. 259–72

Leap, W. 2002a. Not entirely in support of queer linguistics. In Campbell-Kibler, K., Podesva R.J., Roberts, S.J. and Wong, A. (eds) *Language and Sexuality: Contesting Meaning in Theory and Practice*. Stanford, Calif.: Center for the Study of Language and Information, pp. 45–64

Leap, W. 2002b. Studying lesbian and gay languages: vocabulary, text-making and beyond. In Lewin, E. and Leap, W. (eds) *Out in Theory: the Emergence of Lesbian and Gay Anthropology*. Urbana: University of Illinois Press, pp. 128–54

Leap W. 2003. Language and gendered modernity. In Holmes, J. and Meyerhoff, M. (eds) *Handbook of Language and Gender*. London: Blackwell, pp. 401–22

Leap, W. 2004. Language, belonging and (homo)sexual citizenship in Cape Town, South Africa. In Leap, W. and Boellstorff, T. (eds) 2004. *Speaking in Queer Tongues: Globalization and Gay Language*. Urbana: University of Illinois Press, pp. 134–63

Leap, W. Forthcoming. *Gay City: Language, Sexuality and the Politics of Place in Washington DC*. Minneapolis: University of Minnesota Press

Leap, W. and Boellstorff, T. (eds) 2004. *Speaking in Queer Tongues: Globalization and Gay Language*. Urbana: University of Illinois Press

Lemke, J. 2000. Cognition, context and learning: a social semiotic perspective. http://academic.brooklyn.cuny.edu/jlemke/papers/sit-cog.htm (visited on 12.3.2001)

Livia, A. 1995. 'I ought to throw a Buick at you': fictional representations of Butch/Femme speech. In Hall, K. and Bucholtz, M. (eds) *Gender Articulated: Language and the Socially Constructed Self*. New York: Routledge, pp. 245–78

Livia, A. and Hall, K. (eds) 1997. *Queerly Phrased: Language, Gender and Sexuality*. Oxford: Oxford University Press

McDowell, L. 1999. *Gender, Identity and Place: Understanding Feminist Geographies*. Minneapolis: University of Minnesota Press

Manalansan, M. 1994. Searching for community: gay Filipino men in New York City. *Ameriasia Journal* **20** (1): 59–74

Manalansan, M. 1995. 'Performing' the Filipino gay experiences in America: linguistic strategies in a transnantional context. In Leap, W. (ed.) *Beyond the Lavender Lexicon: Authenticity, Imagination and Appropriation in Lesbian and Gay Languages*. Newark: Gordon and Breach Press, pp. 249–66

Manalansan, M. 2003. *Global Divas: Filipino Gay Men in the Diaspora*. Durham: Duke University Press

Manderson, L. and Jolly, M. (eds) 1997. *Sites of Desire, Economies of Pleasure: Sex in Asia and the Pacific*. Chicago: University of Chicago Press

Moonwomon, B. 1995. Lesbian discourse, lesbian knowledge. In Leap, W. (ed.) *Beyond the Lavender Lexicon: Authenticity, Imagination and Appropriation in Lesbian and Gay Languages*. Newark: Gordon and Breach, pp. 45–64

Moonwomon-Baird, B. 2000. What do lesbians do in the daytime? Recover. *Journal of Sociolinguistics* **4** (3): 348–78

Morrish, L. 2002a. Telling tales: outing the Honorable Gentleman. In Patterson, W. (ed.) *Strategic Narrative: New Perspectives on the Power of Personal and Cultural Storytelling*. Lanham, Md: Lexington Books, pp. 147–63

Morrish, L. 2002b. 'Whenever Peter sees a cock-up, he sits on it'. British Broadsheet Press versus Peter Mandelson, 1996–2001. Paper presented at Two-Day Seminar on Language, Love and Sexuality. Kingston University, UK, 8–9 April

Morrish, L. 2002c. The case of the indefinite pronoun: discourse and the concealment of lesbian identity in class. In Litosseliti, L. and Sunderland, J. (eds) *Gender Identity and Discourse Analysis*. Amsterdam: John Benjamins, pp. 177–92

Morrish, L. and Sauntson, H. Forthcoming. *Language and Sexual Identity*. Basingstoke: Palgrave Macmillan

Parker, R. 1999. *Beneath the Equator: Cultures of Desires, Male Homosexuality, and Emerging Gay Communities in Brazil*. New York City: Routledge

Patton, C. and Sanchez-Eppler, B. (eds) 2000. *Queer Diasporas*. Durham and London: Duke University Press

Podesva, R., Roberts, S. and Campbell-Kibler, K. 2002. Sharing resources and indexing meanings in the production of gay styles. In Campbell-Kibler, K., Podesva R.J., Roberts, S.J. and Wong, A. (eds) *Language and Sexuality: Contesting Meaning in Theory and Practice*. Stanford, Calif.: Center for the Study of Language and Information, pp. 175–90

Pratt, M.L. 1987. Linguistic Utopias. In Fabb, N., Attridge, D. and McCabe, C. (eds) *The Linguistics of Writing: Arguments between Language and Literature*. Manchester: Manchester University Press, pp. 48–66

Probyn, E. 1995. Lesbians in space: gender, sex and the structure of missing. *Gender, Place and Culture* **2**: 77–84

Rasmusen, B, Klinenberg, E., Nexica, I. and Wray, M. (eds) 2003. *The Making and Unmaking of Whiteness*. Durham and London: Duke University Press

Sauntson, H. 2002. Examining lesbian conversations as discourses of resistance. Paper delivered at 9th Annual Conference on Lavender Languages and Linguistics, 15–17 February, American University, Washington, DC

Wenger, E. 1998. *Communities of Practice: Learning, Meaning and Identity*. Cambridge: Cambridge University Press

# 2

# 'Everyone Was Convinced that We Were Closet Fags': the Role of Heterosexuality in the Construction of Hegemonic Masculinity

*Jennifer Coates*

## Introduction

At any given time in a culture, there will be many competing masculinities in play, all available to be discursively reproduced by speakers. But of these competing masculinities, one will predominate. It is this form of masculinity – hegemonic masculinity – that I shall focus on in this chapter.[1] My aim is to explore the role of heterosexuality in the formation of contemporary masculinities in Britain, in particular in the formation of hegemonic masculinity, drawing on a database of spontaneous conversation collected over the last 10 years or so.

The concept of hegemonic masculinity was developed by Robert Connell and his colleagues working in feminist sociology. According to Connell (1995), in order to carry off 'being a man' in everyday life, men have to engage with hegemonic masculinity. 'The concept of "hegemony" [ . . . ] refers to the cultural dynamic by which a group claims and sustains a leading position in social life. At any given time, one form of masculinity rather than others is culturally exalted' (Connell, 1995: 77). Hegemonic masculinity maintains, legitimates and naturalises the interests of powerful men while subordinating the interests of others, notably the interests of women and gay men. This position is not fixed but always contestable: the masculinity occupying the hegemonic position is always open to challenge from alternative masculinities. It is an ideal, a normative construction against which males – whatever their class or ethnic allegiance – are measured and, almost invariably, found wanting (Kimmel, 2000: 91).

Key components of contemporary hegemonic masculinity are hard-ness, toughness, coolness, competitiveness, dominance and control (Connell, 1995; Wetherell and Edley, 1998, 1999; Frosh *et al.*, 2002). Although most men do not fit this ideal, the concept of hegemonic masculinity 'captures the power of the masculine ideal for many boys and men' (Frosh *et al.*, 2002: 76).

One significant way in which hegemonic masculinity is created and maintained is through the denial of femininity. The denial of the feminine is central to masculine gender identity (Segal, 1990: 15; Roper and Tosh, 1991: 13; Connell, 1995: 78; Frosh *et al.*, 2002: 77). As Adam Jukes (1993: 43) puts it: 'the exorcism of all one's identifiable "feminine" or "mothering" qualities is essential to assuming masculinity'. Such norms exert great pressure on males in our culture. Men avoid ways of talking that might be associated with femininity and also actively construct women and gay men as the despised other. In a recent research project involving in-depth interviews with boys in 12 London secondary schools, Stephen Frosh and his colleagues claim that one of the canon-ical narratives about masculinity was that 'boys must maintain their difference from girls (and so avoid doing anything that is seen as what girls do)' (Frosh *et al.*, 2002: 77). Being different from girls is far more important for boys than being different from boys is for girls. In contem-porary Western culture, we all recognise that 'being a sissy is a far more serious offence to the gender order than being a tomboy' (Kimmel, 2000: 235).

Avoidance of the feminine is viewed by psychoanalysts in terms of mother–son relations. As Jessica Benjamin (1990: 76) explains, repudi-ation of the mother results in 'a kind of "fault line" running through the male achievement of individuality'. This fault line is implicated in the 'othering' of women and of gay men. Identity construction involves by definition the construction of out-groups as well as the construction of in-groups. We know who is 'we' because 'we' are 'not them' and 'they' are 'not us'. 'The dual others to normative heterosexual masculin-ities in schools are girls/women and non-macho-boys/men' (Frosh *et al.*, 2002: 62). For adult males, the othering of gay men and the denial of homosexuality are particularly salient. Many researchers believe that hegemonic masculinity and heterosexual masculinity are isomorphic (Herek, 1987; Curry, 1991; Cameron, 1997; Gough and Edwards, 1998). It is certainly the case that, at the beginning of the twenty-first century in westernised cultures, 'heterosexual meanings have come to saturate dominant notions of adult "femininity" and "masculinity"' (Thorne, 1993: 155).

# Data

The conversational data in this chapter were collected as part of a wider research project exploring gender differences in language use in Britain. Participants come from a wide range of geographical locations, including urban contexts, such as Belfast and Birmingham, suburban contexts, such as the Wirral and Surrey, and more rural locations, such as Somerset. They belong to a wide range of class and age groups; the majority are white. The database resulting from this project includes all-male, all-female and mixed talk (Table 2.1).[2] This chapter focuses on the all-male data: 32 all-male conversations, audio-recorded with the men's agreement and subsequently transcribed. Participants in all cases were friends; in other words, recordings were made of groups or pairs of men who had a well-established relationship.

The methodology employed in the wider research project is an innovative form of participant observation: after contact was made with a group, they were asked to take responsibility for recording their conversations.[3] The assumption was made that any self-consciousness induced by the presence of the tape recorder would be overcome by the strong normative pressure which such groups exert over their members (see Milroy, 1987: 35). Participants were simply asked to record themselves when they were with their friends. Male participants recorded themselves in a wide range of settings: in their homes, in pubs, in a university office after hours, in a youth club, even in a garden shed in the case of one group of dope-smoking adolescent boys (and also in unexpected places like men's toilets and walking along the street to the chip shop). The pub was, however, by far the most popular setting for all-male talk, a finding which is not surprising, given that 'the pub seems to be a pivotal site for both the expression and reinforcement of traditional masculinities and gendered consumption' (Willott and Griffin, 1997: 115).

*Table 2.1*   The database

|               | All female    | All male        | Mixed         |
|---------------|---------------|-----------------|---------------|
| Conversations | 22            | 32              | 18            |
| Speakers      | 36            | 48              | 52            |
| Hours of talk | 15 hrs 5 mins | 18 hrs 45 mins  | 12 hrs 0 mins |

## An example

At any given time, according to Connell (1995: 77), one form of masculinity rather than others is *'culturally exalted'*. This is the masculinity he calls hegemonic masculinity and is the ideal against which contemporary British men measure themselves. To illustrate the kind of masculinity that is 'culturally exalted' at this time in Britain, I shall look at a typical man's story from my database. Extract 2.1 is a story told by Rob during conversation with friends in the pub. It is one of a series of stories about the workplace – this one focuses on a colleague who had an alcohol problem. Words in italics are contributions from other speakers.[4]

*Extract 2.1*  The Fight
[*Three lower-middle-class men in their twenties in a pub in Somerset talk about an alcoholic engineer at work*]

1   he came in this one time,

2   drunk,

3   and he started ordering me about.

4   With kind of personality I've got

5   I told him to piss off,

6   I wasn't taking any of it.

7   So I was making these um alarm bell boxes,

8   the alarm boxes,

9   you put this bell on and you wire these-

10   can't remember how to do it now anyway but-

11   wiring these up,

12   and he come out,

13   and he sss, sss, sss, <MIMICS NOISE>

14   what he did was he threw this knife at me,

15   this is honest truth,

16   threw a knife at me,

17  and then- and there was this cable,

18  you know um like on the workbenches where you connect the cables into these three points,

19  a bare wire,

20  he fucking chased me with it,

21  and I thought 'Fuck this',

22  and he kept like having a go and teasing me,

23  and I just smashed him straight round the face with a bell box in front of the boss,

24  crack,

25  got away with it as well,

26  I said 'Look', I said, 'he's thrown knives at me',

27  it sounds like something out of a film but it's honest truth.
    [ . . . ]

28  Honestly it was unbelievable.

'The Fight' is a typical first-person male narrative (see Coates, 2000, 2003). It is typical in that it contains the following features: the story constitutes a boast; the narrator presents himself as a lone protagonist who gets involved in conflict, conflict which involves physical violence; the narrator presents himself as a winner; the story is infused with an awareness of power, both the narrator's physical power in relation to the drunken engineer, and also the boss's institutional power, which means the narrator can boast that he *got away with it* in line 25. Other minor points to note are: all the characters in the narrative are male; the setting is the workplace; the narrator goes into detail about technical things such as alarm boxes and cables; the language used includes taboo words (e.g. *piss off, fucking*) and sound effects (e.g. *sss, crack*).

Rob's story focuses on action and, through his story, he presents himself as a winner, someone who will not be pushed around, someone who stands up for himself, and also as someone who gets away with things. His story foregrounds the workplace as a key arena for action, and the storyworld he creates is populated entirely by men: women do not exist in this world. 'The Fight' narrative is a performance of hegemonic masculinity. By this, I mean that Rob uses his account of his fight with the drunken engineer to align himself with dominant norms of masculinity, norms which are exemplified by characters in films popular in Western cultures such as *Rambo* and *The Terminator*. Stories like 'The Fight' are canonical stories of male achievement. When they are told by male narrators to other men, they perform hegemonic masculinity in two ways: first, they perform hardness, coolness, dominance and control (as I have argued, these are key components of hegemonic masculinity); second, they function to maintain difference from women.

What this story accomplishes unambiguously is saying I AM A MAN. The narrator's heterosexuality is not foregrounded in the story, and in this respect the story is typical of those I have collected. Heterosexuality does not have to be foregrounded; it is an assumed component of hegemonic masculinity. Thus, in stories such as 'The Fight', 'compulsory heterosexuality is taken for granted as the cultural norm' (Frosh *et al.*, 2002: 63).

## Hegemonic masculinity and heterosexuality

I shall now move from canonical stories like 'The Fight' to an examination of stories which throw light more overtly on the links between hegemonic masculinity and heterosexuality. I shall look in turn at the following: homophobic talk and talk about homosexuality; the exclusion of women from men's storyworlds; misogynistic talk; boasting to women; collaborative storytelling.

### Homophobic talk and talk about homosexuality

Hegemonic masculine discourses are both misogynistic and homophobic. Deborah Cameron spells out the norm as follows: 'men in all-male groups must unambiguously display their heterosexual orientation' (Cameron 1997: 61). Younger males in my corpus are openly homophobic at times. Extract 2.2 is a story told by Lee, a male student from an upper-working-class background, to a friend about an evening out with his friend Bill:

*Extract 2.2*   Queerie
[*Two male friends, aged 19/20*]

1   and er night before I left to come here right

2   I um ((xx)) Bill ((xx)),

3  I told you this.

4  I was driving down the road

5  and I've just seen this long hair little fucking miniskirt.

6  I've beeped the horn,

7  this fucking bloke's turned round,

8  I've gone 'aaaggghhh!' <SCREAMS>

9  <LAUGHTER>

10  Bill's gone 'what what what?',

11  'it was a bloke',

12  I've gone, 'turn round, turn round',

13  and he's turned round

14  and you could just see these shoes hiding under this car

15  and he must've thought we were just gonna literally beat the crap out of him.

16  [ . . . ]

17  I've driven past,

18  opened the window,

19  'come out, come out, wherever you are,

20  here queerie, queerie, queerie'.

This story does important work in terms of establishing the narrator's identity: he positions himself as uncompromisingly heterosexual both through his initial interest in the person with long hair wearing a miniskirt, and also through his horrified reaction when he realises this person is actually a man. His fantasy that the cross-dresser feared they would *beat the crap out of him* (line 15) hints at the violent feelings unleashed by this encounter. The story ends with the narrator presenting himself as venting his fury at this subversion of conventional gender boundaries by shouting taunts and insults at the man (whether this actually happened or not is beside the point). This story demonstrates how powerful narrative can be as a tool of self-presentation and self-construction: the narrator is at an age when his sexual identity is still fragile and the function of this story is to establish his credentials as a 'normal' heterosexual man.

Extract 2.3 is from a conversation between two 17-year-old boys at one of Britain's most prestigious public schools. They are discussing another boy called Prendergast. Again, these boys are still working to develop a more solid sense of their own masculinity, and this extract shows them struggling with what that means:

*Extract 2.3*   Talking about Prendergast
[*Henry's study-bedroom at boarding school*]

1   Julian:   Prendergast had tea in Mason's room and threw stuff out of the

2              window

3   Henry:    yeah

4   Julian:   were you there?

5   Henry:    yeah

6   Julian:   was he being a massive twat?

7   Henry:    no not really [ . . . ] you know he was just being normal

8              he was going- he was talking about . being raped by Ralph, yeah?

9   Julian:   yeah

10  Henry:    and he was going on about how he didn't see it- think it was

11             actually that disgusting

12  Julian:   he is gay! <INDIGNANT TONE>

13  Henry:    and then- and then we said { . . . } 'didn't you think it was absolutely

14             disgusting?'. he was sit- he was just sitting there like not answering,

15             he was just sort of avoiding the question

This discussion of an absent third person allows them to explore their attitude to homosexuality. Homosexuality is a live topic in British public schools, as it is in all all-male institutions, such as the army and men's prisons. With no women in this social world, and with the dominant discourses insisting that males are biologically programmed to 'need' sexual gratification (Hollway, 1983), the taboos against homosexuality have to be very strong, and in such institutions 'compulsory hetero-sexuality' (Rich, 1980) is rigidly affirmed. The specialised language of such institutions is very revealing: the slang of an in-group is a powerful homosocial bonding mechanism and areas of 'lexical density' centre on women, sexual activity, homosexuality and race. The misogyny, racism and homophobia of such groups can literally be measured by the enormous numbers of pejorative words coined in these areas (see Moore, 1993; Looser, 1997).

In this extract, Henry seems prepared to explore what it means to be *raped*,[5] and to mull over Prendergast's claim that this experience was not necessarily disgusting. Julian, however, is quick to say *he is gay* (line 12). What this statement asserts is that, if someone describes a sexual encounter with someone of the same sex as not *disgusting* (line 11), they must be homosexual. This is a defensive move, and shows Julian's anxiety to close down discussion. He wants to draw a clear line between people who are gay and who consider same-sex activity to be not disgusting, and 'normal' people who *do* consider same-sex activity to be disgusting. Henry's story threatens to breach that neat dichotomy, since Prendergast appears to be a 'normal' boy like Julian and Henry and yet he seems to be saying that his sexual encounter with Ralph was just 'an experience'. Henry's response to Julian's outrage is noticeably disfluent: he in turn feels threatened and he has to re-establish his credentials as a member of the 'normal' camp. He does this by claiming that he and his friends had asked *didn't you think it was absolutely disgusting?* (lines 13–14), a question marked for positive polarity in that it presupposes that it was *absolutely disgusting*.

But despite Julian's strong reaction here, other parts of this conver-sation between these two friends, Julian and Henry, reveal a persistent homo-erotic theme. For example, before Henry embarks on the story about Prendergast, a remark of Julian's casts light on the way the two boys are sitting in Henry's study-bedroom.

*Extract 2.4*  Talk preceding Talking about Prendergast
1  Julian:  ow ow like. OK the neck massage is great
             [*Henry laughs quietly*]

2           but not when done by your feet [*Henry laughs*]

3   Julian:   ng ng ng . . . )

4   Henry:    ng ng ng . . . ) *[both boys mimic the sound of an*
                                *electric guitar]*

To judge from Julian's words, Henry has his feet on Julian's neck while
they talk. The evidence that they are both relaxed about this physical
contact is provided by their making those noises so typical of teenage
boys, sounds imitating an electric guitar solo (made, presumably, while
they pretend to play a guitar).

Later in the same conversation, Julian actually steers the talk round
to a time in the past when they were suspected of being *fags* (i.e. homosexuals).

Extract 2.5   Closet Fags

1   Julian:   I'd- I'd forgotten about that little. episode in M
              when everybody

2             was convinced that we were closet fags

3   Henry:    um that- but that- ((I mean)) that just- that ((was))-
              that's finished

4   Julian:   that was just cos every second minute I was . popping
              along to

5             your room [ . . . ] yeah it's also like the way- you
              know it's what

6             Robert dines off is the fact that .hh Lynch
              climbing into your bed

7             and like no insult but I really couldn't **climb into
              your bed in the

8             morning**

9   Henry:    **yeah that- that was fairly** that was unfortunate I agree

10  Julian:   I really couldn't climb into your bed in the morning

11  Henry:    <LAUGHS>

12  Julian:   I'm sorry, it would have to be very cold

13  Henry:    <LAUGHS> yeah that was unfortunate, does he still
              go on about

14          that?

15  Julian:  yes <BORED DRAWL>

16  Henry:   really?

17  Julian:  yes <BORED DRAWL>

18  Henry:   %god%

[NB: utterances appearing between asterisks ** were spoken at the same time]

This chunk of talk does very important work in negotiating their relationship. They establish that they are not *closet fags*, even though people thought they were. They look at why people made this assumption, and also consider the problems caused for Henry by Lynch's escapade, which according to Julian is still a topic of conversation. Julian's light-hearted banter about why he chooses not to get into bed with Henry in the morning suggests that while it is important for him to state that this is *not* what he wants to do, he still chooses to talk about what he would not do, and to say it twice. He even jokes *I'm sorry, it would have to be very cold* (line 12), implying that in certain circumstances he *would* get into bed with Henry.

For younger speakers, the work of asserting their heterosexuality, that is, of asserting non-homosexuality, is an important part of their everyday construction of themselves as men. These few examples show that this can vary from virulent homophobia (as in Extract 2.2) to more relaxed discussion and negotiation of sexual identity (as in Extract 2.5). In all these examples the dominance of heterosexual masculinity is apparent, as is the tension between heterosocial and homosocial norms.

## Exclusion of women from the storyworld

Another aspect of men's talk that I want to look at is the virtual exclusion of women from the storyworld of men's stories. In both women's and men's storyworlds, the most common character is the narrator themselves. In other words, first-person narratives are the preferred form for all speakers. In relaxed circumstances, we tend to tell stories about ourselves more than we tell stories about significant others (in my database, first-person narratives constitute 72 per cent of women's narratives and 68 per cent of men's). This suggests that women's storyworlds will have a bias to female characters and men's to male characters. But nearly all stories involve other characters beside the protagonist, and

*Table 2.2* Gender of characters in stories told in all-male and all-female conversation

| Gender of characters | Men's stories (%) | Women's stories (%) |
| --- | --- | --- |
| All characters are male | 72 | 1.5 |
| All characters are female | 1.5 | 10 |
| Characters are both male and female | 26.5 | 88 |

third-person stories focus on a character who is not the narrator (even though the narrator may be a participant in the events narrated). In other words, there is plenty of scope even in first-person narratives to portray a world which contains both men and women.

But as we have seen in earlier examples, men's stories often involve no women. The story 'The Fight', discussed above, is a good illustration of this. The main character is the first-person narrator who tells a story about a fight with a (male) workmate, a fight witnessed by the (male) boss. There are no women in this storyworld. Overall, only 28 per cent of the men's stories include women, as Table 2.2 illustrates. This contrasts with the storyworld typical of female narrators, where men are more often present than not (88% of stories in the all-female conversations involve both men and women).

The exclusion of women from the storyworld of men's stories is a disturbing aspect of all-male narrative. These narratives do important ideological work, maintaining a discourse position where men are all-important and women are invisible. This seems to be another aspect of the denial of the feminine.

## Misogynistic talk

It is generally assumed that one of the topics of all-male talk is women, and that much of this talk is misogynistic. In this section, I shall examine two explicitly misogynistic stories from my database, but it is important to note that the conversations I collected contain relatively little miso-gynistic material compared with those collected by male researchers for a variety of research projects. These research projects involved men talking in the 'locker room' before and after sporting events, boys talking about sex, men meeting for a drink and a chat, and men talking about drink and violence (see Wood, 1984; Curry, 1991; Gough and Edwards, 1998; Tomsen, 1997). Much of this material is more sexist and homo-phobic than anything I have collected. For example, the men's talk in my database does not involve explicit talk about male genitalia (Gough and Edwards, 1998), sustained talk about women in terms of body parts (Wood, 1984; Gough and Edwards, 1998), or fantasies about rape (Wood, 1984; Curry, 1991). This might mean that male speakers censor themselves unconsciously when the researcher is female. On the other hand, it could suggest that men are more constrained by hegemonic norms when designing their talk for the ears of a male researcher. Certainly, the more 'macho' elements of hegemonic masculinity are more in evidence in data collected by male researchers, just as they are more in evidence in my data in the all-male conversations than in the mixed conversations.

The two stories I shall focus on here come from the subset of stories told by men which actually include women as characters. I have argued that in conversation men and boys avoid ways of talking that might be associated with femininity, and also actively construct women as well as gay men as the despised other. Misogyny certainly seems to inform men's portrayal of women in some of the stories where women *do* appear.

*Extract 2.6*   This Girl Called Debbie
[*Two male friends aged 19/20, upper working class, narrator = Lee*]

1   I know this girl called Debbie

2   well I used to know her

3   and er-

4   *why did you stop knowing her?*

5   dickhead <LAUGHTER>

6   anyway first time I met her I was sitting in someone's garden having a joint with this bird with my legs like that

7   having a chat with her

8   and suddenly I just felt this like warmth all over my leg

9   I've looked round and she's-

10   no joke I swear to god she had her fucking tits hanging over my leg

11   I just went 'ooh' like that

12   and this girl's just gone.

*Extract 2.7*  The Vibrator
[*Seven male friends aged mid-twenties, lower middle class, narrator = Gary*]

1   I went to this customer's house the other day with um-

2   I was told to go there basically by um the corporate sales director for the Dixon's Stores group [*yeah*]

3   he phoned me up and he said 'You've got to go to this customer

4   cos she's been like trying to write letters to Sidney Smith [*the Managing Director*] and stuff like this [*yeah*]

5   so I get round there and there's like nothing wrong with her computer at all

6   whinging bitch

7   it was quite funny when I was walking out though

8   cos I was walking out-

9   the computer's in her bedroom

10   I was just sort of looking around

11   looked down on the floor under her bedri- bedside cabinet

12   and there was this fucking great vibrator

13   <LAUGHTER>

14   I sort of looked at her and she looked at me and she was like 'oh fuck'

15   <LAUGHTER>

16   *it's not the sort of thing you leave about when you got the engineers coming to do the PC is it?*

17   she had kids as well though

18   fucking kids walking around

19   bloody great vibrator with a sucking cap on the end of it

20   *was she very nice looking?*

21   no she's a big fat pig [*oh*].

Both these stories function as boasts and perform hegemonic masculinity of which heterosexuality is an essential component. Both stories are first-person narratives, and both storyworlds include a female character. But in both the woman is presented in sexual terms. In 'This Girl Called Debbie', the eponymous Debbie is hardly a rounded person: the point of the story is that the narrator felt her breasts on his leg. For the narrator and his friend, it seems that the recounting of such an event is regarded as tellable: it tells us a lot about the internal world of the young men that their sense of their own masculinity depends on their claiming of such encounters. It does not seem to matter what the woman Debbie was like as a person, since what matters in Lee's construction of himself as a heterosexual male is this contact with part of a woman's body. The reduction of women to body parts is a well-documented phenomenon which objectifies women and strips them of human status (see Haywood and Mac an Ghaill, 1997; Gough and Edwards, 1998; Renold, 2000).

In Extract 2.7, 'The Vibrator', the narrator is more sophisticated in his self-presentation. He presents himself as a reliable employee (who carries out promptly the orders of an important senior male) and as a responsible citizen upholding moral standards (line 17: *she had kids as well though, fucking kids walking around*). However, he simultaneously presents himself as a patriarchal male who treats women with contempt with his backstage comments *whinging bitch* and *a big fat pig*, and as a sophisticated, sexually experienced man who knows about vibrators. This complex self-presentation performs masculinity on many levels. But yet again, the woman in the story is unimportant as a person: she is presented in stereotypical terms as a technically incompetent complaining customer – *whinging bitch* – and as a sexual being. While the narrator's attitude to her sexuality is one of disapproval, what matters is that he consigns her to this sexual pigeonhole.

When women are not defined in sexual terms, they tend to be peripheral characters in men's stories, appearing most commonly as wives or mothers. While such references to women are not explicitly misogynistic, they hint at an underlying androcentric world view where women are of little importance. A good example is the following brief extract from the story 'The Good Samaritan':

*Extract 2.8* The Good Samaritan

1  we walked round this boulder

2  and there sitting on the top . was a European couple

3  with their backs to us,

4   as they heard us approach they turned round,

5   and lo it was my Vice Chancellor and his wife.

The point of this subsection of the story is the unexpected meeting between the narrator – a linguistics lecturer – and his Vice Chancellor. The Vice Chancellor's wife is an incidental character. Another example comes in the story 'Strap 'er on':

*Extract 2.9*   Strap 'er on
1   this bloke called Phil at work

2   lives in Taunton

3   [...]

4   and he calls his Mum our Gladys

The reference to the mother is included because the narrator is building up a picture of his strange colleague, Phil: the mother is not a character in the story in any proper sense. The world depicted by the narrator, where Phil behaves in a crazy way, is peopled by men apart from this fleeting reference.

### Boasts in front of women

My database contains all-female and mixed talk as well as all-male talk. I shall now turn to the mixed conversations in my database, that is, to conversations where men and women are talking to each other. I want to show how men's stories in mixed talk function as a form of heterosexual display.

The first example is an extract from a long story and is part of the story's opening. The story is told by Tony to his friend Emily – they are both in their early twenties.

*Extract 2.10*   The Fire Alarm
1   have I told you that story about um . me on cricket tour? [*no*]

2   got no relation to what I've been saying but- [*E LAUGHS*]

3   no, I'll tell you anyway.

4   this must've been when we were about thirteen

5    and we stayed at this really posh school

6    it was in the summer holidays

7    cos it was like the cricket season obviously <LAUGHS>

8    and um- and we're all like in a corridor

9    [...]

10   and um- and we're just like pissing about in the corridor playing cricket

11   [...]

12   I've bowled this ball

13   and it's hit the top of this chair which we used as a wicket

14   and it's gone-

15   it's only a tennis ball

16   and it's hit like . the main alarm [*E LAUGHS oh dear*]

17   and it's evacuated the-

18   I'm not joking

19   must be about a hundred and fifty people in this building [*E LAUGHS*]

20   and um . this is like two in the morning [*bloody hell*]

This story is clearly a boast, just like 'The Fight' (Extract 2.1). The difference is that in all-male talk, stories are often boasts, but the narrators are overtly competing with each other to tell the best story; they use storytelling as a way of jockeying for position. But in a story such as 'The Fire Alarm', the male narrator is not competing with his female friend in terms of individual prowess. Tony does not expect Emily to respond with a storytelling of her own sporting achievements. Tony tells his story to impress Emily and to be indulged by her.

Men's assumption that women will indulge them and listen to their stories of youthful escapades is borne out in this particular conversation. The conversation contains a total of 20 narratives. Of these, 15 are told by Tony, four by Emily, and one is a joint effort. Not only does Tony dominate the conversation in terms of narrative, he uses these

narrative opportunities to construct a dominant form of masculinity and is supported in doing this by Emily.

Extract 2.11 is a story from a different type of conversation, one involving a middle-aged lecturer (Michael), his female partner (Suzanne) and a close male friend (Bill) during a meal at Michael and Suzanne's house in Islington. This story is also a boast; it emerges from general conversation about wine and wine-drinking. Extract 2.11 is from the opening of the story. Michael's words are printed in normal font; Suzanne's in *ITALIC CAPITALS*; Bill's in *italics*. The storyteller is Michael.

*Extract 2.11*   Buying Wine in Cornwall

1   funnily enough we went to an inn in Cornwall

2   which had a most impressive display of . wine bottles on the wall [*mhm, MHM*]

3   um . well you may see Bill after you've finished

4   and um .

5   *these were empty bottles*

6   no no, they were full I mean

7   and they had a- a-

8   and- and . it was recommended as a place to eat by various guidebooks

9   so we had a meal there

10   and got chatting to the owner

11   cos I thought his wine was very good

12   and very reasonable- very reasonably priced [*yes*]

13   and so well we have a list

14   so er -

15   [ . . . ]

16   paradoxically . I- I've ordered um four cases of wine from Cornwall

While this narrative displays the emotional restraint typically associated with well-educated middle-aged men (Seidler, 1989: 63;

Jackson, 1990: 156; Pleck, 1995), it is still in essence a boast. The narrator/protagonist presents himself as someone who cleverly spots that a Cornish innkeeper has a good palate and orders four cases of wine from him. This is a narrative of achievement, but achievement in a social context where being a hero is acted out in terms of wine connoisseurship rather than engagement in physical contest with another man (as in 'The Fight').

After Michael has finished his narrative, Bill tells a minimal narrative about wine-buying which aligns him very positively with Michael's point of view and performs solidarity between the two men. It also functions to position him as another wine connoisseur. Extract 2.12 gives Bill's story and Michael's response to it. Bill's words are in *italics*; Michael's in normal font.

*Extract 2.12*  Oddbins in Upper Street

1   *well I went to the Oddbins in Upper Street to get the bottle that I brought*

2   *I wasn't wildly impressed with what they had there* [no, it's um-]

3   *they're trying too hard in too many directions*

4   yeah, ((that's)) my sense

5   you see whereas with this chap [in Cornwall] he just- . he buys what he likes

6   [ . . . ]

7   I thought we'll . see if his palate is as extensively good as-

8   it was certainly good on the Chablis and- and on Côtes du Rhône

9   so I was thinking well- if it extends across the range

10  I'll put you on the mailing list

The chief recipient of the story 'Buying Wine in Cornwall' is, at first glance, a male. But a better analysis of Extracts 2.11 and 2.12 is to see them as a performance of masculinity by two male friends to a female audience. These two examples show how complex recipient design can be, with the primary narrator – recipient duo (Michael and Bill) being attended to in turn by another recipient, Michael's partner. The fact that the primary duo consists of male speakers, while the secondary recipient is female, is highly salient to the narrative's design. Suzanne, apart from helping to clarify a particular point in Michael's story (not shown in Extract 2.11), does not make any contribution to the narrative, but her silent presence is vital to our understanding of what Michael and Bill are doing, which is in essence a form of hegemonically masculine (heterosexual) display (see Dunbar, 1996). So in Extracts 2.10, 2.11 and 2.12, men and women collude in the construction of hegemonic masculinity and in the maintenance of conventional heteronormative gender relations.

## Collaborative storytelling

I have argued that telling stories to a female audience allows these British men to indulge in a form of heterosexual display. But telling stories in mixed company also allows the men to discuss topics which they avoid in all-male talk – topics such as death, fear, concern for small animals. Even more striking, it allows the men to tell stories collaboratively. This is something that occurs only rarely in all-male talk, though it is common in all-female talk. Collaborative storytelling is symbolic of closeness and connection – it is presumably avoided by men in talk with other men because displaying closeness with another male is dangerous and could be construed as 'gay'.[6]

But in mixed talk involving heterosexual couples, men and women share in the telling of stories. I'm going to focus on two examples which occur in sequence. They come from a conversation involving two couples, Diane and Ian, and Jean and Martin. What is remarkable about this sequence of two stories is that both stories are collaboratively constructed, with Jean and Martin telling the first and Diane and Ian telling the second. Jean's words are in normal typeface, Martin's in *italics*.

   *Extract 2.13*   Kittens 1
1   we looked out of our window today

2   we saw two little kittens didn't we?

3   | I thought 'what the hell is that doing out there'

4   | *dashing past the window yeah, tiny*

5   **cos I thought i- it was too young to be out

6   one of them was like that

7   just chucked in the garden**

8   ***only one of them that big and one was just a little bit bigger there***

9   *it just- they had the-* \*\*

10  I thought   |'((xxxxxxxxxxx))'

11               |*chasing each other round the garden*

12  I knocked next door,

13  I said 'have you got two new kittens?',

14  and he said 'yeah',

15  and I said 'Have they escaped or something or what?',

16  'They're alright as long as they don't go that way',

17  like pointing to the road,

18  I thought well can't really guarantee that really can you?

19  *no the road is a- it's a busy road.*

Jean and Martin's story is followed directly by another one, told by Ian and Diane, again on the subject of kittens. The story is initiated by Ian, who makes the topical link with the first story, but Diane provides the second line, and from then on they construct the story collaboratively, with occasional contributions from Jean and Martin. Extract 2.14 is from this (longer) story. 'Jazz' is Ian and Diane's cat. Ian's contributions are in normal typeface; Diane's in *italics*; Jean's in *ITALIC CAPITALS*.

**Extract 2.14**   Kittens 2

1  it's like that stupid bat who lived next door to me in . Allen Close

2  *she had a cat that could*   |*never have been more than five weeks old*

3                       |she- she had a . ((little)) cat that big

4  *no way maybe even four weeks old*

5  like that

6  *NOT WITH THE MOTHER?* [no] *OH THAT'S AWFUL*

7  ((there)) there and sh- she put it out for the day

8  |((xxxxxxxxxxxxxxxx))

9  |*((put it out there))*

10  *and Jazz used to bring it home*

11   |she just put it out

12   |and it is so tiny

13   *it couldn't even get through the cat flap*

14   it couldn't   |reach up into the cat flap

15                    |that's how . tiny he was

16   [ . . . ]

17   *he was completely black and just absolutely . adorable wasn't he?*

18   and on one day 'bug doosh' <SOUND EFFECT>

19   through there   |in the catflap ((2 words))

20                    |and one day he actually got through

21   *and i- he was- he was hanging through the catflap with his little paws dangling*

22   |he was like <RUNNING NOISE>

23   |but . he couldn't get the rest of his body through

24   and he got through the cat flap

25   and that was it

26   he used to come   |in and out and then out

27                        |they went up and down the stairs

28   |they w- it didn't want to go

29   |we used to feed him and everything

30   and she used to put it out all day like

31   I mean this thing was like . just could not survive

32   *I used to get in from work and ((take it from)) the door and feed him and everything*

'Kittens 2' is a classic example of collaborative narration. The story is co-narrated by two speakers who share the floor to give an account of a shared experience, using repetition of words and phrases and simultaneous speech to tie their contributions together.

Extract 2.14, like 2.13, shows that male speakers can perform alternative versions of masculinity in certain contexts. Ian and Martin both choose to collaborate in narratives where the topic is kittens and where key themes are care and concern about vulnerable creatures. Such themes are not characteristic of narratives produced in all-male talk. What seems to be crucial about the circumstances of this conversation is that both men (Ian and Martin) are in stable partnerships with women, and the four speakers are also friends with each other.

But if we examine Ian and Diane's contributions to 'Kittens 2' carefully, we can see that as co-narrators they still take up conventional heteronormative gender positions relative to each other. Diane's contributions draw on a nurturing or maternal discourse; examples are *Jazz used to bring it home* (line 10), *we used to feed him and everything* (line 29), *I used to get in from work and ((take it from)) the door and feed him and everything* (line 32). They also pay attention to the kitten's adorability and smallness: *he was [..] just absolutely adorable wasn't he?* (line 17), *that's how tiny he was* (line 15), *with his little paws dangling* (line 21). Ian contributes more narrative clauses than Diane (compare lines 11 and 12 where Ian's narrative clause *she just put it out* is said at the same time as Diane's evaluative line *and it is so tiny*). Ian's contributions focus more on the kitten achieving its goals: *and within the week he learned how to get there* (from the omitted central section); *and he got through the cat flap and that was it* (lines 24–5). So Ian and Diane simultaneously perform coupledom through collaborating in storytelling and also maintain gender distinctions through subtle differences in the perspectives they adopt as co-narrators.

Another point here is: why is it that men *only* co-construct stories in mixed talk with female speakers? The mixed conversations are full of collaborative narration, involving heterosexual couples, fathers and daughters, mothers and male family members, as well as mothers and daughters, sisters, female friends. But there are no examples in the mixed conversations of men collaborating with other men to tell a narrative. Why should men avoid collaborative talk in the company of male peers and in mixed company? Is it the case that, given the homophobia which is an integral part of hegemonic masculinity, men avoid ways of talking which display closeness with men for fear of being accused of being gay? And in mixed talk do men choose to co-construct talk with a female partner to display their non-gayness? In other words, the phenomenon of men co-narrating stories with a female partner confirms that heterosexuality is at the heart of dominant versions of masculinity. When male speakers co-narrate a story with a woman partner, they are performing heterosexual coupledom and so are also by definition performing hegemonic masculinity.

## Conclusions

In this chapter, I have explored the links between heterosexuality and hegemonic masculinity in a contemporary British cultural context. I have used examples from a database of spontaneous conversation to illustrate the form of masculinity which is culturally exalted at this point in history in Britain, and to demonstrate that this hegemonic form is unambiguously heterosexual.

The last ten years have seen a huge outpouring of books focusing on masculinity. These books are the result of work in a wide range of disciplines: sociology, anthropology, psychology, media studies, literary criticism. But whatever their disciplinary framework, many of these analyses have conflated gender and sexuality without question. This is because heterosexuality is an intrinsic component of the dominant ideology of gender. 'This ideology holds that real men axiomatically desire women, and true women want men to desire them. Hence, if you are not heterosexual you cannot be a real man or a true woman [ . . . ]' (Cameron and Kulick, 2003: 6–7). But this link between sexuality and gender – between sexuality and masculinities and femininities – is too often overlooked. It is one of the aims of this chapter, and indeed this book, to flag up this link and to argue that the analysis of gender entails an analysis of sexuality.

This chapter has focused on hegemonic masculinity, but it is important to remember that the hegemonic position is only one among many competing masculinities; it is always contestable. One of the issues exposed by this chapter is the constant tension between hegemonic, heterosexual masculinity and the subversiveness of non-heterosexual alternatives. 'Homosexual desire', as Connell (1995: 58) puts it, '[ . . . ] is certainly a bodily fact, and one that disrupts hege-monic masculinity.' Lynne Segal (1990: 137) has argued that the stability of contemporary heterosexual masculinity depends on the obsessive denunciation of homosexuality. While homophobia has a huge impact on gay experience, it also structures the experience and identities of heterosexuals, since heterosexual men live in fear of being 'perceived as unmanly, effeminate or worst of all gay' (Kimmel, 2000: 239). It is for this reason that we see British men in their everyday talk striving to align themselves with the culturally dominant heterosocial norms as part of their performances of themselves as men.

# Notes

1. This chapter is based on the keynote lecture I gave at the conference 'Love is a many splendoured thing: language, love and sexuality' held at Kingston University in April 2002. I subsequently gave a revised version of the paper at the 10th Lavender Languages and Linguistics Conference at American University, Washington, DC in February 2003. I am grateful to participants at these two conferences for helpful feedback. I am indebted to Margaret Gottschalk, Kira Hall, and the editors of this volume for comments on this written version of the paper. I would also like to acknowledge the support of the following grant-giving bodies who made my research into men's narratives possible: the British Academy (small grant); the Arts and Humanities Research Board (research leave); the English Department, Roehampton University (study leave).

2. I am enormously grateful to all those who agreed to allow their conversations to be used in this project. All names have been changed. Some of the recordings were made initially by other researchers, including students taking my Conversational Narrative course at Roehampton. I would like to put on record my gratitude to the following for giving me access to these recordings: Alex Bean, Keith Brown, Noni Geleit, Jacqueline Huett, Emma Ogden-Hooper, Janis Pringle, Andrew Rosta, Karl Stuart, Mark Wildsmith, John Wilson.

3. I started using this methodology in 1985. Other sociolinguists who have collected conversational data using a similar approach are Rampton (1995) and Wilson (1989).

4. Transcripts of narratives are presented in numbered lines, each line corresponding to one of the narrator's breath-groups or intonation units, typically a grammatical phrase or clause (Chafe, 1980).

5. The boys' use of the word 'rape' is problematic: there is no way of knowing exactly what had taken place between 'Ralph' and 'Prendergast', but frequent listening to this passage on the tape suggests to me that the word does not have the same (extremely negative) meaning as it would have in, for example, a feminist context. The word 'rape' here does not seem to mean that any physical violation has taken place. Henry's choice of this word may be influenced simply by his wish to imply that Prendergast had not *chosen* to take part in this sexual encounter.

6. Interestingly, Deborah Cameron (1997) looks at an example of all-male talk that does display collaborative features, but she shows how it is simultaneously competitive (two of the men dominate discussion), and the predominant topic of conversation is non-present students who are despised for being 'gay'. In other words, her example of collaborative talk involving men is explicitly homophobic, so the males involved need not fear being accused of homosexual tendencies.

# References

Benjamin, J. 1990. *The Bonds of Love*. London: Virago

Cameron, D. 1997. Performing gender identity: young men's talk and the construction of heterosexual masculinity. In Johnson, S. and Meinhof, U.H. (eds) *Language and Masculinity*. Oxford: Blackwell, pp. 47–64

Cameron, D. and Kulick, D. 2003. *Language and Sexuality*. Cambridge: Cambridge University Press

Chafe, W. 1980. The deployment of consciousness in the production of narrative. In Chafe, W. (ed.) *The Pear Stories: Cognitive, Cultural and Linguistic Aspects of Narrative Production*. Norwood NJ: Ablex, pp. 9–50

Coates, J. 2000. 'So I thought "Bollocks to it" ': men, stories and masculinities. In Holmes, J. (ed.) *Gendered Speech in Social Context*. Wellington, NZ: Victoria University Press, pp. 11–38

Coates, J. 2003. *Men Talk: Stories in the Making of Masculinities*. Oxford: Blackwell

Connell, R.W. 1995. *Masculinities*. Cambridge: Polity Press

Curry, T. 1991. Fraternal bonding in the locker room: a pro-feminist analysis of talk about competition and women. *Sociology of Sport Journal* 8: 119–35

Dunbar, R. 1996. *Grooming, Gossip and the Evolution of Language*. London: Faber and Faber

Frosh, S., Phoenix, A. and Pattman, R. 2002. *Young Masculinities*. Basingstoke: Palgrave

Gough, B. and Edwards, G. 1998. The beer talking: four lads, a carry out and the reproduction of masculinities. *The Sociological Review* 46 (3): 409–35

Haywood, C. and Mac an Ghaill, M. 1997. 'A man in the making': sexual masculinities within changing training cultures. *The Sociological Review* 45 (4): 576–90

Herek, G.M. 1987. On heterosexual masculinity: some psychical consequences of the social construction of gender and sexuality. In Kimmel, M.S. (ed.) *Changing Men: New Directions in Research on Men and Masculinity*. London: Sage, pp. 68–82

Hollway, W. 1983. Heterosexual sex: power and desire for the other. In Cartledge, S. and Ryan, J. (eds) *Sex and Love: New Thoughts on Old Contradictions*. London: Women's Press, pp. 124–40

Jackson, D. 1990. *Unmasking Masculinity*. London: Unwin Hyman

Jukes, A. 1993. *Why Men Hate Women*. London: Free Association Books

Kimmel, M.S. 2000. *The Gendered Society*. Oxford: Oxford University Press

Looser, D. 1997. Bonds and barriers: a study of language in a New Zealand prison. *The New Zealand English Journal* 11: 46–54

Milroy, L. 1987. *Observing and Analysing Natural Language*. Oxford: Blackwell

Moore, B. 1993. *A Lexicon of Cadet Language*. Canberra: Australian National Dictionary Centre

Pleck, J. 1995. Men's power with women, other men, and society: a men's movement analysis. In Kimmel, M.S. and Messner M.A. (eds) *Men's Lives* (3rd edn). Boston: Allyn & Bacon, pp. 5–12

Rampton, B. 1995. *Crossing: Language and Ethnicity among Adolescents*. London: Longman

Renold, E. 2000. 'Coming out': gender, (hetero)sexuality and the primary school. *Gender and Education* 12: 309–26

Rich, A. 1980. Compulsory heterosexuality and lesbian existence. *Signs: Journal of Women in Culture and Society* 5: 631–60

Roper, M. and Tosh, J. 1991. Introduction. In Roper, M. and Tosh, J. (eds) *Manful Assertions: Masculinities in Britain since 1800*. London: Routledge, pp. 1–19

Segal, L. 1990. *Slow Motion: Changing Masculinities, Changing Men*. London: Virago

Seidler, V. 1989. *Rediscovering Masculinity: Reason, Language and Sexuality*. London: Routledge

Thorne, B. 1993. *Gender Play: Girls and Boys in School*. Buckingham: Open University Press

Tomsen, S. 1997. A top night: social protest, masculinity and the culture of drinking violence. *British Journal of Criminology* **37** (1): 90–102

Wetherell, M. and Edley, N. 1998. Gender practices: steps in the analysis of men and masculinities. In Henwood, K., Griffiths, C. and Phoenix, A. (eds) *Standpoints and Differences: Essays in the Practice of Feminist Psychology.* London: Sage, pp. 157–73

Wetherell, M. and Edley, N. 1999. Negotiating hegemonic masculinity: imaginary positions and psycho-discursive practices. *Feminism and Psychology* **9** (3): 335–56

Willott, S. and Griffin, C. 1997. 'Wham bam, am I a man?': unemployed men talk about masculinities. *Feminism and Psychology* **7** (1): 107–28

Wilson, J. 1989. *On the Boundaries of Conversation.* Oxford: Pergamon Press

Wood, J. 1984. Groping towards sexism: boys' sex talk. In McRobbie, A. and Nava, M. (eds) *Gender and Generation.* London: Macmillan, pp. 54–84

# 3
# 'This Sex Thing Is such a Big Issue now': Sex Talk and Identities in Three Groups of Adolescent Girls

*Pia Pichler*

## Introduction

In this chapter, I shall demonstrate that the sex talk of adolescent girls can constitute a rich resource for the discursive construction of identities that transcend sexuality and highlight the complex interplay between gender, ethnicity and social class. I will present results from a study analysing informal talk about a wide spectrum of sexual experience from three friendship groups of British girls from different ethnic, cultural and socio-economic backgrounds. My linguistic analysis of the girls' talk has a twofold aim. Firstly, it examines the construction of heterosexuality from a cross-cultural perspective, combining foci on both local and extralocal dimensions of identity.[1] Secondly, it seeks to investigate sex and sexuality in relation to gender norms and practices and, therefore, shows how the girls in my study use their sex talk not only to identify as heterosexual or to signal varying degrees of sexual experience, but also to carry out important gender work. In fact, even talk about desire, which, according to Kulick (2000: 270), 'makes sexuality sexuality' is used by the Bangladeshi and white/mixed British girls in my study to position themselves in relation to dominant discourses about gender from their respective sociocultural backgrounds.[2] Although Kulick (2000: 270) warns that research should not 'vaporize sexuality into gender', Kulick's more recent collaboration with Cameron (2003) acknowledges the strong link between sexuality and gender. Cameron and Kulick (2003: 142) argue that 'while gender does not subsume sexuality, it is clear that no absolute separation between them is possible. An investigation of either will involve the other as well. Whenever sexuality is

68

at issue, gender is also at issue – and, importantly, vice versa.' For the purpose of this chapter, I shall maintain a conceptual differentiation between sexuality and gender, however, my data strongly suggest that it is neither possible nor desirable to exclude gender and identity from a discussion on sex and sexuality (see also Morrish and Leap, Ch. 1 this volume).

I shall first give a brief overview of previous research on girls' sexuality, followed by a section on my methodological approach, including information on participants, data collection, transcription and analytic frameworks. Before analysing several conversational extracts, I discuss a range of explanations for the different types of sex talk apparent in the three groups of girls I studied. I propose that the girls use their sex talk as a resource for renegotiating sociocultural norms that influence their construction of (hetero)sexual and gender identities and I develop this argument in the remainder of the chapter.

## Previous research on girls' sexuality

Previous research on adolescent female sexuality has largely focused on girls' disempowerment. Lees's (1993) ethnographic study of 15–16-year-old London girls in the 1980s found that girls felt that it was important to preserve their sexual reputation, but on the other hand they also felt pressured by their peers into finding a boyfriend. In her interviews, Lees discovered that the girls had adopted a discourse that stigmatises active female sexuality, a finding that appears to be supported by Hollway's (1995: 87) argument that 'there is no emancipatory discourse of women's heterosexual desire'. However, the presentation of women as sexually repressed has been challenged in more recent research. Segal (1997: 81) admits that many young women still feel pressured into having (heterosexual) sex, but opposes the equation of female sexuality with passivity, highlighting the 'diversity and fluidities of heterosexual experiences'. Evidence of young women's efforts to construct themselves as agents when talking about their sexual experiences can be found in the recent sociological studies of Frith and Kitzinger (1998), and Jackson and Cram (2003). Both studies acknowledge the importance of treating interview data not only as 'a transparent window on to people's beliefs and behaviours' (Frith and Kitzinger, 1998: 317), but as a resource for the interviewees to construct their identities.

My own study also views the sex talk of young women as a resource to construct identities for themselves. However, in contrast to the above studies, I do not elicit the girls' views on sex(uality) in interviews, but study extracts of spontaneous talk in which the girls addressed the topic themselves. I believe that this approach is better suited to determine the role that the topics of sex and sexuality play in same-age friend-ship groups of adolescent girls. Whereas in interviews with an adult researcher adolescent girls can present themselves as 'either unaware or embarrassed to talk about sex openly' (Lees, 1993: 115), my own data show that the girls' talk is rich in references to sex and to sexual experience. Moreover, the fact that I do not impose my own agenda on the girls' interaction generates data that highlight significant differ-ences in how the three friendship groups approach sex talk and allows me to explore these differences in relation to the girls' membership in contrasting sociocultural groups.

## Data collection, transcription and analysis

I obtained my data from three groups of adolescent British girls who taped their conversations for me in my absence. The girls were all attending year 11 at their respective schools (ages 15–17), but differed in their social class, cultural and ethnic backgrounds. Whereas groups 1 and 2 attended a state school in the East End of London, the girls in group 3 were pupils at a reputable public school in the West End of London. Group 1 consisted of five British Bangladeshi girls, group 2 of three white British/European girls and one black Nigerian/white British girl and group 3 of four public school girls of largely white British/European descent.[3] Four of the five girls in group 1, and two of the four girls in group 2 were eligible for free school meals, which is usually due to the parents receiving income support or job seeker's allowance. On the other hand, the parents of the girls in group 3 were all in paid employment ranging from textbook writing and marketing to working as a neurologist, holding a managerial post with the BBC and owning an art gallery. My initial assessment of groups 1 and 2 as working class and group 3 as upper-middle class was thus based on the traditional criteria of parental occupation and schooling, although my analysis will clearly show that the girls are very much agents in renegotiating the meaning of social class in contemporary Britain.

My analysis will draw on the spontaneous conversational data from all three groups as well as on the information that I gained from one of the girls in group 1. This 'in-group informant' helped me to translate the Bengali (the standard language in Bangladesh) and Sylheti (a language spoken in northern Bangladesh) utterances into English and provided me with her own interpretations of the data and with rich and insightful details about herself and the other girls, their families and communities.[4]

I chose to represent my data on a stave system, which, similarly to a musical score, uses alignment of utterances within a stave to signal simultaneity and thus allowed me to capture multi-party talk more clearly. All of the Sylheti and Bengali utterances have been converted into Roman script and translations are given at the end of each stave. Transcription conventions are provided at the end of this chapter.

Although I conceptualise sexual identities as discursive constructs rather than as fixed social categories, I view the discursive repertoire of an individual as being influenced by and influencing the norms and practices of micro and macro communities. My analytical focus is, therefore, on both local and extralocal dimensions of discourses that are negotiated in the three groups of girls, that is, on the discourse practices that reflect the beliefs and norms of smaller (friendship) and larger-scale (sociocultural) groups.

My largely qualitative analysis of the talk on a discursive level is linked to a microlinguistic investigation. Thus, my assessment of the girls' positions in relation to specific discourses is based on an examination of the structure and organisation of talk, on lexical choices, paralinguistic and non-verbal cues and, at times, on phonetic and grammatical features. These analytic features were relevant both to my focus on discourses and to my exploration of conversational frames in the sex talk of the girls. The concept of frame (Bateson, 1987) has been developed in Deborah Tannen's discourse analytic work (Tannen, 1993; Tannen and Wallat, 1993). I shall define frames as different speech activities, such as joking, teasing, debating or arguing, and broadly categorise them as either playful frames or serious frames. For the purpose of this chapter it was relevant to determine whether sex talk had been framed as 'play' vs 'non-play' (Bateson, 1987: 179), or as personal self-disclosure vs impersonal academic debate.

My comparative analysis of the discourses and conversational frames adopted by the girls aims to explore the identities that the girls in the three groups accomplish in their sex talk and to examine whether and how these are linked to larger-scale sociocultural norms.

## Different types of sex talk

Although I take a predominantly qualitative approach to my analysis, the varying importance of the topic 'sex' for the three groups of girls is first evident on a quantitative level. Pat, Susan, Natalie and Jenny in group 2 dedicate about 23 per cent of their total recording time to sex talk, whereas Ardiana, Dilshana, Rahima, Varda and Hennah in group 1 spend approximately 6.4 per cent and Daniela, Elizabeth, Nicky and Jane in group 3 only 3.3 per cent of their time talking about sex and related issues.

The qualitative analysis of my data shows that the girls in the three groups cover different subtopics in their sex talk and, moreover, approach these subtopics in contrasting ways. Personal self-disclosure about penetrative sexual experience only features in the talk of Pat and her predominantly white working-class friends (group 2), who deal with this and other sex-related topics with an astounding openness and directness. The Bangladeshi girls (group 1) only discuss penetrative sex in the context of porn movies, and their personal sex talk centres on boys' nudity, kissing and even pregnancy. This sex talk is characterised by the girls' frequent switches between serious conversational frames and teasing or boasting activities. This strategy allows them to preserve face and to reconcile culturally opposing discourses. In the upper-middle-class group (group 3), on the other hand, the topic of sex takes a significantly more marginal role than in the two working-class groups. They talk about sex freely, but without engaging in any personal self-disclosure.

## Explanations for different types of sex talk

It could be suggested that these differences are due to the fact that some of the girls have not had sex or do not even date. However, the correlation between actual sexual experience and quantity (and quality) of sex talk is not that straightforward. Although the number of the girls that appeared to have boyfriends varied in each group (from 1 in the upper-class group to 3 in the two working-class groups), it seems that in all three groups only one of the girls had possibly had sex. Moreover, my data will show that the girls' readiness to self-disclose or take up liberal positions in sex talk does not necessarily increase with their sexual experience.

I have also considered the question whether the girls in group 3 might have refrained from engaging in (personal) talk about sex, because they were the only group who knew me also as a part-time member of staff at their school. In fact, only one of the students had ever been taught by me, and most of them perceived me as a 'lower status' member of staff and were allowed to address me by my first name, as I had held the position of a language assistant in the first of my two years at their school. More importantly, my data indicate that the girls' greatest concern was not the confidentiality of their own 'taboo' experiences, such as sex or drugs, but more the confidentiality of their 'gossip' about fellow students or other members of staff. I also consider it to be an advantage in this respect that group 3 was the only one that actually carried out all the recording at home as the girls had not found enough time to be undisturbed at school.[5] I believe that this home environment as well as the fact that the speakers are friends who are used to conversing with each other could have largely offset any negative effects my status as a member of staff might have had on the girls' sex talk.

Thus, although I accept that the girls' contrasting experiences with boyfriends (and to a lesser degree sex) or my status as a member of staff could have had some influence on the characteristics of each group's sex talk, I shall argue that their different approaches cannot fully be explained by these circumstances. Instead, I suggest that the different approaches to the topic of sex need to be linked to the different sociocultural norms and practices that are displayed and renegotiated in all of the three groups of girls.

## Sex talk as a resource for identity construction

In the remainder of the chapter, I will explore several conversational extracts which indicate that the sexual and gender identities constructed by the girls in their sex talk both reflect and shape the sociocultural backgrounds of the three groups. I shall begin by discussing the playful sex talk of the working-class Bangladeshi girls, and then discuss data from the other working-class group of girls before turning to the sex talk of the white middle-class public school girls.

### Playful sex talk: good girls vs bad girls

It has been claimed that Asian girls refrain from talking about sex, as this is taboo by their religious and cultural standards (Wilson, 1978; Jamdagni, 1980; Aggarwal *et al.*, 2000). My own data both confirm and contradict these claims: Dilshana, Ardiana, Hennah, Rahima and Varda engage in some personal sex talk, however, mostly in a playful conversational frame, such as teasing or boasting.

#### Sex talk in a playful frame

The following extract is from a longer conversation about sex in which the girls first express their disgust about certain sexual practices (such as anal sex and group sex) displayed in pornographic films, then engage in a boasting competition about who has watched porn movies most often and finally shift their sex talk onto a more personal level.

*Extract 3.1*  Group 1 – 'Blue Films'

(20)

A    =(yeah it) was so- ugh it was disgusting

R                                            =[(but you

D    I know= =[(xxxxxxx

(21)

A                                            {amused}oh: yeah

R    don't know you might enjoy it if you were there]

D    xxxxxxxxxxxxxxxxxxxxxxxxxxxxxx UGH:::::::::)]

(22)

A    Rahima we know you've been through it [we know you've

R                                          {laughing}[ no I don't think

(23)

A    done it].hhh        {-laughs-}

R    so I] don't think so I don't think so (-) but still

(24)

R    (.) it's **their** man [(they're doing it innit >it's them

D                {slow tease}[someone's been through it

||

||

?H                      (no)

?V    (xxxxxxxx)

(25)

A                                        [someone']s been through

R    the ones who xxxxxx<)]

D    over]=                        =here some[one ha:s]{slow tease}

(26)

A    it {teasing}haven't they:: (-) [it] is Rahi:::ma:{mock}

R                                    [what]

||

||

?V                                              this thing

(27)

A    childish}

D              (.) what was it={staccato}ip dip

||

||

?V    isn't- (.) (%xxx%)

Extract 3.1 shows that the girls explore one another's views about and experience in sex predominantly in a playful frame. The only attempt to approach the topic in a serious discussion is made by Rahima in staves 23–24 *but still it's their man* .... However, the contextualisation cues (Gumperz, 1982) of Dilshana and Ardiana's reactions in staves 24 and 25 suggest that they want to keep the conversation on a playful key. Thus, Ardiana and Dilshana's repeated accusations that Rahima has *been through it* or in other words, has had sex, are clearly marked as teasing by the girls' playful tone of voice in staves 21, 22, 24, 25, 26, the laughter in stave 23, the childlike slow, drawling voice and the lengthened vowels in staves 24–25. Moreover, the fact that the girls simply repeat their accusations and denials, instead of giving explanations for their claims, is also reminiscent of childlike teasing (see Rahima staves 22–23: *I don't think so*; Dilshana and Ardiana staves 24–26: *someone has been through it* . . . ; and Extract 3.2, below). Goodwin (1990: 158–63) found that children 'recycle positions', that is, repeat their challenges rather than offer an explaining account, in order to sustain their playful disputes. Thus, the repetitions of specific utterances in this sequence support the interpretation of this dispute as a playful activity which is enjoyed by the girls.

However, the playful frame does not only provide the girls with a fun activity, it also gives them the opportunity to position themselves as sexually experienced 'bad' girls. I use the stereotypical and culturally salient binary of 'good' girls vs 'bad' girls to capture the identities that Ardiana and her friends are constructing for themselves in their talk and argue that the former implies 'a denial of [ . . . ] sexuality' (Orellana 1999: 73), which is frequently positioned as appropriate behaviour for young women and, therefore, constitutes a dominant gender norm. Interestingly, in this group these 'bad' girl identities are largely restricted to non-serious frames, such as Dilshana's following playground rhyme, which is the culmination of the tease.

*Extract 3.2*  Group 1 – 'Blue Films'
(27)
D      {*staccato*}=ip dip dog shit fucking (bastard silly git)

(28)
A                {*amused*}it's **you** .hh [it's **you**] it's you it's you
D      you are not IT {*laughing*}no [no no] .hhhh

(29)

A    [Dils]hana it's you Dilshana          =yes it is (-) yes it
D    [ no no ]*{laughing}*          (-) nn*{negating}*
||
||
H                              (xxx)          (xxxx) (-) (can you
                                                  *{banging noise}*

(30)

A    is=
D        =I know I haven't been through it I would never do it
||
||
H    hear it)
     *starts}*

(31)

A                              (1) when do you wanna get married
D    until I get married then
||
||
V                              (watch the light)
     *{banging noise continues}*

This playground rhyme serves a dual purpose. On one hand, the use of expletives adds toughness to the 'bad' girl identity Dilshana has been constructing for herself. On the other hand the rhyme also takes the focus off Rahima as the main target of the playful accusations. Thus, Dilshana defends Rahima's innocence, but at the same time she implies that somebody else might have had sex. Ardiana's reaction acknowledges this dual function of the rhyme. She ceases to tease Rahima and redirects her mock accusations at Dilshana, thus orienting to the bad/tough girl identity displayed by Dilshana. The end of the teasing frame is signalled by Dilshana in stave 30, when she switches from her laughing voice into a serious voice to reaffirm her denial of having had sex, thus adopting a 'good' girl position.

### 'Good' girls vs 'bad' girls: the construction of bicultural femininities in sex talk

As I have argued in Pichler (2001), I view the sexual 'bad' and the non-sexual 'good' girl identities as rooted in two very different discourses, which are not only gendered, but also culture-specific. The norms regarding young women's sexual behaviour in these two discourses contrast sharply with each other. One is a discourse which views dating and sexual intercourse as an essential part of adolescence and represents the norms of British working-class youth culture (see group 2 for further evidence). The other I identify as a traditional Bangladeshi discourse, which objects to dating, as it constitutes a threat to a girl's reputation. Positioning themselves as sexually experienced, therefore, helps Ardiana and her friends to align themselves with the norms of British working-class youth culture. The other discourse, however, which allows the girls to negotiate 'good' girl identities, celebrates the conservative value of sexual innocence in young girls.

I believe that this discourse of female chastity constitutes the dominant norm in many cultures. However, I argue that for many Asian girls their sexual innocence is of particularly high importance as not only their own, but also their entire family's reputation and honour depend on it. Wilson (1978), who carried out the first study on Asian women in Britain, argues that a woman's *sharam* (shame, modesty, shyness) is absolutely essential for her good reputation, which in turn is linked to the *izzat* (honour) of the entire family (Wilson, 1978: 99–104). The continuing influence of the concept of *izzat* in a number of Asian communities in Britain has since then been confirmed by sociological and anthropological research (Jamdagni, 1980; Ballard, 1994).

In a conversation with my Bangladeshi 'in-group informant', it transpired that she was not herself familiar with the (originally Persian/Urdu) term *izzat*, but very much so with the concept. For example, she told me that it was important for girls who are older than 15 not to be associated with 'guys'. In a different conversation, she explained to me that girls are not supposed to be dating and that, if their parents find out about it, the girl would either be married to the boy she has been with or get taken abroad to get married as the parents 'don't wanna face the shame'.

Although my data demonstrate that these Bangladeshi friends do in fact talk about boys and sex, it also appears that not all of them enjoy the topics. In this conversation, two of the girls hardly participate in the sexual teasing, but pursue a separate conversation. Hennah's and Varda's silence could signal their opposition to the topic under discussion, which would suggest that they position themselves more clearly in the dominant discourse of their Muslim Bangladeshi cultural background than the other girls. However, by tackling the issue of sex in a teasing activity, Ardiana, Dilshana and Rahima protect their own as well as their listeners' face. It allows them to reduce the risk of offending others and of being stigmatised as 'bad' girls, as the truth value of any of the propositions made in the teasing can easily be denied. At the same time this strategy confirms the girls' awareness of cultural norms that restrain both the sexual and the gender practices of girls in the British Bangladeshi community. Thus, the switching in-between playful and serious frames allows the girls to synthesise both sexual and non-sexual (heterocentric) identities and a range of culture-specific gender practices, and to accomplish in this way what I call 'bicultural femininities'.

## Self-disclosing sex talk: self-determined girls

It could be suggested that the Bangladeshi girls' preference of a playful frame for their sex talk is a sign of adolescent embarrassment, rather than a strategy to reconcile bicultural discourses. In addition, it could be claimed that the 'good' girl identities these Bangladeshi girls construct for themselves are influenced by a universally powerful discourse of female chastity, rather than a discourse of *sharam*. However, the different quality of the sex talk of the other working-class group in my study suggests otherwise.

The sex talk of the white/mixed British working-class girls is striking both on a quantitative and on a qualitative level. The girls approach the topic of sex predominantly from a serious frame, in spite of self-disclosing very intimate details about themselves in their conversations.

### *Direct approach to topic*

In this group a personal question about sexual experience does not result in a switch to a non-serious floor but is instead answered fully and directly.

*Extract 3.3*  Group 2 – 'The First Time'
(1)
N  %>did you \do *[high p.]* it with him

(2)
P                                    no:: I didn't (.) I didn't do
N  (with Simon)<%

(3)
P  anything
N  (1) %(you never shagged him xxxxxxxxxx)%

(4)
P                *I didn't I didn't do nothing I [promise you] [if
N                               [(alright no] I'[m
*Pat seems to be smiling weakly*

(5)
P    I did]         I would tell you
S                                   (.).hhh
?S                       alright (-)/mm
N    just saying)]

In Extract 3.3, Natalie asks Pat whether she had sex with her former boyfriend. Although the reduced volume and the faster speed of utterance delivery of Natalie's question in staves 1–2 and the smiling or amused tone of voice that Pat adopts in her reply in stave 4 may reveal a level of embarrassment, the girls do not switch into a teasing or boasting frame. Instead, they embark on a serious discussion about heterosexual practices and relationships (see Extracts 3.5 and 3.6, staves 6–16, below). This suggests that the girls in this group position sex talk as less problematic than the Bangladeshi working-class girls.

*Self-disclosure*

The sex talk of Pat, Jenny, Susan and Natalie is very personal, containing many instances of self-disclosure, both about their sexual experience and about their lack of it. Thus, Susan admits to wondering whether thicker (and, therefore, safer) condoms might constitute a problem in case *your womb is tight*. In the subsequent discussion, Natalie self-discloses about what appears to have been her own first sexual experience.

Extract 3.4   Group 2 – 'Contraceptives'
(29)
P                                             [so when the f]irst
?S   XXXXXXXXXXXXXXXXXXXXX I'm only like [I'm only like]

(30)
P    time you have sex you can't have some (-) **big fat**

(31)
P    (-) (%dick%) *{laughs}*
S                 (xxxxxxxxxxxxxxxxxxxxxxxxxxx
N                 (yeah but remember the first
?                      (xxxx

(32)
S      xxxx)
?N     time you have sex you [don't]          properly
L      xxxx)
?                            [*[brief laugh]*]

(33)
P                                            =yeah
S                            (.) yea[h]
N      you don't feel like     [(you)] just had sex=

Whereas Susan is concerned about the thickness of the condom material, Pat seems to suggest that the real problem is the thickness of the penis itself (staves 30–31). In both cases, however, the girls self-disclose about their anxiety in relation to the size of the penis in relation to their vaginas. Again there are paralinguistic cues (such as laughter in stave 31, hesitations in stave 30 and the reduced volume in stave 31) that signal Pat's embarrassment. However, again this embarrassment does not lead to a topic change, as it would have done in the Bangladeshi group. On the contrary, after the girls have relieved their feeling of unease about the topic, the discussion is resumed on a more serious level again. In staves 31–33, Natalie positions herself as an expert when she asks the others to *remember* that first time sex does not feel like proper sex. This expert stance also goes hand in hand with a self-disclosure, as Natalie's utterance indicates not only that she has already experienced sex, but also that her first time actually did not feel as if she had just had sex.

This extract confirms the personal and direct approach of the girls from group 2 towards the topic of sex. Although the girls (and in particular Jenny) do show embarrassment of varying degrees when they self-disclose, they never refrain from pursuing the topic further. Moreover, Natalie's self-disclosure shows that girls with personal sexual experience do not need to be afraid of being stigmatised, but instead can claim an expert stance and, therefore, status within the group.

### Pro-sex discourse of British working-class youth culture

This pro-sex discourse does not need to be framed as playful teasing, nor does it have to be balanced by a discourse that establishes sexual innocence as the norm. In contrast to the Bangladeshi girls, the group of white British working-class girls construct an open display of active heterosexuality as appropriate and even desirable gendered behaviour.

Interestingly, Pat, Susan, Jenny and Natalie are actually conscious of this pro-sex norm and at times appear to perceive it even as a pressure.

*Extract 3.5*  Group 2 – 'The First Time'
(6)
S    it is a big pressure (really) when you're (with someone

(7)
P        [yeah of course .hh]      {clicks tongue} look
S    in a) [relationship=]      =but~

(8)
P    right (.) as soon er cause we're fifth- like (all) older

(9)
P    than fifteen this sex thing is such a big issue now

In stave 6, Susan first reveals that she, and presumably other adolescents, can feel pressured into having sex. Whereas Susan appears to be referring to pressures within a relationship, Pat interprets Susan's utterance as a description of peer pressure. Pat's interpretation becomes evident in staves 8–9, when she suggests that sex has become a big issue for herself and others from the age of 15 onwards. Her use of the first-person plural pronoun 'we' indicates that she is referring to a group that she is part of and the following staves confirm that she is referring to her peer group. Thus, the discourse that encourages and even rewards sexual experience with status appears to be linked to a group of adolescents with specific sociocultural (working-class) and ethnic (predominantly white British) affiliations.

As the conversation continues there is more evidence of the girls' awareness of and resistance to this dominant pro-sex discourse within their peer group.

*Extract 3.6*  Group 2 – 'The First Time'
(15)
P    everyone's talking about it and they're like

(16)
P    {raucous voice}["oh have you done (anything yet)"
N                        [(in] this day xxxxxxxxx)
?J                    [(I don'[t)]

It seems that Pat is mocking a teenage-like enquiry about the sexual experience of another teenager in stave 16. The sexual overtone of the raucous voice Pat adopts reinforces the content of her utterance. The utterance content suggests that working-class girls can feel the pressure to have sex just like working-class boys.

In his study of Glaswegian working-class boys, Wight (1994: 721) confirms public belief that male adolescents do not like to admit to 'being virgins'. Wight explains this by pointing to male peers and family members as well as to the media that 'construct vaginal sexual inter-course as a normal, and essential, element of masculinity, as highly pleasurable, legitimate and something that many boys of their age are probably engaged in' (Wight, 1994: 721).

My own data suggest that having or not having 'done it' has also become a defining characteristic of adolescent British working-class femininity. In contrast, this discourse does not belong to the repertoire of my group of upper-middle-class girls. It seems to me that the high significance which, according to the girls in group 2, many of their peers attribute to their first experience of sexual intercourse, is indicative of a dominant norm in British working-class youth culture. However, unlike Wight's working-class boys, Pat and some of the other girls in the group are distancing themselves from this dominant discourse, marking their opposition both on a content level and by paralinguistic cues, such as her changed voice (stave 16).

### Conflicting discourses: morality, romance, liberalism and self-determination

The most powerful acts of resistance against the pro-sex discourse of their peer group are displayed by Susan, who, at the same time, challenges the dominant discourse of female virginity by arguing that *your virginity ain't a big thing at all* and ridiculing people who *go on like it's- (.) .hh li::ke a million Dollars that you are throwing away*. Although the girls' reactions to Susan's liberal stance show that they do not want to dismiss the importance of first-time sex altogether, they rarely invoke an overt discourse of sexual morality, but instead foreground their individual romantic desires.

*Extract 3.7* Group 2 – 'The First Time'
(52)
P     (saying) for (like [inci]dent) if you did (lose
S                  [yeah]

(53)
P     vigi-) virginity with John you can say .hh "I lost

(54)
P     with- my virginity to someone I was with for a

(55)
P     long time and I loved him" .hhh yo[u can't] just
S                                     [yeah]

Similarly to the girls' jokes about locations that they would not choose for their 'first time' (such as the back of a car, the back of a street or a pub toilet), Extract 3.7 contains an element of sexual morality. Pat postulates that it is better for a girl to be in a long-term loving relationship with the first boy she sleeps with. Wendy Hollway (1984: 65) calls this (feminine) romanticisation of sex the 'have/hold discourse', arguing that it reflects the Christian approach to sex as a means of reproduction within marriage. My own data do not confirm that this romantic sex talk of Pat and her friends signals a concern about premarital virginity. Moreover, it seems to me that this romantic discourse, in which first-time sex with a loving/loved partner is constructed as a special and worthwhile event, does not highlight the passivity of girls, as some researchers have maintained (Walkerdine, 1984; Lees, 1993). This romantic discourse allows for a greater degree of individual agency and power than a discourse of premarital chastity (especially when linked to family honour, as in group 1), because it encourages the girls to make their own choice about when, where and with whom they want to have sex. In fact, I would argue that this romantic discourse is less influenced by sexist discourses that link (female) sexual restraint to the preservation of a 'good' girl reputation than by the girls' concern about the fulfilment of their own romantic needs and desires.

Throughout their sex talk Pat, Susan, Natalie and Jenny demonstrate that, rather than complying with the sexual pressures from their peer group or the norms and restraints of public or parental sexual morality, they want to prioritise their own wishes and determine their own personal lives. This discourse of self-determination is made explicit when Pat states *it's up to **you** it's not what your mum says* or when Susan says *people do what they wanna wa- erm do like .hh their relationships's (.) theirs innit*. However, although the girls make it clear that they want to make their own choices about their 'first time', the central role of (hetero)sexual experience and practice remains largely uncontested by the group and thus becomes a marker of the adolescent working-class femininities that the girls construct in their talk.

## Impersonal sex talk: knowing girls

In contrast to the two working-class groups, the topic of sex is less prevalent in the talk of the four white upper-middle-class girls. In the following section, I argue that the quantitative and the qualitative characteristics of group 3's sex talk should not be interpreted in the light of the girls' lack of sexual experience. Instead, I shall demonstrate that the few instances of the girls' knowledgeable, but impersonal sex talk are affected by and affect a set of dominant sociocultural norms and play a significant role in the girls' discursive construction of their sexual and gender identities.

### 'Academic' sex talk

Nicky, Daniela, Jane and Elizabeth frequently engage in what I would define as 'academic' debates about topics such as society, science and literature. Their rare attempts at approaching sex-related topics also tend to be set within such academic frames. Thus, they discuss male promiscuity as a subtopic in their lengthy 'scientific' debate about human nature, they talk about paedophilia on the basis of the book/film *Lolita* and they read out quasi-pornographic material from a book by the Marquis de Sade.

The academic sex talk allows the girls to construct themselves as knowledgeable and uninhibited in relation to sex, without presenting themselves as sexually active. This type of sex talk accomplishes identity work that goes far beyond sexuality. Daniela and her friends position themselves as academic liberals and cool connoisseurs of literature, which highlights the effect of the dominant discourse of (academic) knowledge that both reflects and shapes the public school middle-class background of the girls. At the same time, however, the appropriation of this discourse of knowledge for the purpose of sex talk allows the girls to position themselves in opposition to the British cultural gender stereotype of the prudish and sheltered middle-class girl.

### Sex talk about others

The girls also construct themselves as (sexually) uninhibited in their non-academic sex talk, which, however, largely centres on other people's experiences.

*Extract 3.8*  Group 3 – 'Sexual Experience of Peers'
(2)
E                                    (1) they **didn't**
D    no they d- didn't have sex (1)                no:

(3)
E    that's quite sur[prising]
D                    [cause she] wouldn't (.) or something


In Extract 3.8, Elizabeth talks about the sexual experience of her peers openly and without assuming a moralistic or prudish stance. By expressing her surprise about the fact that one of their fellow students has not had sex with her boyfriend, Elizabeth signals that she considers sexual relations in a heterosexual relationship in her age group to be the norm.

However, the girls' open and relaxed approach to their non-academic sex talk is restricted to what they appear to define as normal, that is, heterosexual. This is particularly evident when their sex talk becomes more personal.

*Extract 3.9*  Group 3 – 'Sexual Experience of Peers'
(28)
J    (2.5) the strangest girl in the entire (year xxx

(29)
J    **that**) is Linda (1)                          she is (-)
?N                    (Lin[da's) a] freak (1)
D                (1)    [(Linda)]

(30)
J    [%(xxxx)%]
E    [she said] she (-) first had sex when she was like

(31)
J            [she] **did** and she kissed me on the lips once
E    twel[ve]

(32)
N    >she kissed me on the lips<
E    hhhhh*{amused}*

(33)
J     she kissed (<u>xxxxxxxxxxx</u>)*{laughing, laughs}*
E     <u>hhhhh</u>*{amused}*
?D          *{laughs}*            *{laughing}*<u>when</u>

(34)
N        (Jane)
J     she was <u>after your</u> **arse***{laughing, laughs}*

(35)
N     (she was after)] your arse she kissed Jane first
J                        (xxxxxxx)
D     <u>when</u> ]*{laughing}*

(36)
N     yeah               (xxxxxxxxxx)
J     after [(<u>you left</u>)]*{laughing, laughs}*
D        [<u>when</u> *{laughing}*]

Linda's strangeness seems to be – at least partly – due to her sexual transgressions, which consist of her comparatively young age of having sex for the first time and of her alleged 'lesbian' approaches. In stave 31, Jane reveals that Linda had kissed her on the lips once, an act that is clearly interpreted as a sign of sexual interest and/or orientation. When it turns out that Jane is not the only member of the group who has been kissed on the lips by Linda (see stave 32), a playful competition between the two recipients of the kisses develops in staves 34–36. This competition is reminiscent of the sexual teasing in group 1, which allowed the Bangladeshi girls to present themselves as heterosexually experienced 'bad' girls. This could suggest that it is equally face threatening to admit to homosexual experiences in group 3, as it is to admit to heterosexual experiences in group 1. At the same time, however, the teasing frame allows Jane and her friends (who express amused interest in the incident) to signal coolness rather than indignation about the 'lesbian' kisses. Thus, whereas the Bangladeshi girls use the teasing frequently to switch between discourses of their bicultural backgrounds (one denying their active sexuality and the other one encouraging it), Jane uses the same strategy to reconcile demands of coolness from within her own peer group with a heterocentric discourse. However, both groups of girls use teasing as a strategy to balance dominant and culture-specific discourses about 'normal' sexual and gender practices with other and frequently opposing norms upheld in their friendship groups.

*Childhood sex talk*

The only stretch of data in which the girls deal with a sex-related topic from an exclusively personal perspective is a 3 minute 30 seconds long conversation in which they reveal how and when each of them first learned about sex. Similarly to their academic debates about sex, this type of sex talk positions 'knowledge' as a dominant discourse for the group.

*Extract 3.10*   Group 3 – 'I don't Know how I Learned about it'
(9)
D     (-) (it's funny xxxxxxxxx) I don't remember **ever**

(10)
D     being told about sex (so) I don't know how I learned

(11)
N                  [I] (.) I read it .hh (in a) (.) children's
E                              (xxxxxxxx) children are
D     about [it]

(12)
N     encyclopaedia
E     very (xxxxxx)
D                  = I **know** I think I just sort of **knew**=

It is particularly characteristic of Daniela, Jane, Elizabeth and Nicky to present themselves as knowledgeable or 'enlightened' about sex, even at an early age. Daniela's knowledge about sex appears to be 'innate' (stave 12). By arguing that she did not need to be informed about 'the facts of life' as a child, Daniela not only indicates that she was wise and mature beyond her years, but also that not even as a child did she consider sex to be a scandalous or improper topic. Nicky, on the other hand, appears to have displayed her characteristically scientific mind already during her early childhood by supplying herself with the necessary information from a children's encyclopaedia.

The powerful effect of the discourse of knowledge is also evident in the following example.

*Extract 3.11*   Group 3 – 'I don't Know how I Learned about it'
(29)
N     XXXXXXXX House) >and we're talking about< I was lik:e

(30)
N     (1.5) five six yeah (-) and (I) used to go "how do you

(31)
N     get pregnant" .hh and then I said "is it because (.)

(32)
N     they hold hands and they make a wish"
?E                                                    {snort/chuckle}

(33)
N     and like my brother [(xxxxxxxxxxxxx no that's what
E                              [you didn't really believe that
?D                                 [(xxxxxxxxxxxxxxxxxxxxxxxxxxxxxxx

(34)
N     I honest]ly thought when I was like five yeah=
E     did you]
D     xxxxxxx)                                      =that's

(35)
N                     =erm (.) and they used to laugh at me
D     quite sheltered=

When Nicky reveals the unrealistic views about procreation she had as a child in stave 32 the other girls do not judge this innocence positively. Thus, Nicky's depiction of herself as naive is openly challenged by Elizabeth in staves 33–34 *you didn't really believe that did you*. Daniela, whose first reaction is indecipherable due to its simultaneity, also expresses her surprise when referring to Nicky's view as *quite sheltered* (stave 35). These reactions show that the subject position of an innocent girl is not one that is encouraged by the group. It would conflict with the group's efforts to construct themselves as knowledgeable and is thus rejected.

The girls' knowledge about sex tends to be paired with a display of coolness or lack of inhibition about the potentially embarrassing and taboo nature of sex talk. The following example shows one of the most explicit attempts of one of the girls at presenting herself as knowledgeable and cool rather than as naive and prudish.

*Extract 3.12*   Group 3 – 'I don't Know how I Learned about it'
(65)
E       and my mum goes "do you know what sex is" (-) and I

(66)
E       go 'yup' and she goes "what" and I go .hh {cool}"the

(67)
E       man puts his willie (.) in the woman's fanny" and

(68)
N                               {laughs}
J                               {laughs}
E       she goes "yeah"
D                               {laughs} {amused}hhhh
?       {chuckle}

The fact that Elizabeth knew about sex before her mother told her, and, even more so, the explicitness of this knowledge paired with a lack of childlike simplifications or euphemisms, present Elizabeth as a mature and uninhibited child, a position which is supported by her cool tone of voice in staves 66–67. Elizabeth also portrays her mother as very liberal by signalling that she was not shocked about her daughter's knowledge about sex.

Again, however, the group has established clear boundaries of this most personal type of sex talk. These are reached when Elizabeth attempts to direct the conversation towards the future and their personal sex life.

*Extract 3.13*   Group 3 – 'I don't Know how I Learned about it'
(80)
N       my mum had trust[ed us
D                       [my brother on- only started to

(81)
N       [(not alone)-]
D       [tell me about] his sex life like (-) this gap year

(82)
N       (1) did he (tell you xxxxxx)
E       *(1) (xxxx) what time did he have like how old was
*+ *sucking noise - eating mints*

(83)
E      he when he first did it
D                                  like (-) fifteen or something

(84)
E      *{sucking noise}*]                        I'm gonna be about
D      (or)]          (.) something like that

(85)
E      twenty I expect .hhh           *{sucking noise}*
D                     (1.5) (%xxxx%)               oh God

(86)
D      it was just so amazing when my brother went to France

After Daniela reveals that her brother was 15 years old when he first had sex, Elizabeth self-discloses about when she expects to have her first sexual experience. However, this self-disclosure is not mirrored by any of the other girls. Neither do the other girls comment on Elizabeth's prognosis about her future sex life in any other way. It is particularly interesting that Daniela, who has a boyfriend, does not display any more interest in a hypothetical discussion about their future sex lives than the others, as her abrupt topic change indicates.

It seems that this exchange is significant in two ways. Firstly, it shows that the group does not encourage the development of sex talk into a more personal direction. Secondly, this group norm is respected or even reinforced by Daniela, who has a steady boyfriend, which suggests that the girls' avoidance of personal sex talk cannot sufficiently be explained by a lack of experience in relation to boyfriends or sex. This extract suggests that the girls do not want to discuss their personal sex life with each other, even if this discussion would be a hypothetical one. This constitutes the most important boundary of the group's acceptability of sex talk. The girls do not hesitate to speak about the sex life of other people they know. They also tend to present themselves as enlightened and liberal when discussing their childhood views on sex and/or other sex-related topics in their academic debates. However, they refrain from approaching the topic on an explicitly personal level.

## Conclusion

My data from three groups of British girls clearly confirm the culture-specificity of sex talk and its importance for the construction of adolescent identities. Thus, the girls in all groups do not only use their sex talk to position themselves as more or less heterosexually experienced, but they also use it as a resource to accomplish a wide range of identities that are affected by the girls' membership in specific sociocultural groups.

In spite of their ethnic and cultural differences, the girls in both working-class groups display an interest in the sex life of other members of their group. They ask one another questions about their sexual experiences and generally signal their interest in the topic from a personal point of view. Both groups show their familiarity with a discourse that values and encourages sexual experience among adolescents; group 2 even comments on this discourse explicitly. I have argued above that this discourse appears to draw on dominant norms of British working-class youth culture, and I believe that its main purpose is to establish (active) heterosexuality as an important aspect of adolescent working-class identities for both girls and boys.

This pro-sex discourse is absent in the talk of group 3, which supports my argument of its class-specificity. It appears that the white upper-middle-class girls in my study are not affected by any pressures to present themselves as sexually active. Instead, the subject positions of the public school girls are shaped by the discourses of knowledge and academic liberalism, which allow the girls to present themselves as enlightened and progressive. However, the girls' acceptance of what they perceive as non-normative sexualities is restricted to their academic talk, and their (limited) personal talk about sexual experiences, such as 'lesbian' kissing, shows that they construct heterosexuality as the norm.

In group 1, the girls' attempts to position themselves as sexually experienced British working-class adolescents have to be balanced with their desire to position themselves as sexually inactive in the Bangladeshi discourse of *sharam/izzat*, which discourages sexual relationships and values a girl's premarital chastity, as it preserves her good reputation and in turn her family's honour. Thus, the girls switch in-between both discourses, framing their sexual bad girl identities almost exclusively in teasing or boasting activities.

All of these examples show the link between (hetero)sexuality, gender and sociocultural identities. In their sex talk, the girls voice discourses that are not only gendered, but are also indicative of the girls' ethnic and social class backgrounds. Thus, the girls' emphasis on, dismissal of or even shame about their sexual experiences can be linked to gender norms that vary according to their social class and culture affiliations, promoting either *sharam*, or romantic self-fulfilment or academic liberalism.

At the same time, the identities that are accomplished by the girls in their sex talk are not exclusively determined by the dominant discourses of their respective socio-economic status and ethnicity. Instead, they all show clear signs of agency, resulting in the local renegotiations of class and culture-specific norms about sexuality and gender. Thus, the Bangladeshi girls have found a way to present themselves as bi- rather than monocultural. The white/mixed race working-class girls' emphasis on self-determination and fulfilment of their romantic desires challenges the pro-sex discourse of their working-class peers, as well as public and parental discourses of feminine sexual morality. In spite of not fore-grounding their sexual experience, the white upper-middle-class girls do not voice a discourse of sexual morality, but use their sex talk to signal that they are not sexually inhibited or prudish middle-class girls. Thus, my comparative approach to the three types of sex talk has allowed me to show that the girls' discursive negotiation of sexual and gender identities is characterised by a constructive tension between dominant sociocultural norms and practices and the girls' efforts to construct alternative positions for themselves. It is this dialectic between local and extralocal dimensions of discourses about sex and sexuality that, in my view, should be central to any investigation of sexual identities and desires across cultures.

## Key to transcription symbols

| | |
|---|---|
| Group 1: | A (Ardiana), D (Dilshana), R (Rahima), V (Varda), H (Hennah) |
| Group 2: | P (Pat), S (Susan), N (Natalie), J (Jenny) |
| Group 3: | D (Daniela), E (Elizabeth), N (Nicky), J (Jane) |
| ? | identity of speaker not clear |
| *{laughter}* | non-verbal information |
| <u>xxxxx</u>*{laughing}* | paralinguistic information qualifying underlined utterance |
| [ . . . . . ] | beginning/end of simultaneous speech |
| (xxxxxxxx) | inaudible material |
| ( . . . . . . ) | doubt about accuracy of transcription |
| " . . . . . . " | intertextuality: speaker uses words/voice of others |
| CAPITALS | increased volume |
| % . . . . . . % | decreased volume |
| **bold print** | speaker emphasis |

| >...< | faster speed of utterance delivery |
|-------|-------------------------------------|
| - | incomplete word or utterance |
| ~ | speaker intentionally leaves utterance incomplete |
| / | rising tone |
| \ | falling tone |
| yeah::::: | lengthened sound |
| = | latching on |
| (.) | micro pause |
| (−) | pause shorter than one second |
| (1); (2) | timed pauses (longer than one second) |
| /..../ | phonetic transcription |
| .hhh; hhh | in-breath; out-breath |
| speaker A | |
| ‖ | two different conversations develop |
| | simultaneously in same stave |
| ‖ | |
| speaker B | |

## Notes

1. As the girls in the study all identify as heterosexual I will not attempt to generalise my findings to other types of sexual identity. Any references to 'sex' and 'sexuality' in this chapter are, unless otherwise stated, references to heterosexuality.

2. In his more recent publication with Cameron, Kulick mirrors his 2000 quote by stating that 'limiting an examination of sexuality to "sexual identity" leaves unexamined everything that arguably makes sexuality sexuality: namely, fantasy, repression, pleasure, fear and the unconscious' (Cameron and Kulick, 2003: 105). From this quote it appears that the focus of Cameron and Kulick's examination of sexuality remains firmly on 'these other dimensions of sexual experience' which the authors sum up 'under the general heading of "desire"' (Cameron and Kulick, 2003: 106). However, the overall argument of the book has actually shifted to accept that '[s]exual identity is certainly an aspect of sexuality' (Cameron and Kulick, 2003: xi).

3. All of the girls (and schools) gave their permission for their data to be used by me and all of the names have been changed to preserve the participants' anonymity. *Group 1*:
Ardiana, Dilshana, Rahima, Varda and Hennah
15/16 years old at time of recording
British Bangladeshi girls
attended year 11 at School C, a comprehensive school in London's East End
*Group 2*:
Pat, Susan, Natalie and Jenny
16/17 years old at time of recording
3 British/white European girls; 1 Nigerian/white British girl

attended year 11 at School C
*Group 3*:
Daniela, Elizabeth, Nicky and Jane
16/17 years old at time of recording
3 British/white European girls; one from Persian/English background attended
year 11 at School P, a public school in the West End of London
4. For the purpose of this chapter, I shall not be drawing on any of my other
sources of data, such as my informal observations of the girls in their school
environment, the group interviews or the questionnaires.
5. Although I had originally been concerned about this change to my research
design, I later accepted it as a consequence of the different role school plays
in the life of the public school girls in contrast to the other two groups who
found time for their talk at school. I, therefore, argue that the change in setting
should be interpreted as the girls' accommodation to their natural space for
doing friendship talk, rather than as a regrettable difference in context that
renders the data incomparable.

# References

Aggarwal, O., Sharma, A. and Chhabra, P. 2000. Study in sexuality of medical
college students in India. *Journal of Adolescent Health* 26 (3): 226–9
Ballard, R. 1994. Introduction: the emergence of Desh Paradesh. In Ballard, R. (ed.)
*Desh Paradesh. The South Asian Presence in Britain*. London: C. Hurst and Co.
Publishers, pp. 1–34
Bateson, G. 1987. A theory of play and fantasy. In Gregory B. (ed.) *Steps to
an Ecology of Mind. Collected Essays in Anthropology, Psychiatry, Evolution and
Epistemology*. London: Jason Aronson Inc., pp. 177–93
Cameron, D. and Kulick, D. 2003. *Language and Sexuality*. Cambridge: Cambridge
University Press
Frith, H. and Kitzinger, C. 1998. 'Emotion work' as participant resource.
A feminist analysis of young women's talk-in-interaction. *Sociology* 32 (2):
299–320
Goodwin, M.H. 1990. *He-said-she-said: Talk as Social Organisation among Black
Children*. Bloomington: Indiana University Press
Gumperz, J. 1982. *Discourse Strategies*. Cambridge: Cambridge University Press
Hollway, W. 1984. Women's power in heterosexual sex. *Women's Studies International Forum* 7 (1): 63–8
Hollway, W. 1995. Feminist discourses and women's heterosexual desire. In
Wilkinson, S. and Kitzinger, C. (eds) *Feminism and Discourse: Psychological
Perspectives*. London: Sage, pp. 87–105
Jackson, S. and Cram, F. 2003. Disrupting the sexual double standard: young
women's talk about heterosexuality. *British Journal of Social Psychology* 42:
113–27
Jamdagni, L. 1980. *Hamari, Rangily Zindagi: Our Colourful Lives*. Leicester: National
Association of Youth Clubs
Kulick, D. 2000. Gay and lesbian language. *Annual Review of Anthropology* 29:
243–85
Lees, S. 1993. *Sugar and Spice: Sexuality and Adolescent Girls*. London: Penguin

Orellana, M. 1999. 'Good' guys and 'bad' girls: identity construction by Latina and Latino student writers. In Bucholtz, M., Liang, A.C. and Sutton, L. (eds) *Reinventing Identities. The Gendered Self in Discourse*. Oxford: Oxford University Press, pp. 64–82

Pichler, P. 2001. The construction of bicultural femininities in the talk of British Bangladeshi girls. In Cotterill, J. and Ife, A. (eds) *Language across Boundaries*. London: Continuum in association with BAAL, pp. 25–46

Segal, L. 1997. Feminist sexual politics and the heterosexual predicament. In Segal, L. (ed.) *New Sexual Agendas*. Basingstoke: Macmillan, pp. 77–89

Tannen, D. 1993. Introduction. In Tannen, D. (ed.) *Framing in Discourse*. Oxford: Oxford University Press, pp. 3–13

Tannen, D. and Wallat, C. 1993. Interactive frames and knowledge schemas in interaction: examples from a medical examination/interview. In Tannen, D. (ed.) *Framing in Discourse*. Oxford: Oxford University Press, pp. 57–76

Walkerdine, V. 1984. Some day my prince will come: young girls and the preparation for adolescent sexuality. In McRobbie, A. and Nava, M. (eds) *Gender and Generation*. Basingstoke: Macmillan, pp. 162–84

Wight, D. 1994. Boys' thoughts and talk about sex in a working class locality of Glasgow. *The Sociological Review* **42** (4): 703–37

Wilson, A. 1978. *Finding a Voice. Asian Women in Britain*. London: Virago Press

# 4
# The Semantics of Desire: Exploring Desire, Love and Sexuality through Metaphor

*Sakis Kyratzis*

## Introduction

Lakoff and Johnson (1980a: 454) suggest that 'since communication is based on the same conceptual system in terms of which we think and act, language is an important source of evidence for what that system is like'. This chapter will, therefore, use linguistic data (from two conversations between young Greeks) in order to explore the ways in which we conceptualise and think about desire and sexuality. In doing so, I will show how cognitive linguistic tools (and especially metaphor) can be used to enrich studies of sexualities.

Although the study of metaphor has a longer tradition than most of the other aspects of linguistic analysis (starting from Aristotle), progress has not been that spectacular, due mainly to the fact that for a long time metaphor was considered to be a marginal feature of language. Metaphor was thus studied mainly in relation to literature, having a rhetorical function. Most theories of metaphor (even more recent ones) are based on either examples taken from literature or on fabricated, simple and out of context examples, like 'Man is a wolf' or 'Some marriages are iceboxes' (the latter taken from Glucksberg, 1989). Although these examples are a good starting point, they potentially constrain the scope of these theories and represent only a limited aspect of the metaphorical phenomenon.

More recently, it has been argued that metaphor is omnipresent and not just limited to literary language, and theories of metaphor have appeared arguing for or against the integration of metaphor in the study of language in general. Current theories of metaphor acknowledge the cognitive aspects of metaphor and, although they were developed recently, their roots can be traced as far back as Aristotle. Lakoff and

Johnson's (1980b) book *Metaphors We Live By*, however, was the one to draw the world's attention to the cognitive potential of metaphor. They set out to investigate the role of metaphor in the way we perceive and structure reality in our minds. Their main goal was to prove that metaphor plays an important role in understanding: this means that metaphor is not just a matter of language, as is usually suggested, but of thought as well. Their main argument is that metaphors are the 'filters' that help us structure abstract concepts so that we can understand them; in this sense, our conceptual system is to a large extent metaphorical and, consequently, the way we live is largely based on metaphor.

Metaphorical processes involve the bringing together of two concepts; hence, metaphor can be defined as understanding one thing in terms of another (Lakoff and Johnson, 1980b). The relationship between these two concepts that are brought together by the metaphor and are caused to interact can be represented by the two-spaced model (see Figure 4.1).

In its initial stages, the cognitive theory of metaphor suggests that the source domain is a well-structured, familiar concept, whereas the target domain is usually unfamiliar and abstract and, therefore, in need of structure. Via metaphor, cross-domain mappings are created from the source domain to the target domain. Via these correspondences, knowledge, inferences and structure (in other words, frames or cognitive models) are transferred from the source to the target domain. The result is a better understanding of the target domain with the help of the source domain; we talk and think about the former in terms of the latter. For instance, the classic example provided by Lakoff and Johnson (1980b) is that of arguments. Expressions such as *Your claims are **indefensible*** and *His criticisms were right **on target*** show that there is an underlying metaphor (ARGUMENT IS WAR) that creates cross-domain mappings from the source domain-WAR to the target domain-ARGUMENT. Consequently, we think, reason and behave in arguments *as if* we were in a war.

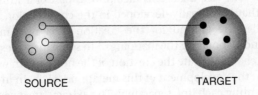

SOURCE                               TARGET

*Figure 4.1*  The two-spaced model

Lakoff and his collaborators paved the way for several studies in conceptual metaphor which have shown its importance in the understanding and handling of abstract concepts in a number of areas, varying from physics and medicine to politics, philosophy and maths (see Johnson, 1987; Mio and Katz, 1996; Lakoff and Johnson, 1998; Lakoff and Muñez, 2000; Lakoff, 2002, among others). Moving away from these areas and towards more day-to-day topics, this chapter explores how metaphor is used dynamically in *everyday* discourse as a tool for attaining meaning, especially in defining sexual desire and sexuality. In the data examined, participants are *struggling* for meaning and one of the ways they find possible to express themselves is through metaphor, because metaphor is the tool that allows for new meaning to emerge through well-known concepts. This chapter follows this endeavour and provides a combined semantic–pragmatic exploration of the way sexual desire and sexuality evolve cognitively within the conversations. Moreover, it will consider how the social and cultural context may influence the way these concepts are perceived.

The extracts that will be presented in this chapter are taken from two transcribed conversations.[1] The first was held in Athens among five young Greek journalists (one woman and four men) aged between 22 and 36 (group 1). The topic of the conversation was celibacy. The second conversation took place in Thessaloniki. The participants of this conversation were four young students (two men and two women) from various disciplines, aged between 24 and 26 (group 2). The topic of this second conversation was love, sex and relationships in general.

## The trysting fields

The first set of examples concentrate on how the object of desire, the body, is conceptualised in Greek culture. In the conversation about celibacy, there is one pervasive metaphor in the conversation which presents the body as a field. This metaphor is part of a string of related metaphors that is gradually developed in the conversation. Each metaphor provides the ground for the creation of a new metaphor by extending and elaborating the mappings.[2] In some instances, metaphors outside this chain facilitate the creation of the new link. In what follows, I will present the development of this metaphorical chain in the conversation, presenting each link separately. The extracts are given in order of appearance.

The first link of this metaphorical chain provides the basis on which the FIELD metaphor can be developed. It can be found in the following extract:

*Extract 4.1* Group 1

S What's happening in the province? There's thirst for sex! I know it because I have a heap of friends in the country who are looking for someone to fuck and they don't find anyone.

Y Yes, but we shouldn't forget that in the country there is always the marriage in the end.

This is an instance of the basic metaphor SEX IS WATER, according to which, the body is in need of sex as it needs water to survive, thus stressing the importance of sex in the overall balance of the body. This metaphor is the equivalent of SEX IS FOOD, which is basic to both the English and the Greek language (people can *hunger for sex* or they can be *sex-starved* – or simply *be hungry*. For more on the FOOD metaphor in other cultures, see Emanatian, 1995, 1999).

This difference in the way sexual desire is conceptualised in English and Greek can be explained by the fact that metaphors (and consequently our conceptual system) are culture-specific and partly constrained and defined by our experience (Lakoff and Johnson, 1980b; Lakoff, 1985). Water is probably a more important element in the Greek culture than in the British culture. This might explain why it functions as a source domain in basic metaphors, such as SEX IS WATER. Shortage of water in Greece makes it a valuable commodity and it is this sense of value and indispensability that is transferred onto the concept of SEX in the aforementioned metaphor.

The SEX IS WATER metaphor is the first link of the chain of metaphors that is present in this conversation. In this metaphor, only sex is seen metaphorically. The following extract is one step further:

*Extract 4.2* Group 1

K Those who have sex from morning till night are boring types, they preoccupy themselves with the various positions they have or haven't tried and they don't think of anything else. Celibacy makes you stronger.

S The body, though, is like a field, it needs watering. I think, K, that you're referring to people who might channel their energy into creative things.

This is the first instance of the BODY AS A FIELD metaphor in the conversation. This metaphor is semi-conventional in Greek. There is a tradition (mainly literary – dating back to Plato; see Theaetetus, 149e) where the female body is seen as fertile ground ready to be sown and produce its crop (so female body = field, semen = seed). The metaphor that is present in this conversation, however, is somewhat different, more general. The body is not gender-specific, it can refer to both men and women, and sex is water irrigating the field. So there is a level of abstraction from the more traditional version of the metaphor: from female body to body (in general) and from semen to sex (in general). The BODY AS A FIELD metaphor is grounded on a common experience in Greek culture, i.e. irrigating a field. In the British culture, where fields are not typically irrigated, the BODY AS A FIELD metaphor might seem somewhat strange, and indeed a different metaphor, such as SEX IS FOOD, might represent more aptly the importance of sex in one's life (which also indicates the priority of food over water in this culture).

It was mentioned earlier that the BODY AS A FIELD is the next link in the chain of metaphors to be added to the SEX IS WATER metaphor. In both cases, sex is seen metaphorically as water but in the former the body is also conceived metaphorically as a field. This mapping is more conceptually productive than the SEX IS WATER one: in viewing the body as a field, apart from understanding the need for sex as watering (something which is also present in the SEX IS WATER metaphor), it also provides the possibility for the creation of cross-domain associations that would allow concepts like fertility, sowing, barren ground, etc. to be used in relation to sex and the body. It also provides the ground on which new metaphors can be built by extending the original one. This is what happens in Extract 4.3:

*Extract 4.3*   Group 1

S   The pressure that a celibate youth accepts today is very big. There is prejudice. It is considered as an abnormality and a disability whenever there is a period in your life that you don't experience sex. But this is how others see it, how do we see it?

D   believe that nothing's really happened. Let's relax and it will pass.

S   This phase resembles a bit to letting land lie fallow. You know, every 5–6 years the farmers don't sow a field so that it won't be

exhausted. They leave it not sown and it rests and the following
year it produces its best crop.

Y   This holds true on the brave assumption that sex exhausts you.

If the body is a field, then it can also lie fallow, which is a new way of
viewing a period of celibacy in one's sex life. Although this metaphor has
its origins in the BODY AS A FIELD metaphor (of which it is an extension),[3]
the triggering of this metaphorical extension is provided by another
metaphor which is presented by S in his first turn. It is a conventional
way of conceiving one's life as a path or as a journey consisting of
various stages. S puts forward the idea that celibacy is one of these
stages, and especially one that stands out as an *abnormality* in a level
path, or as a *disabled* person among others that do not have a disability.
The combination of this metaphor with the BODY AS A FIELD provides the
basis for the extension of the latter (in lines 5–7): the natural cycle of
a field comprises stages of sowing, watering and reaping. Letting a field
lie fallow is an interruption of this natural cycle, an abnormal stage in
the life of a field. Celibacy is such an abnormal stage in sex life. Putting
together all the implications of these metaphors, we have:

- from agricultural life:
  fields need watering (it is normal) ⇒ fields are sown, watered, reaped
  regularly (it is normal) ⇒ letting a field lie fallow is not a normal
  stage in the field's life
- from human life:
  the body needs sex (it is normal) ⇒ people have sex regularly (it is
  normal) ⇒ celibacy is not a normal stage in one's sex life
- what brings together these two domains:
  the body is a field, therefore celibacy is letting a field lie fallow (since
  both are abnormal stages in both the agricultural and the human
  life cycle)

This illustrates how metaphor shapes our reasoning and can be used
in argumentation. In this case, the new metaphor that has been
introduced not only casts further light on how desire is conceptualised
by this group, but it is also used to make a point about the lack of sexual
desire: it can have positive aspects since it can be seen as an intermission
during which the body can rest and then, renewed and relaxed, resume
its normal rhythm. Instead of presenting these points explicitly,

S chooses to put them forward by using a novel metaphor. The metaphor is presented and then the mapping is made explicit. This is done because, when a new metaphor is introduced in the conversation, the participants may not see instantly which parts of the source domain are mapped on the target domain, and consequently they may be uncertain as to how exactly they should restructure their experience and in what new way they should look at the target concept. S, in spelling out the mapping, directs his audience straight to the points he wishes to exploit from the metaphor in order to illustrate his opinion, in this case that celibacy can be something good, something necessary and something that has a beginning and, most important, an end, and can be inserted in the normal course of things. This is exactly the power of new metaphor. Since its mappings are not crystallised in our minds (like in conventional metaphors), they can be easily manipulated by the speakers to illustrate their point. In this case, the concept of celibacy is seen in a new light: although in human life it has negative connotations, by bringing it together with letting land lie fallow (which has positive connotations in agricultural life) our perception of celibacy is restructured in a more positive way.

Moreover, the above example shows that personal experience and knowledge can affect the creation of metaphor and consequently the conceptualisation of desire, sex and so on. Taking a closer look at the CELIBACY IS LETTING LAND LIE FALLOW metaphor one will notice that it is not accurate: when land is lying fallow, it continues to be watered (so the scientists tell me). S may or may not be aware of this fact, and indeed neither are most people. Metaphors are based on folk theories that one believes in, rather than on exact scientific knowledge. What links this metaphor, however, to the BODY AS A FIELD one is the fact that S considers celibacy to be an abnormal stage in one's sex life, just like he considers letting land lie fallow to be an abnormal stage in a field's life cycle. Notice, however, that this is his own *personal* belief system (that might be shared by his interlocutors). Of course it should be kept in mind that even personal beliefs are culturally and socially induced. Letting land lie fallow might seem as an abnormal stage in the field's cycle, because this is how we have learned to see it. In other words, it is the cultural background of this particular group that suggests that a field's purpose is to be sown and to produce crops, and not to lie fallow, but also that a person should be sexually active.

Finally, closing the chain of the BODY AS A FIELD metaphors, later on in the conversation, this metaphor that was initially introduced tentatively by S (see Extract 4.2) is picked up by another speaker and is being used as an established metaphor (in the context of this particular conversation, of course):

Extract 4.4   Group 1
Y   The body has to be watered everyday or else you're fixed on the idea to fuck everyday and you think that you're having a good time?

To sum up, the development of this metaphorical chain can be represented in the following way:

| Metaphor | | Feature | | New metaphor |
|---|---|---|---|---|
| | | necessity | ⇒ | WATER |
| WATER | + | cycle | ⇒ | FIELD |
| FIELD | + | interruption | ⇒ | FALLOW FIELD |

It can be seen how each metaphor provides the basis for the next, and how by elaborating and adding new features a new metaphor is produced. Notice how the further down the chain we move the less conventional the metaphors become. Following the development of this metaphorical chain in the conversation, it becomes apparent that the members of this group view sexual desire and sex as a biological necessity (such as thirst for water), and also as an important part of the reproductive cycle (just like ploughing and sowing a field). It is interesting to note that these metaphors seem to present sex as an obligation, externally imposed, rather than as an intrinsic quest for pleasure. The conjecture that can be made here is that perhaps these views derive from the more conservative side of Greek culture, which sees sex linked to marriage and propagation (something that is alluded to in Extract 4.1) – the fact that these elements are present in the way these concepts are perceived by young journalists is perhaps an indication of how deeply embedded in Greek culture traditional values are.

## The chains of love and desire

The extracts in the previous section revealed the way the speakers *think* about the object of sexual desire. Analysing the various metaphors of the body used by the speakers provided an insight in the way desire is conceptualised. This section will focus on the attempt by the speakers to *define* love and sexual desire. Since these are two complex and abstract concepts that notoriously defy definition, the speakers, in their struggle to pin down their main characteristics, resort to a variety of metaphors, each focusing on different aspects.

A large part of the second conversation was devoted to the differentiation between *eros* and *agape* (two concepts that do not have direct equivalents in English). *Eros* refers to sexual love and passion, whereas *agape* is a deeper and more lasting love. The most common way in which speakers define these concepts in the data is by using the CONTAINER metaphor. According to Lakoff and Johnson (1980b), the basis of container metaphors is provided by the fact that we ourselves are in a way containers, bounded from the rest of the world by our skin. This in–out orientation is projected onto other physical objects that are bounded by surfaces. Psychological states, activities, actions and events can also be conceptualised as containers, as is revealed by expressions such as *He's **in** love*. In the conversation about love and relationships, speakers, in order to define what *eros* is, turn the concept into a box in which they put all its defining characteristics, thus creating what I term a 'metonymic definition', i.e. a definition that is the sum of the concept's parts. So, things that one can find in *eros* are: selfishness (*E: What fills up eros is selfishness*), self-affirmation (*Y: Eros has inside it the element of self-affirmation*), difficulty (*E: It must have a, the notion of difficulty inside it*), and sexual arousal (*Y: Can there be eros without sexual arousal?*).

Apart from metonymic definitions, speakers also resort to *defining metaphors* in order to describe more accurately the difference between *love* and *eros*. By 'defining metaphor' I mean a metaphor that, according to its creator, encapsulates all the basic characteristics of the concept she or he is trying to elucidate. For instance, a part of the conversation was devoted to the idea of time in relation to *eros* and *love*. The former is transient, whereas the latter is more lasting and is born out of *eros*. Two metaphors were introduced that incorporate these features:

*Extract 4.5*　Group 2

Y　Eros is meant to be possessive

S　Whereas love isn't?

Y　Possessive and volatile, it evaporates like methylated spirit

*Extract 4.6* Group 2

Y  Why does eros have to go for love to arrive? Can't they co-exist?

E  No. It's a form of evolution, one can't exist with the other. Why? Because eros is such a strong thing and so egotistical that you can't ...

Y  Do you see eros then as the fire and love the clay object that comes out of it?

The two metaphors in these extracts summarise in a way the conversation up to that point and also reveal the speakers' understanding of these two concepts. The METHYLATED SPIRIT metaphor puts forward the notion of transience that speakers relate to *eros*, whereas the CLAY OBJECT metaphor encapsulates a number of features discussed previously in the conversation: the intensity of *eros* (*eros* is fire), the transience of *eros* (fires die down), the relationship between *eros* and love (*eros* precedes love, and the latter is the product of the former), and the resilience (but also fragility) of love (clay objects last for longer than fires, but they can be broken).

A more complex way to outline the boundaries of these concepts is by the dynamic development of *chains* of defining metaphors. As the conversation develops, new characteristics emerge that have to be included in the definition, and the metaphors are constantly reworked to fit the new data. In this way, metaphors are either elaborated, extended or even replaced by more accurate ones. It should be stressed that this is done in a collaborative way among the speakers: a metaphor that is being introduced by one can be passed on to and reshaped by another. The metaphors that are presented below have to do with the difficulties and consequences of lust and desire and come from the discussion on celibacy.

Overall in the conversation, sexual desire appears to be equated to some form of struggle. A chain of metaphors is gradually developed with each link highlighting a different aspect of this struggle. The links of this chain are (in order of appearance): STRUGGLE ⇒ HUNT ⇒ DRUG ⇒ RAGE ⇒ ANIMAL. The first example (Extract 4.5) illustrates how a defining metaphor is born. The most common way in which such metaphors come about in the data is the following: during the conversation one speaker introduces a defining feature of the concept of sexual desire; this prompts either the same or another speaker to produce a metaphor that, in a way, summarises what has been said so far and also incorporates the new feature. This is what happens in Extract 4.7:

*Extract 4.7*   Group 1

D   If someone is only concerned with pornography, they are satisfied with themselves and they don't go to the trouble of going out and meeting new faces that will appeal to them.

S   Why? Is it some sort of a struggle to find someone to have sex with?

K   It's definitely some sort of struggle and many might be tired of the whole process of getting done up, going to the club, posing for harpooning someone and not being successful in the end.

D characterises the whole process of finding a sexual partner as tiresome (*they don't go to the trouble of going out*). The word used in Greek (*kopos*) also means tiredness and exertion. S, led by these defining elements introduced by D, creates the defining metaphor SEX IS STRUGGLE that incorporates the features of trouble, hard work and weariness, but also gives structure to the concept of sex. This metaphor is introduced tentatively by S in the form of a question. This tentativeness is also present in the expression *some sort of* that is used by both S and K. This is an indication that the speakers are struggling to make meaning in relation to desire: in a sense, they are searching in the dark and when they find something, they are not sure if this is what they were looking for. This uncertainty is exemplified by S's choice to introduce the metaphor in the form of a question. He is seeking agreement or confirmation from his interlocutors that he has used an accurate metaphor, in other words, a metaphor that is cognitively relevant for the others too. This is what K does in his turn (*It's definitely some sort of struggle*); he then proceeds to explicate why seeking a sexual partner is some sort of struggle, and in so doing, shows why this metaphor is cognitively relevant to him. This is how the first link (i.e. the STRUGGLE metaphor) of the chain is created.

In Extract 4.7, the transition to the second link, the HUNT metaphor, is also present. K uses a conventional metaphor in Greek, *harpooning someone*, which means to pick someone up. People (usually men) who chat others up in bars are typically referred to as 'harpoons' (*kamaki*). This conventional metaphor is consistent with the STRUGGLE metaphor: the HARPOON metaphor incorporates the features of trouble and hard work (also present in the STRUGGLE metaphor), but it also includes the action of seeking and getting someone. The HARPOON metaphor can be considered as the link between the STRUGGLE metaphor and the HUNT metaphor, which sees sex or the sexual partner as an animal, and is exemplified more clearly in the following extract (the extended version of Extract 4.3):

*Extract 4.8* Group 1

S  This phase resembles a bit to letting land lie fallow. You know, every 5–6 years the farmers don't sow a field so that it won't be exhausted. They leave it not sown and it rests and the following year it produces its best crop.

Y  This holds true on the brave assumption that sex exhausts you.

S  Indeed, the hunt for sex is often debilitating. Especially if loneliness has made you a sex-addict and you take to the streets and the bars to quench your thirst and you can't – like Tantalus who was cursed by the gods.

The HARPOON metaphor lies at the conventionalised corner of the Greek speaker's metaphorical system and provides the ground for the less conventional HUNT metaphor. There are two versions of the HUNT metaphor: (a) one, which views sexual desire in general as an animal (which is the case in this extract), and is attested in expressions like *the hunt for sex*, and (b) a more specific version, which presents the sexual partner as an animal (which will be presented later on in Extract 4.9); an expression pertaining to this version would be *sex is hunting*. The HUNT metaphor is introduced by S in his second turn, but it is interesting to trace its origins and to see how its gradual development is concurrent with a move away from the FIELD metaphor (presented in the previous section) to the STRUGGLE metaphor. In his first turn, S uses the word exhausted literally (in Greek) to refer to fields.[4] The same word is used metaphorically by Y to mean 'tired'. It is this feature of weariness that connects the two chains (the FIELD and the STRUGGLE chains) and prepares the ground for S to introduce the HUNT metaphor, which, as was mentioned before, combines the STRUGGLE metaphor with the effort of finding a sexual partner. The difficulties that characterise a STRUGGLE are also attested by the word *debilitating* (which is related to the word *trouble* used in Extract 4.7 above to refer to the process of finding someone). This meeting of the two chains (the FIELD and the STRUGGLE) occurs once more (this time more clearly) in Extract 4.9:

*Extract 4.9*    Group 1
S   Are the celibate cowards?

Y   Not just that! They are the ones that might at some point feel tired with the barren struggle of love.

Again, tiredness is present, the STRUGGLE metaphor which was introduced tentatively is now more conventionalised in the expression *struggle of love* and it is characterised by the conventional metaphor *barren*, taken from the FIELD chain, to mean futile.

So far I have presented two of the five links of the STRUGGLE chain of defining metaphors: the STRUGGLE metaphor (which incorporates the characteristics of 'weariness' and 'hard work') and the HUNT metaphor (which combines the characteristics of 'weariness' and 'hard work' with the element of 'seeking'). In Extract 4.8, the third defining metaphor of the chain is also present: SEX IS A DRUG. It is attested in S's words *sex addict*. I think that this metaphor is yet a step further in the STRUGGLE chain of metaphors. S introduces it to incorporate all the characteristics that are represented by the HUNT metaphor (exhaustion, seeking), as well as the obsession or madness that is usually associated with love or sex. Lakoff and Johnson (1980b) showed that LOVE IS MADNESS is one of the basic metaphors for the English language highlighting the lack of control experienced by people in love; this metaphor is also present in the Greek language. In this extract, it is combined with the HUNT metaphor to give the DRUG metaphor: the elements that are combined are 'exhaustion' and 'seeking' from the HUNT metaphor with 'obsession' and 'dependence' from the MADNESS metaphor.

In the following extract, the MADNESS metaphor provides the basis for the fourth link of the chain, the RAGE metaphor.

*Extract 4.10*    Group 1
S   Let me ask you something else: has it ever happened to you that randiness has hit you so hard that you would consider much more easier going out and humiliating yourself rather than going crazy by it?

D   You can wank and it will pass . . .

S   Yes, but sometimes the rage to pocket with some human body is so strong, that wanking, as an act, doesn't cross your mind.

S introduces the madness aspect of sex or desire, which then, in combination with the ANIMAL metaphor, gives the RAGE metaphor (*the rage to pocket with some human body*). The word used in Greek is *lissa*, which literally means rabies. This word is typically used to mean fury or mania, but it is also used literally to refer to mad animals. In this context of hunting for sex and going crazy with randiness, this metaphor is rather revealing of the emotions experienced by someone with unfulfilled desires. It is also significant that, although love and desire are conventionally connected with madness, in these metaphors madness is defined more narrowly as relating to animals. In trying to find the essence of desire, the speakers appear to be stripping the concept of its social aspects and focusing on its more biological/physical level. This is something that is taken to extremes in the following extract (Extract 4.11).

The RAGE metaphor is combined with an interesting and unusual novel metaphor which counterbalances the animal and violent aspects discussed thus far by representing togetherness and sexual intercourse as *pocketing* with someone. This could be the cosiest metaphor of sex in the conversation, due mainly to its evocation of enclosed warm places and human proximity. This metaphor is even more striking in its context, where it is contrasted with images of madness and even violence. The violent aspect of sex is the last the participants of this conversation include in their definition of sex. It is attested in S's words *randiness has hit so hard*, but it is more explicitly portrayed closer to the end of the conversation, where the discussion culminates in a delirium of metaphors and the long quest for a fitting metaphor for sexual desire finally ends in the creation of the final link of the STRUGGLE chain: the ANIMAL metaphor.

*Extract 4.11* Group 1

S   We're not talking about love! We're talking about fucking! We're talking about blind randiness that hits you like a thunderbolt and you feel like an animal, defenceless – you want to pounce on anyone and without looking at their face, to fuck. The panting during sex, to me, is more powerful than any love call. It's the moment when you lose yourself, you lose your conscience and that moment of unscrupulousness is the lightest in the history of man. There is no conclusion to be drawn, but in these vast topics it's already something to raise the issue.

In the conclusion of the conversation, a final definition of sexual desire is attempted that combines the characteristics that were highlighted by other defining metaphors in previous parts of the discussion. Sex is distinguished from love and is then metonymically equated to randiness (in other words, the symptom stands for the disease). As in the previous extract, randiness is associated with violence, but also it is viewed as something that comes from the outside. This is related to the object of desire, the stimulus, as it were, or the cause of sexual arousal. In this case, the violent aspect of sex is highlighted even more than in the previous extract as randiness is seen as a thunderbolt, i.e. a strong external natural force that electrocutes you, but also as blindness. Desire is often associated with blindness. This metaphor could stem from the more conventional SEEING IS UNDERSTANDING (see Lakoff and Johnson, 1980b) metaphor and, therefore, blindness can be associated with irrationality or instinctual behaviour, which is sometimes the result of strong desire – S's words also attest to this, when he says that the moment you fulfil your desire is *when you lose yourself, you lose your conscience*. I think instinctual behaviour is the common ground between animals and strong desire (something that was alluded to in the RAGE metaphor), and the two domains that are brought together in the ANIMAL metaphor. However, in this extract, sexual desire is no longer the animal: the person possessed with desire becomes an animal. It was said earlier that there are two versions of the HUNT metaphor: one that sees sexual desire as a hunted animal and another that sees the sexual partner hunted by a human. In this extract, it could be said that desire transfers the animal characteristics it acquired through the general version of the HUNT metaphor onto the person that is obsessed with desire, thus taking the metaphor a step further: both partners are depicted as defenceless animals, one hunting the other with only one purpose, sex. This is the final defining ANIMAL metaphor. In this definition of sex, love is excluded and the concept is stripped down to its instinctual level, where even the *love call* is equalled to *the panting during sex*. This 'natural' final definition of sexual desire is the normal outcome of the STRUGGLE chain of metaphors since it combines all the characteristics suggested by the speakers: endeavour, intensive seeking, fury, violence and pure blinding instinct.

To sum up, the metaphors of the STRUGGLE chain are related to each other by the fact that each link is created on the basis of the previous one: in this metaphorical mathematics, adding a new defining feature creates a new metaphor:

| Metaphor | | Feature | | New metaphor |
|---|---|---|---|---|
| | | trouble | ⇨ | STRUGGLE |
| STRUGGLE | + | seeking | ⇨ | HUNT |
| HUNT | + | madness | ⇨ | DRUG |
| HUNT | + | instinct | ⇨ | ANIMAL |
| ANIMAL | + | fury | ⇨ | RAGE |

As can be seen, the metaphors used in this conversation present sexual desire as non-human and irrational, echoing again (see previous section) more traditional moral views that prefer desire to be suppressed if disastrous consequences are to be avoided.

## The homosexual cake

The final section focuses on conceptualisations of sexual identity. The following extract comes from the second conversation. The current topic is sexuality, and someone suggested the metaphor 'sexuality is a two-sided object'. In Extract 4.12 below, Y elaborates and extends the metaphor, and creates new ones to explain what he feels sexuality is:

*Extract 4.12* Group 2

Y These two sides are not necessarily equally distributed

L No

Y I believe that each person has a percentage

L Of course

Y It could be zero, ninety-nine

E Yes

Y Or whatever

E Can I ask you something?

L I don't know about zero though

Y But I . . .

D OK then, one per cent

Y OK then, one that can appear at some unsuspected time

E I can't understand this low percentage you put

Y   This little happens because ...

E   It happens but ...

Y   It's like the ingredients ...

E   That's what I'm saying

Y   It's like the ingredients of a cake

[...]

L   I don't believe that there is black and white

E   To take only one side

Y   There is no black and white in nature

L   Look, when you say one per cent ...

E   Yes, I agree

L   It's almost black and white. One per cent equals nothing ...

D   What is one per cent? I didn't understand

L   One equals none

Y   Do you doubt whether each person can have a different percentage of the two materials – heterosexual and homosexual?

The TWO-SIDED OBJECT metaphor stems from the fact that sexuality is generally thought to consist of homosexuality and heterosexuality. Y elaborates on the metaphor by adding the characteristic of inequality between the two sides, thus introducing the concept of quantity in sexuality. This is a necessary premise for the argument he tries to put forward, namely that sexuality is defined on the basis of the strength of presence of the homosexual and heterosexual elements in a person. However, an unequally sided object is an awkward image and not a very easily manipulated metaphor. The notion of quantity is more adequately represented by the PERCENTAGE metaphor: numbers are more appropriate in discussing quantities than sides. The PERCENTAGE metaphor, although less abstract than the UNEQUALLY SIDED OBJECT, is too absolute: talking about one's sexuality in numbers raises objections (see E's turns, for instance). What is, therefore, needed is a metaphor that encapsulates the characteristics of quantity or percentage, but one that presents them somewhat blurred.

This is how the CAKE metaphor is introduced: a person's sexuality is like a cake and, according to its ingredients, one can have a homosexual or a heterosexual cake. With the aid of this metaphor, absoluteness has been replaced by predominance and exact percentages that might raise brows need not be introduced. Although this is a successful metaphor for Y's argument, it is not taken up by the other interlocutors, maybe because it is not a serious or scientific one; the PERCENTAGE metaphor and its entailments are what sticks in their minds, because it is the most clear and easily managed metaphor from the ones Y introduced. The characteristic of absoluteness, which pertains to the PERCENTAGE metaphor, is the basis for the COLOUR metaphor: absolute percentages are projected onto the two ends of the colour spectrum, black and white, which are as definite as numbers. L uses this metaphor to shoot down Y's argument, who actually agrees that *there is no black and white in nature*. What L is saying is that arguing for absolute percentages in sexuality is like arguing for black and white in nature. To resolve this matter Y combines the PERCENTAGE metaphor and the CAKE metaphor (in the more general form of *materials*) which creates a more acceptable metaphor for sexuality. To sum up, the characteristics and the metaphors encapsulating them that are introduced to define sexuality in this conversation are:

| Metaphor | | Feature | | New metaphor |
|---|---|---|---|---|
| | | division | ⇨ | TWO-SIDED OBJECT |
| TWO-SIDED OBJECT | + | inequality | ⇨ | UNEQUALLY SIDED OBJECT |
| UNEQUALLY SIDED OBJECT | + | quantity | ⇨ | PERCENTAGE |
| PERCENTAGE | − | absoluteness | ⇨ | CAKE |

This example illustrates how, in metaphorical mathematics, new defining metaphors can be created not only by adding, but also by subtracting characteristics. It also shows that a helpful and successful metaphor is not always sustained, because there might be other more powerful ones competing with it. The CAKE metaphor had all the necessary ingredients, but it was overshadowed by the PERCENTAGE metaphor. This is probably because the latter is a more established metaphor in the speakers' conceptual systems. What is interesting to note, however, is that this group rejects crystallised metaphors that represent traditional conceptualisations of sexuality: the TWO-SIDED OBJECT metaphor is the first one to be contested, because it does not fit with the speakers' belief that sexuality is not bipolar. The same applies to the COLOUR metaphor in its black/white manifestation. The alternative metaphors suggested, such as the CAKE and MATERIALS metaphors, all highlight what appears to be the most important feature of sexuality for the speakers: fluidity. The reason why the PERCENTAGE metaphor therefore prevails is because it is close to traditional values (by allowing exact quantification) but also it can accommodate more contemporary views of sexuality (by allowing different percentages for each person).

## Conclusions

This chapter shows how cognitive linguistics can help access the ways in which desire and sexuality are conceptualised using language as the main source of evidence. Combining cognitive linguistics with the socio-psychoanalytical approach to language and desire put forward by Cameron and Kulick (2003) will provide a more comprehensive view of the concept: the former shows how the concepts of desire and sexuality are structured in our conceptual system, the latter provides an account of how they are enacted.

The analysis of the examples of metaphoric expressions relating to desire and sexuality in this chapter also showed how the cognitive approach not only reveals the way we think about these concepts but also how our perception is influenced by our culture. There is a long debate as to which came first, cultural or cognitive models (see, for instance, Kövecses, 1999), but as Gibbs (1999: 156) suggests, all these debates 'tend to disappear if we embrace the possibility that all cognition is embodied in cultural situations'. The truth is that concepts that are culturally important will also be linguistically visible and they will influence perception and conceptualisation.

This was evident in the data. A long tradition of considering sex and sexuality as taboo topics in Greek culture (and in others as well) has resulted in conventional metaphors that highlight their negative aspects (e.g. biological necessity rather than pleasure, fury and madness rather than reason). This finding is in line with similar studies that focus on the Anglo-Saxon culture. Deignan (1997: 40) conducted a survey of conventional metaphors of desire in the English language (drawing her data from the British National Corpus) and her findings show that:

> We fear desire, possibly for its potential to disrupt the established patterns of our lives; desire is talked of metaphorically as a wild animal, and as the dangerous elements of water, fire and electricity; [ ... ] we project [desire] linguistically onto objects or forces outside ourselves. Thus desire appears uninvited and takes us over; we are not responsible. This both reflects our physical

perception of desire and allows us to disclaim responsibility for 'sinful' desire.

These are certainly the entailments of some of the metaphors discussed in this chapter. However, there are some important culture-specific differences. For instance, the concept of water is used in both cultures in relation to desire. In Deignan's data it is associated with desire in a negative way, as in the example *It is so easy to tip over and fall into a torrent of passion that sweeps you away* (Deignan, 1997: 25). In the Greek data, however, water is associated with desire in a positive way, as an invaluable element of survival. This can be attributed to the way these two cultures experience water: one has it (or used to have it) in abundance, sometimes in catastrophic quantities; the other, however, has limited access to it and, therefore, water is considered to be a valuable commodity.

Finally, this chapter has also shown how the conceptualisation of desire and sexuality can evolve. Deignan focused only on conventional metaphors and mostly on literary data and was thus unable to comment on how these established metaphors can be challenged. The data from this chapter were conversational, and, therefore, provided the possibility to observe the creation of new metaphors. These new data show how conventional metaphors of love, desire and sexuality still exist in the conceptual system of younger generations, but they now have to compete with new metaphors that highlight different aspects of these concepts. New metaphors are created *dynamically* and *collaboratively*, and this is an indication that speakers are unhappy with the established metaphors that delineate these concepts and that they are looking for new ones that represent more successfully the way they see sexuality. This was illustrated by examples such as the FALLOW FIELD metaphor that presented celibacy in a new light, or the CAKE metaphor that tried to incorporate the notion of fluidity in the conceptualisation of sexuality. Future studies of language and sexuality should focus on what new metaphors reveal about the way the conceptualisation of desire and sexuality has evolved in specific cultural contexts.

## Notes

1. The extracts will be presented translated from Greek. Any significant difference between the English and Greek texts will be flagged. Metaphors are referred to in SMALL CAPS.

2. By 'mappings' I mean the correspondences that are created by the metaphor between the two conceptual domains that are brought together.
3. 'Metaphorical extension' is a term introduced in Lakoff and Johnson (1980b) and further elaborated in Lakoff and Turner (1989). In a metaphor, not all aspects of one domain are mapped onto the other, because that would be a tautology. Therefore, there is always an 'unused part' of the metaphor. For instance, in the BODY AS A FIELD metaphor what is transferred from the FIELD domain to the BODY domain is irrigation and not, say, fertilising, pruning or letting land lie fallow. By using the 'unused part' of the metaphor a novel metaphor is created, according to Lakoff and Johnson (1980b).
4. The original meaning of the verb 'to exhaust' is 'to drain' in both English and Greek. Although in English the word has lost its original meaning, and only the metaphorical meaning remains, in Greek both meanings survive, the metaphorical being the primary one.

# References

Cameron, D. and Kulick, D. 2003. *Language and Sexuality*. Cambridge: Cambridge University Press

Deignan, A. 1997. Metaphors of desire. In Harvey, K. and Shalom, C. (eds) *Language and Desire: Encoding Sex, Romance and Intimacy*. London: Routledge, pp. 21–42

Emanatian, M. 1995. Metaphor and the expression of emotion. The value of cross-cultural perspectives. *Metaphor and Symbolic Activity* 10 (3): 163–82

Emanatian, M. 1999. Congruence by degree: on the relation between metaphor and cultural models. In Gibbs, R.W. Jr and Steen, G.J. (eds) *Metaphor in Cognitive Linguistics*. Amsterdam: John Benjamins, pp. 205–18

Gibbs, R.W. Jr 1999. Taking metaphor out of our heads and putting it into the cultural world. In Gibbs, R.W. Jr and Steen, G.J. (eds) *Metaphor in Cognitive Linguistics*. Amsterdam: John Benjamins, pp. 145–66

Glucksberg, S. 1989. Metaphors in conversation: how are they understood? Why are they used? *Metaphor and Symbolic Activity* 4 (3): 125–43

Johnson, M. 1987. *The Body in the Mind. The Bodily Basis of Meaning, Imagination, and Reason*. Chicago: The University of Chicago Press

Kövecses, Z. 1999. Metaphor: does it constitute or reflect cultural models? In Gibbs, R.W. Jr and Steen, G.J. (eds) *Metaphor in Cognitive Linguistics*. Amsterdam: John Benjamins, pp. 167–88

Lakoff, G. 1985. Metaphor, folk theories and the possibilities of dialogue. In Dascal, M. and Cuyckens, H. (eds) *Dialogue: an Interdisciplinary Approach*. Amsterdam: Benjamins, pp. 57–72

Lakoff, G. 2002. *Moral Politics: How Liberals and Conservatives Think*. Chicago: University of Chicago Press

Lakoff, G. and Johnson, M. 1980a. Conceptual metaphor in everyday language. *Journal of Philosophy* 7 (7): 453–86

Lakoff, G. and Johnson, M. 1980b. *Metaphors We Live By*. Chicago: The University of Chicago Press

Lakoff, G. and Johnson, M. 1998. *Philosophy in the Flesh. The Embodied Mind and its Challenge to Western Thought*. New York: Basic Books

Lakoff, G. and Muñez, R. 2000. *Where Mathematics Comes from: How the Embodied Mind Brings Methematics into Being.* New York: Basic Books
Lakoff, G. and Turner, M. 1989. *More than Cool Reason: a Field Guide to Poetic Metaphor.* Chicago: The University of Chicago Press
Mio, J.S. and Katz, A.N. (eds) 1996. *Metaphor: Implications and Applications.* Mahwah: Lawrence Erlbaum Associates

# 5
# Queering Language: a Love that Dare not Speak its Name Comes Out of the Closet[1]

*Yvonne Dröschel*

## Introduction

It has long been established that social conditions are reflected in the way identities and practices are encoded, resulting in a plethora of distinct and describable linguistic features (Gumperz, 1982; LePage and Tabouret-Keller, 1985; Mühlhäusler and Harre, 1990; Eckert and McConnell-Ginet, 1992, 1999; Hall and Bucholtz, 1995). As a critical component of gay male interaction, linguistic practices are particularly revealing about the changing nature of homosexual subcultures and the relationship between language and sexuality. One way of introducing the differences between the social identities and activities through which male sexual relations and identities have been constituted is to review the changes in the vernacular terms used by gay men to refer to themselves and to their experiences, as well as to reconstruct how gay men have used different linguistic tactics to negotiate their position in society (cf. Leap, 1996; Harvey, 1997). This is precisely the aim of this chapter. The key research question I will be addressing is 'how do a sample of British and American gay men negotiate and construct their sexual identities through their knowledge and use of gay slang?' While I do not intend to provide a comprehensive account of the use of slang by gay men, it is hoped that the research presented in this chapter will give some preliminary insights into how British and American gay men use slang as a means of ordering their experiences and constructing their sexual identities. Although many individuals at any given time, as one might expect, use gay slang along with a range of other resources to construct their identity, the broad contours of lexical evolution reveal much about the changes in the organisation of male sexual practices and identities. Some of these sociocultural changes will also be highlighted throughout this chapter.

This chapter, then, is primarily a sociolinguistic account of the covariation between slang vocabulary and sexuality and provides a description of a range of lexical strategies through which gay male sexual identities have been constructed in British and North American contexts. Even though a certain theoretical continuity between male and female homosexuality undoubtedly exists (Butler, 1993), I will be focusing on gay male identities and use the term *gay* only in this restricted sense. I believe that a study that conceptualises lesbian and gay identities together would ignore significant differences in gender and identity practices which are manifested in the cultures of the two groups and hence the language they use. Thus, by limiting myself to gay male informants, I seek to draw attention to the gay/straight male variable without the added complication of gender.[2]

In the following pages, I will briefly sketch the development of gay slang in Great Britain over the past 50 years, giving special attention to Polari, an opaque slang vocabulary which was most commonly used by gay men in the 1950s and 1960s and has now become almost obsolete. Polari is mainly a lexicon derived from a variety of sources including lingua franca, the Romance-based pidgin dating from the Crusades (Hancock, 1973), rhyming slang, backslang, Italian, Occitan, Yiddish and Cant. Used by itinerant actors and showmen in the eighteenth century, in the nineteenth century Polari had become an in-group language among theatrical and circus people and by the mid-twentieth century became associated with gay slang (cf. Cox and Fay, 1994; Baker, 2002, for a detailed discussion of the origins of Polari).

By comparing some gay speech strategies through time, I seek to explore some of the social and ideological factors underlying issues of language and sexual identity from a diachronic perspective and aim to show that the last three decades have seen the emergence of a gay style that opts for equality and legitimate agency in a normatively heterosexual society. From this vantage point, I then draw on my own data and investigate social and context-related factors determining word choice by gay men in Britain and North America today. The point I wish to make, then, is that the use of gay slang has always been highly unstable, both from a diachronic and a synchronic perspective. As Harvey (1997) points out, this lack of stability seems to be a consequence of highly charged social and ideological issues which are paramount in the construction of gay identities.

I am interested, then, in exploring the extent to which the slang used by gay men both in terms of self- and other-identification, but also in terms of labelling experiences, has changed and why it has done so. To achieve these research aims, I employ an ethnographic methodology of questionnaires with two groups of male gay speakers of English: gay men living in England and gay men living in North America. In addition, I obtain data from heterosexual men and women living in England, in order to find out how much of the colloquial vocabulary used by gay men is deployed as non-gay slang. Since the parameters and features of gay male vocabulary use change from city to city, person to person and day to day, this account is mainly an attempt to open up interest in areas of further research that are still largely unexplored within sociolinguistics.

## Theoretical frameworks

Analysing the language of a group that is defined in terms of its sexuality calls into question the very definition of sexuality labels such as *gay*. In order to analyse how identities and membership in social groups are constructed through language, it is necessary to make some basic theoretical observations about the characteristics of the community and to define the criteria that constitute group membership. One of the primary issues for delineating the gay community typically revolves around trying to specify who might or might not belong to it. Although most discussions concerning the category *gay* refer to both biological sex and sexual orientation, all definitions of a gay speech community based on such criteria remain problematic. Frameworks based on the assumption that there is some 'genuine' or 'authentic' gay male culture usually define the gay community as primarily consisting of men who explicitly self-identify as gay, and the sexual category *gay men* is only too often limited to overtly claimed identities. For reasons such as these, it has been argued that the entire notion of identity categories and the communities based on such categories are inadequate for an analysis of gay language and behaviour. Butler (1993: 227), for example, has maintained that, for a less rigid definition of the community, the definition of membership has to remain vague:

> As much as identity terms must be used, as much as 'outness' is to be affirmed, these same notions must become subject to a critique of the exclusionary operations of their own production: For whom is outness a historically affordable option? Is there an unmarked class

character to the demand for universal 'outness'? Who is represented by which use of the term, and who is excluded? (Butler, 1993: 227)

The boundaries of the gay community are fluid, and a definition of sexual practice may not adequately reflect any real concept of how people define their own identities, multiple membership or marginal participation in the community. Since the traditional identity category *gay* is problematic, we need to find frameworks that allow for diversity in identity categories and group membership, integrating various forms of participation in the community as well as the participants' subjective perception of who is a member. Nevertheless, identity categories have played an important role for minority groups in their struggle to obtain equality. The deconstruction of such categories may depoliticise sexuality and the study of it, which is potentially disempowering to marginalised groups (see, for example, Morrish and Leap, this volume).

I suggest that one of the primary ways in which members of gay communities can be characterised (and, thus, are able to identify one another) is through a combination of a number of linguistic styles which make up a distinctive gay repertoire to which gay men may or may not revert in particular situations. In other words, it is not membership in the abstract concept of the gay community that makes the language of its members unique, but rather a set of conventionalised meanings that can be exploited in uniquely gay ways (cf. Leap, 1996). These meanings include those created and negotiated in the use of gay-associated slang vocabulary.

## Methodology

In order to obtain first-hand information about the most common features of gay male use of slang vocabulary, the productive and receptive knowledge of Polari and significant similarities and differences between American and British gay slang, I conducted a sociolinguistic survey in the form of a questionnaire. The questionnaires were distributed to gay acquaintances in England and circulated through gay mailing lists both in England and America. In addition, I asked straight male and female informants in England to fill in the questionnaires in order to obtain information about the use of Polari terms in non-gay colloquial speech. I focused on Polari as a specifically British form of gay slang in order to investigate changes in British gay slang and to establish the extent to which American gay slang may have contributed to these changes. The survey covered all age groups from 20 to 65, as well as various educational and socio-economic backgrounds. It is interesting to note that twice as many English-speaking North American as British gay men were willing to fill in the questionnaires and thereby provide information about themselves and their use of gay slang. The significantly larger number of responses obtained from American residents might reflect the higher politicisation of American gay communities, which also seem to have a much stronger presence on the Internet.

The questionnaires were designed to gain information, firstly, about slang words used to *describe* gay men and, secondly, about slang words that are *used by* gay men. The first section of the questionnaire focused on the personal background of the informant: age, gender, sexuality, level of urbanisation, proximity to gay culture and interest in language in general. Part two of the questionnaire required respondents to list terms they use to refer to gay men and specify whether they consider these terms to have neutral, negative or positive connotations, as well as whether this usage is intimate, private or public. In addition, they were asked to make some metalinguistic comments about the reasons why they use these terms. A final question required the respondents to list terms referring to gay men they consider abusive if coming from an outsider (a person unacquainted with or hostile to gay people), but neutral or positive if coming from an insider (gay people, friends) and, if possible, to explain their classification. For the third part of the questionnaire, I compiled a list of 90 possible lexical items which were either part of my own word stock or taken from several glossaries available on the Internet. The word list consists of about 70 per cent of terms that can be traced back to Polari, reflecting my interest in the present usage of these terms in both British and American gay slang, but also includes other colloquial terms referring to sexual experiences and identity categories. The respondents were asked to tick on this list those lexical items they are familiar with, to specify whether they use these terms themselves, and to give a brief definition of the meaning of those terms that are known to them. From this list, the most commonly known and frequently used terms were extracted to obtain information about the current word stock of gay slang, as well as about differences and similarities between American and British usage. Furthermore, I was interested in finding out whether any Polari terms have passed into American usage.

Of all the questionnaires I had distributed only a third were returned completed. With such a small percentage of questionnaires being returned, it is clear that this survey is limited in various ways and that much more detailed work remains to be done in this area. By focusing solely on vocabulary items, the survey was limited in scope and with tens rather than thousands of people, it was limited in extent. Also, by using an uncontextualised test-like research instrument, the survey is biased in that gay male vocabulary is usually used informally in specifically defin- able contexts, so that producing it in the context of the questionnaire is extremely difficult. Despite these shortcomings, some initial conclu- sions about gay male vocabulary and the attitudes of its speakers, and the current status of Polari and crossovers from British and American gay slang can be drawn.

A profile of the typical respondent for this study emerged from the data collected: 40.8 per cent are in the 30–39 years age group and 22.2 per cent are in the 20–29 years age group; 52 per cent currently reside in North America and 33 per cent live in England; 66.7 per cent consider themselves members of the middle class. The majority of respondents identify as gay (straight: 4; gay: 23, with 1 bisexual and 1 specifying that he identified himself as 'queer'). The most common respondent is therefore a middle-class gay man in his thirties.

In the remainder of this chapter, I will firstly discuss the gay men's use of Polari terms, as an example of gay slang. This will move on to a discussion of how gay slang appears to be used as a means of negotiating and affirming gay male identities. This discussion includes an examination of the slang words used to describe gay men and the words used by them. I will then compare the responses of the British and US informants to see if any notable cross-cultural similarities or differences can be drawn.

## Gay slang as a mirror of social change

### Polari

Before discussing the respondents' use and knowledge of Polari terms, it would be useful to provide a very brief outline of the history and development of Polari as a form of gay slang.[3] It is in Polari, which is not so much an entire language, but rather a vocabulary of coded expressions and words, that we find the most exclusive use of gay slang. Even though Polari is one of the richest and most effective slang vocab- ularies, as a form of gay slang it is still the least acknowledged and has been studied by only a few linguists (Cox and Fay, 1994; Lucas, 1994; Baker, 2002).

Polari as a gay slang was confined to England (Baker, 2002). As a spoken vernacular (Baker, 2002), it has gradually disappeared with only a little having been passed on, so that the corpus of words that can still be pieced together is frustratingly limited. A satisfactory analysis of the slang, its development, and past and present status in the gay community would be an almost impossible task, were it not for the fact that some items have remained part and parcel of current gay slang or have been absorbed into general non-gay colloquial speech. Polari can be defined as an 'antilanguage' generated by an anti-society in Halliday's (1978: 165) sense, representing the 'acting out of a distinct social structure [ . . . ] the bearer of an alternative social reality' and a set of values opposed to the dominant social order. Trudgill (1992: 10) defines an antilanguage as:

> A variety of a language, usually spoken on particular occasions by members of certain relatively powerless or marginal groups in a society, which is intended to be incomprehensible to other speakers of the language or otherwise to exclude them. [ . . . ] Exclusivity is maintained through the use of slang vocabulary, sometimes known as argot, not known to other groups, including vocabulary derived from other languages.

Hence, Polari as an antilanguage was one of the identifying signs of belonging to the margins of society; it was a secret code unintelligible to outsiders. With an important affinity to theatricality, Polari was not only a series of linguistic signs which served to disclose information and identify members while protecting individuals or communities; more importantly, it also provided a form of social cohesion which constructed and gave structure to the gay community at a time when homosexuality was still heavily criminalised and gay men were forced to hide their sexual identity. By the mid-twentieth century, Polari had been established as a recognisably gay form of slang. Words such as *omee-palone* 'male homosexual' and *ecaf* 'face' had become part of the gay subculture, representing a mixture of theatrical manoeuvres and self-protection against unwelcome revelations in public.

However, Polari not only helped to protect homosexual identity, but also served as a linguistic strategy for undermining and parodying the ludicrousness of heterosexual norms when gay culture was becoming more visible in the 1950s and 1960s. The peak of Polari usage, curiously enough, coincided with its popularisation in a non-gay context by the

BBC Radio Series *Round the Horne*, which developed a cult surrounding Polari through using catchphrases, such as 'How bona to vada your dolly old eek.' The code of Polari as presented on national radio was used to provide all kinds of information on homosexual lifestyle and activity and, as Lucas (1994: 107) points out, satirised '[t]he British obedience to codes and dress, behaviour, patriotism, manliness and femininity'. Polari almost died out towards the end of the 1960s. The number of people in general and gay men in particular who are familiar with Polari and still use a relative large corpus of Polari items is constantly decreasing. The three respondents who identified and defined the term *Polari* were all British gay men over 30 and only two of them were able to recognise all of the Polari terms included in the questionnaire. Moreover, those who are still actively using Polari terms are rarely acquainted with more than 20 odd expressions, which reflects Hancock's (1973) conclusion that it is somewhat problematical to equate a know-ledge of such a small number of Polari words with a knowledge of Polari itself. Given that a considerable number of Polari terms have passed into non-gay slang, it is not surprising that expressions such as *bevvy, naff, manky* and *savvy* were equally familiar to British gay and straight respondents. There is thus some indication that most of the few Polari expressions that have survived are no longer confined to exclus-ively gay usage, but have equally become part of non-gay colloquial usage.

Polari almost disappeared in Great Britain at a time when the contro-versy about the legitimacy and usefulness of any kind of gay slang became increasingly heated, especially in America. According to Lucas (1994: 108), gay radical groups came to regard such code adoption as a self-ghettoising mentality which contributed to the continuing domin-ance of the heterosexual society, and thus maintained the marginalisa-tion of the gay community. The concept of being gay as a politicised and socialised homosexual slowly started to take root, and homosexuals began to shed their own perception of themselves as social deviants, sexual perverts or outlaws, images that had been promoted by medical, religious and legal circles. Lucas (1994: 108) argues that Polari could not meet the requirements of a newly emerging gay identity which became increasingly less clandestine, adopting a more radical perspective and actively fighting against the self-ghettoisation of the gay community and for its social and political rights. Largely based on the growing strength of their political identity, the ways of being gay had drastically changed, a change that is mirrored in the linguistic strategies pursued by gay men.

## Current Polari terms

The results of the study reveal that the British gay men above 60 with an academic background and a certain level of urbanisation are clearly the most familiar with Polari, while the younger gay men are completely ignorant of its existence and use. Those that do know some have very little receptive knowledge of Polari items and productively use only a few Polari terms, most of which have passed into wider colloquial use. Many Polari terms have even become part of current British gay slang, *trade* 'sexual partner', *cottage* 'public toilet' and *troll* 'wander over' being some popular examples. Some expressions have crossed over into general colloquial slang, for example, *naff* and *bevvy* are receptively known by a wide range of younger British people, be they straight or gay. However, some items have undergone a complete change of meaning as they have passed from gay use into wider slang. The evaluation of the questionnaires filled in by heterosexual respondents confirms Hancock's conclusion that some Polari terms have been adopted into general slang: *naff* 'boring, unfashionable', *balonie* 'nonsense', *barney* 'fight', *bevvy* 'drink', *clobber* 'clothes', *manky* 'bad, poor, tasteless', *scarper* or *to do a Johnny Scarper* 'escape', *savvy* 'streetwise', *camp* 'effeminate'. The changing face of Polari has meant that some original Polari terms have changed their meaning: *bevvy* originally meant a tavern or a pub and not a drink and *naff*, which used to refer to straight men, has changed its meaning to 'boring, unfashionable'.

Although the American gay respondents claimed to be familiar with a considerably smaller range of Polari terms, both their receptive knowledge and their productive use of some of the items was higher than expected (see Table 5.1). However, the terms most current in American gay slang identified by the respondents cannot be attributed exclusively to Polari (e.g. *bimbo, camp, dish, cruise*) and might even have been originally coined in America.

## Constructing and affirming gay identities

### The disruptive force of gay slang: the strategy of reappropriation

As expected, Polari and more general forms of gay slang often contain many words referring to male homosexual identity. Some of these 'identity words' are used in a derogatory and discriminatory way in non-gay contexts but take on more positive, and even celebratory, meanings when employed by gay men themselves. The linguistic redefinition of pejorative terms and, hence, the disruption of dominant linguistic

*Table 5.1* Polari terms (American gay men)

| Item | Total | Receptive knowledge | Productive use |
|---|---|---|---|
| Bagadga | 1 | – | 0 |
| Batter | 3 | 2 | 1 |
| Bijou | 1 | 0 | 1 |
| Bimbo | 12 | 4 | 9 |
| Camp | 13 | 10 | 3 |
| Dish | 14 | 8 | 6 |
| Dish the dirt | 12 | 7 | 5 |
| Doll/dolly | 6 | 4 | 2 |
| Fab | 10 | 3 | 7 |
| Mince | 6 | 3 | 3 |
| Ogle | 6 | 3 | 3 |
| Polari | 2 | 0 | 2 |
| Savvy | 7 | 0 | 7 |
| Troll (verb) | 3 | 0 | 3 |
| Cruise | 10 | 10 | 2 |
| Scarper | 1 | 0 | 1 |
| Swish | 5 | 4 | 1 |
| Tat | 1 | 1 | 0 |
| Molly | 2 | 0 | 2 |
| Aunt | 3 | 0 | 3 |

systems, is a strategy used by many marginalised groups as, for example, black people in America who use the term *nigger* as an in-group marker (cf. Kennedy, 2002). It had already been pursued in the earlier stages of gay slang, but became a principal preoccupation of radical-activist gay movements in the 1970s, when metaphors of disruption were used as a reaction to stereotypes about gays and served to rebuke societal judgements. This strategy of recharging old words is sometimes referred to as *queering*, described by Leap (1996: 22–3) as 'the appropriation for ourselves [gay men] of objects, activities, and identities found in everyday experience and the representation to others of those objects, activities, and identities as queered appropriations'. One of the American gay respondents underlined the liberating aspect of reclaiming pejorative language:

*Extract 5.1*
Queer, fag, fairy are all negative from an outsider but not an insider. I believe there is something liberating about gay people co-opting

terms that have been used to oppress and marginalizing them, similar to how African-Americans use the term nigger. (AGM2)

Concomitant with the association of reappropriated terms of abuse as an expression of resistance to homophobic abuse and marginalisation is the view that these terms express a degree of familiarity and group membership:

*Extract 5.2*
Any negative epithet works when recycled among our friends. (AGM7)

*Extract 5.3*
If an outsider uses the term faggot, it seems derogatory, but if a gay person uses it to another gay person it seems like a term of familiarity. (AGM10)

However, the comments the informants made about the use of terms such as *queer* or *fag* illustrate that the reappropriation of pejorative terms might have lost some of its force and is contested by some gay men:

*Extract 5.4*
I don't really subscribe to the 'reclamation' point of view, although I can see how others would. (BGM4)

*Extract 5.5*
I despise the term queer and fag and never use the terms – very negative and derogatory. (AGM5)

*Extract 5.6*
Faggot, queer, and fruit always sounds negative, even when used by gay men. (AGM7)

It becomes apparent from these commentaries that the issue of reappropriation is ideologically charged. The differential interpretations of such reclaimed terms illustrate that, as Harvey (1997: 63) so aptly puts it, 'meanings exist in a constant state not merely of diachronic flux but also of synchronic contestation'.

One of the sections of the questionnaire required the respondents to list and comment on terms, expressions or phrases referring to gay men they consider abusive if coming from an outsider (a person unacquainted with or hostile to gay people), but neutral or positive if coming from

*Table 5.2* Most frequent terms of reference

| Item | Total | Positive | Negative | Neutral |
|---|---|---|---|---|
| Fag | 11 | 1 | 7 | 3 |
| Queen(s) | 9 | 2 | 3 | 1 |
| Queer | 8 | 4 | 2 | 2 |
| Puff(s)/poof(s) | 4 | 2 | 1 | 1 |
| Faggot | 3 | 1 | 2 | – |

an insider (gay or gay-friendly people). Table 5.2 contains those terms most frequently mentioned by the respondents, indicating whether they were considered as having positive, negative or neutral connotations. Table 5.2 illustrates that there is no overall consensus among gay men as to which term is the most appropriate and that personal, group and societal issues underlie and determine the differential use of terms of reference. Although some terms, notably *queer*, have lost their negative meaning for some gay men and acquired connotations of positive self-identification, many others argue that even the ironic or parodic use of pejorative terms may help to maintain exactly those stereotypical images society holds about gay men. Moreover, some terms formerly associated with gay pride may gradually become restigmatised and turned into a cliché. As the respondent cited below argues, these terms may then be used by some gay men to distance themselves from others in terms of disapproval often with respect to overtly effeminate behaviour:

*Extract 5.7*
Will use queen or puffs when referring to very effeminate, annoying gay men. Note – I have effeminate friends who are not annoying – it's only the annoying ones who I use this label at, and never to their faces. (BGM4)

Some informants pointed to the fact that the connotations of any term of reference, but most notably terms such as *fag, faggot* and *queer*, depend on the tone of the speaker and the context in which it is used. This is true for terms of self-reference that have been appropriated by other minority groups, and similar opinions are often voiced about the term *nigger*, which is considered highly abusive when used by white people, but accepted as an in-group expression. There seems to be no overall agreement as to which terms should generally be avoided and which are acceptable, since many of them have both intimate and abusive reference. However, some of the respondents were whole-heartedly opposed to even the intimate use of terms such as *fag, faggot, fairy* and *queen*, since they considered these expressions to be extremely negative in nature. As one of the respondents pointed out, some gay men perceive these terms as positive, only when coming from an insider:

Extract 5.8
I believe that there is something liberating about gay people co-opting terms that have been used to oppress and marginalise them. [ . . . ] However, of course, I consider these terms to be negative if used by a straight person. Even if they are not used with negative intentions, for instance if a straight person is trying to demonstrate that they are comfortable or knowledgeable about gays, I would still find it negative and patronising. (AGM2)

Since the respondents report that some of these words are used by straight speakers as pejorative terms for gay men, their meaning is not fixed, and some have been fully appropriated as positive terms of iden-tification, while others have retained some of their negative potential. The most controversial word in this regard seems to be *queer*. The results show that the term *queer* clearly enjoys higher popularity among English gay men than it does among Americans. All of the English informants classified the connotations of *queer* as positive or neutral and only two respondents above 60 declared that they did not actually use *queer*, because it used to have a negative meaning when they were younger. Even though the American respondents under 30 recognised that the term *queer* can have positive connotations, all but one stated that they did not use it, because its negative connotations are still overriding. English gay men seem to be more in favour of using the term *queer* when referring to their sexual identity, a finding that is particularly interesting in view of the fact that *queer* was regularly used during gay parades in America. Those gay men in the survey who objected to the word *queer* did so because of its negative connotations: 'odd', 'eccentric', 'strange' and 'perverted', i.e. because it presupposes the normative character of heterosexuality and opposes gay men to 'normal' men, encouraging the idea that homosexuality involves a certain degree of perversion. One of the informants pointed out that while *homosexual* and *gay* are now relatively free of any possible negative connotation and can, therefore, be used in any environment, *queer* still sounded negative to him, since it was always pejorative when he was growing up.

It is interesting that younger English gay men seem to be less concerned with 'political correctness' and regularly use terms such as *queen* or *fag* when making a sarcastic or humorous comment about another gay man. Of the 12 American respondents, 10 considered the use of *fag, queen* and *fairy*, etc. as being generally abusive:

Extract 5.9
I despise the term queer and fag and never use these terms since they are very negative and derogatory. (AGM6)

Only two younger gay male respondents indicated that these terms may be used jokingly by gay men and were abusive only when coming from straight people. All of the English respondents, however, labelled these terms as neutral or positive when coming from other gay men, and indicated that they frequently used them in in-group conversations or when gossiping about someone.

Extract 5.10
I use fag, dyke, queer and queen only when I am in a private setting with other gays and we are talking as 'members of a family'. (AGM6)

It seems, then, that such terms are used mainly in in-group contexts. Even though rejection of reappropriated terms is not consistent across the group of gay male respondents, concerns about their negative connotations appear to outweigh considerations of challenging the heterosexual cultural value system by redefining pejorative terms used by homophobes.

The following statement reflects the notion that a large part of gay slang mirrors stereotypes held by the dominant society and is used to denigrate certain types of inappropriate behaviours or attitudes.

Extract 5.11
Big Mary what I call my flat mate and anyone (gay/str8, male/female) if they are behaving in a certain way, i.e., effem- inate/camp/screaming. Screaming queen I usually use this when talking with gay/gay-friendly friends about someone who is on the scene camping it up usually when I am annoyed, i.e., oh god, not another screaming queen! (BGM6)

The irony of this comment lies in the fact that the phrase *camp it up* is used to qualify a particular 'type' of homosexual, i.e. that of the overtly feminine gay man. The speaker constructs his own identity in terms of disapproving and forcefully distancing himself from 'effeminacy' as an undesirable property often perceived by heterosexual homophobes to be stereotypical of all gay men.

Moreover, gay slang itself, to a certain extent, singles out minorities not only with respect to sexual behaviour and identity, but also in terms of ethnicity or race, as the invention of terms such as *rice queen* (a gay man who is attracted to Asian men) and *dinge queen* (a gay man who is attracted to black men) illustrate. Most of the gay men who answered the questionnaire, both American and British, were familiar with such expressions, but nevertheless indicated that they were increasingly reluctant to use them, because they perceived them as derogatory and racist. It seems, then, that constructing gay identities on the basis of social and racial difference is considered to be counterproductive in the pursuit of equality.

## From a secret code to a classificatory language

In recent decades, gay slang seems to have undergone a shift away from a relatively homogeneous code allowing gay men of various social and political backgrounds to communicate with each other towards a more intelligible slang that, as Farrell (1972: 98) puts it, focuses on the function of 'ordering and classifying experience within the homosexual community, particularly those interests and problems which are of focal concern to the [individual] homosexual'. Although such a classification system was clearly already inherent in Polari, as it is for most anti-languages, it has become more elaborate and now seems to be of focal concern. Gay vocabulary no longer primarily provides for a secret code which is unintelligible to outsiders, but rather is now a register that deals primarily with types of homosexuals, their sexual and social activities, as well as stereotypical behaviour patterns and attitudes, as illustrated in my results. The term *gay*, for instance, could once be used as a secret code word by gay men to identify each other secretly in a heterosexual setting, since the term was not always associated with homosexuality. Chauncey (1994: 17–18) explains the use of *gay* as follows:

> A properly intoned reference or two to a 'gay bar' or to 'having a gay time' served to alert the listener familiar with homosexual culture, as one gay writer explained in 1941. [ . . . ] Similarly, in 1951 the Cyrano Restaurant let gay men know they were welcome while revealing nothing to others by advertising itself as the place 'where the Gay Set Meet for Dinner'.

In Britain, this shift away from a secret code understood only by the initiated is clearly reflected in the loss of the once secret Polari terms which are today understood only by a dwindling number of gay men or have made their way into general colloquial speech. Nevertheless, the need for a classification system proper for the gay subculture persists, although it no longer reflects a concern with secrecy and separation from non-gay culture as it once used to. On the contrary, such classification today reflects the growing heterogeneity of the gay community, comprising individuals with a wide range of concerns and interests. Gay men today use a particular term of reference not to keep their sexual identity secret, but because it seems to be most appropriate in describing their identity, and to distinguish between members and non-members of gay subcultures. Accordingly, only one informant stated that he uses words such as *gays, gay men, fag, faggot*, etc.

*Extract 5.12*
in order to express myself clearly and to delineate the in-group from the out-group in terms of approval or disapproval. (AGM4)

Various gay subgroups have conflicting ideas about the most useful terms of reference and no longer simply self-identify as *homosexual* or *gay*, but make use of the increasing variety of terms of self-reference existing at present. Table 5.3 lists the most frequently mentioned terms of reference (more than one occurrence). The different interpretations of these terms illustrate that they have a range of connotations so that there is no general consensus as to which term is the most appropriate one. A comparison between British and North American English speakers (Tables 5.4 and 5.5) shows that both groups consider the term *gay* as having either positive or neutral connotations. Moreover, *gay* was the term most frequently cited by all respondents.

The most striking difference is found with respect to the term *queer*: the proportion of respondents considering the term to be positive in meaning is much higher among the North American than the British group. Although this study is too limited to provide a detailed account of the distribution of the term *queer*, it allows for the conclusion that there is no general consensus as to which term of reference is the most 'politically correct', reflecting the increasing heterogeneity of the gay community. Using *queer* may be perfectly acceptable for one group of gay men, and totally rejected by another. The following comments illustrate this differential interpretation:

*Table 5.3* Terms of reference

| Item | Total | Positive | Negative | Neutral |
|---|---|---|---|---|
| Gay | 16 | 8 | – | 8 |
| Fag | 11 | 1 | 7 | 3 |
| Queen(s) | 9 | 2 | 2 | 5 |
| Queer | 8 | 3 | 2 | 2 |
| Gay men | 8 | 3 | – | 5 |
| Homosexual | 7 | 1 | 1 | 5 |
| Gays | 5 | 1 | 1 | 3 |
| Puff(s)/poof(s) | 4 | 2 | 1 | 1 |
| Faggot | 3 | 1 | 2 | – |
| Her/she | 2 | 1 | 1 | – |
| Mary/Big Mary | 2 | – | 1 | 1 |
| Sister | 2 | 2 | – | – |

*Table 5.4* English speakers in North America

| Item | Total | Positive | Negative | Neutral |
|---|---|---|---|---|
| Gay | 11 | 6 | – | 5 |
| Fag | 10 | 1 | 7 | 2 |
| Gay men | 7 | 3 | – | 4 |
| Homosexual | 6 | 1 | 1 | 4 |
| Gays | 5 | 1 | 1 | 3 |
| Queer | 5 | 1 | 2 | 2 |
| Queen(s) | 4 | 1 | 1 | 2 |
| Faggot | 3 | 1 | 2 | – |
| Her/she | 2 | 1 | 1 | – |
| Puff(s)/poof(s) | 1 | 1 | – | – |
| Mary/big Mary | 1 | – | – | 1 |
| Sister | 1 | 1 | – | – |

*Table 5.5* English speakers in England

| Item | Total | Positive | Negative | Neutral |
|---|---|---|---|---|
| Gay | 5 | 2 | – | 3 |
| Queen(s) | 5 | 1 | 1 | 3 |
| Puff(s)/poof(s) | 3 | 1 | 1 | 1 |
| Queer | 3 | 3 | – | – |
| Homosexual | 1 | – | – | 1 |
| Fag | 1 | – | – | 1 |
| Gay men | 1 | – | – | 1 |
| Mary/Big Mary | 1 | – | 1 | – |
| Sister | 1 | 1 | – | – |

*Extract 5.13*
Queer is what gay activists seem to like to use; I might use it when talking to them. (AGM1)

*Extract 5.14*
I really don't use queer unless others around me use it; only in private gay settings. (AGM6)

The terms of reference used most frequently are *gay* and *homosexual*, both of them being perceived as more neutral than the term *queer*. Some respondents even pointed out that they preferred to use *gay* because it did not limit their identity to sexual interests and thus sounded less clinical:

*Extract 5.15*
I use gay because it is the most neutral term available. It is not offensive and it is commonly understood by everyone. [ . . . ] I only use homosexual and lesbian in political or social discussions, generally involving heterosexuals. They are neutral terms but they are somewhat clinical, dry terms. (AGM6)

## The Americanisation of British gay slang

Although there is only little solid documentation concerning the differences between American and British gay slang, it is revealing that most of the terms known to all the American respondents were also used by the British informants, with the exception of a few isolated terms such as *bear* (a large and usually hairy gay man) and *hustler* (a gay prostitute). Both items were known by all and used by a large majority of the American respondents, while only three of the younger (aged between 26 and 40) British respondents indicated that they were familiar with the terms even though they did not use them themselves. In addition, two of the British respondents pointed out that *hustler* was of American origin. On the other hand, many British terms, notably those having passed into British gay slang through Polari, such as *swish* (smart, fashionable), *mince* (walk effeminately), *bevvy* and *naff*, were not recognised by any of the American respondents, although these words have already passed into non-gay colloquial speech in Britain. Hence, it seems that the American gay subculture has far more influence in Britain than is true of the opposite direction. As Cox and Fay (1994: 285–6) state:

The cultural differences between the USA and Britain are mirrored in linguistic differences, no more so than in Gay culture. Because of the open upfront attitudes of North Americans in comparison to the reticence of the British, the verbalisation of activities common to both societies occurs more in the USA than in Britain. Gay men cruise parks in both countries, but only American Gayspeak has a term, green queen, to describe them. Similarly, the open public face of Gay culture in cities such as San Francisco and New York, resulting for example in the bathhouse scene, has produced US-only terminology to describe that scene, e.g., a bathsheba or our lady of the vapours. We note that social categorization, e.g., Safeway queen and fashion reference have higher frequency in Britain than in the USA, and sexual categorization and body references seem less frequent in Britain. However, the Gay scene in Britain becomes increasingly Americanized as the common use of buns, cruise, and pecs illustrates.

The gay parades in America had set in motion a more upfront attitude that was subsequently adopted in England (as well as in other countries). As a consequence, language had become a means of fighting for political and social goals, rather than just remaining a secret language. With changing sensibilities, the need for a new colloquial lexicon arose, a lexicon which met a variety of interests and differentiates various attitudes and types of homosexuals. Gay slang had long principally served to aid the cohesion of gay minority groups, marginalised because of their different sexual identity, and provided them with a feeling of security and belonging, as well as, to a certain extent, security against hostility and outside interference. The current gay lexical repertoire now seems to act predominantly as a means of distinguishing gay men's affiliations within the minority group and, although this is true only for certain subgroups, as a means of defiance towards abuse from outside. A greater shift towards a redefinition of linguistic strategies is clearly recognisable in current gay slang. Harvey (1997: 78) argues that gay men today no longer exclude themselves by the use of an opaque linguistic repertoire as was the case with Polari, but 'are colonising the lexical universe of "straight" English itself in what is no doubt a reflection of their increasing self-confidence and sense of identity'. In my data, there is some preliminary evidence that gay men have become more sensitive to social and ideological factors and draw on a wider range of lexical items to suit the shifting cultural context.

# Conclusion

The research conducted for this chapter was not intended to provide comprehensive and conclusive data about the colloquial vocabulary or slang used by gay men, but rather to give some insights into the ways in which gay men's experience, and their accompanying linguistic practices, have been affected by social change.

The growing heterogeneity of the gay community has naturally resulted in a gradual diversification of vocabulary use, with gay men signalling their group affiliation to diverse communities of practice by using different subsets of the linguistic repertoire available in the gay communities. Gay men display idiosyncratic speech styles as a way of constructing their identities, and do this by relating themselves, positively or negatively, to the people around them, projecting affiliation or distance through language. By verbally encoding their experiences, as well as by naming and renaming themselves and others, gay identities are constructed in a wide variety of ways. Different experiences of sexual, cultural and political identities emerge in controversies and arguments around issues of identity and the public negotiation of gay experience. The unstable and often controversial use of lexical items illustrates the lack of consensual meaning as a consequence of this diversifying process.

In this chapter, I have aimed to deconstruct the paradigm of gay vocabulary as a single way of speaking and to show how gay individuals explore and constantly recreate the lexical system in order to construct their identities. Gay male communities are diverse and fluid social categories and contexts, and even though speakers of gay slang may share familiarity with forms of gay practice and the linguistic representations that those forms command, they may have little else in common. It is now misleading to speak about a *single* gay slang, since cultural background, age, occupation, ethnic identity and socio-economic status, as well as variables such as degree of integration into the heterosexual community and political activism and cultural contexts of language use, structure the conditions of social, cultural and linguistic attitudes of gay men.

The crossover of gay terms into general non-gay colloquial slang may reflect the gradual lowering of sociocultural barriers to homosexuality and the gradual opening up of Western heterosexual cultures towards homosexual needs and concerns. Moreover, it is often impossible to distinguish between slang terms used by homosexual and heterosexual speakers, and the large number of currently popular slang phrases shared by heterosexual and homosexual speakers makes it difficult to determine in which direction borrowing has taken place. 'Gay vernacular' is a living and growing language. While some words may gradually change their meanings or become obsolete, new ones are introduced. Gay slang consists of a variety of linguistic strategies gay men may combine to encode a whole plethora not only of sexual, but also of cultural and political experiences and identities.

## Key for speaker codes

BGM 4 = British gay male. Age group: 26–30
BGM 6 = British gay male. Age group: 26–30
AGM 1 = American gay male. Age group: 31–35
AGM 2 = American gay male. Age group: 36–40
AGM 3 = American gay male. Age group: 36–40
AGM 4 = American gay male. Age group: 41–45
AGM 5 = American gay male. Age group: 51–60
AGM 6 = American gay male. Age group: 41–45
AGM 7 = American gay male. Age group: 36–40
AGM 10 = American gay male. Age group: 31–35

## Notes

1. Sedgwick (1990: 74) relates Lord Alfred Douglas's public declaration 'I am the Love that dare not speak its name' to 'St. Paul's routinely reproduced and re-worked denomination of sodomy as the crime whose name is not to be uttered'.
2. I do, however, acknowledge that the links between gender and sexuality are important to constructions of sexual identity and have been explored elsewhere in this book (see, for example, Morrish and Leap, this volume).
3. For the origins of Polari, cf. Hancock (1973).

## References

Baker, P. 2002. *Polari – the Lost Language of Gay Men*. New York: Routledge
Butler, J. 1993. *Bodies that Matter: on the Discursive Limits of 'Sex'*. New York: Routledge
Chauncey, G. 1994. *Gay New York*. New York: Basic Books
Cox, L.J. and Fay, R.J. 1994. Gayspeak, the linguistic fringe: Bona Polari, Camp, Queerspeak, and beyond. In Whittle, S. (ed.) *The Margins of the City: Gay Men's Urban Lives*. Aldershot: Arena, pp. 103–27
Eckert, P. and McConnell-Ginet, S. 1992. Think practically and look locally: language and gender as community based practice. *Annual Review of Anthropology* 21: 461–90

Eckert, P. and McConnell-Ginet, S. 1999. New generalizations and explanations in language and gender research. *Language in Society* 28 (2): 185–201

Farrell, R.A. 1972. The argot of the homosexual subculture. *Anthropological Linguistics* 14: 97–109

Gumperz, J.J. (ed.) 1982. *Language and Social Identity*. Cambridge: Cambridge University Press

Hall, K. and Bucholtz, M. (eds) 1995. *Gender Articulated: Language and the Socially Constructed Self*. New York: Routledge

Halliday, M.A.K. 1978. *Language as a Social Semiotic: the Social Interpretation of Language and Meaning*. London: Arnold

Hancock, I. 1973. Shelta and Polari. In Trudgill, P. (ed.) *The Languages of the British Isles*. Cambridge: Cambridge University Press, pp. 384–404

Harvey, K. 1997. 'Everybody loves a lover': gay men, straight men and a problem of lexical choice. In Harvey, K. and Shalom, C. (eds) *Language and Desire: Encoding Sex, Romance and Intimacy*. London: Routledge, pp. 60–82

Kennedy, R. 2002. *Nigger: the Strange Career of a Troublesome Word*. New York: Pantheon Books

Leap, W. 1996. *Word's Out: Gay Men's English*. Minnesota: University of Minnesota Press

LePage, R.B. and Tabouret-Keller, A. 1985. *Acts of Identity: Creole-based Approaches to Language and Ethnicity*. Cambridge: Cambridge University Press

Lucas, I. 1994. *Impertinent Decorum: Gay Theatrical Manoeuvres*. London: Cassell

Mühlhäusler, P. and Harre, R. 1990. *Pronouns and People: the Linguistic Construction of Social and Personal Identity*. Oxford: Blackwell

Sedgwick, E. 1990. *The Epistemology of the Closet*. Berkeley: University of California Press

Trudgill, P. 1992. *Introducing Language and Society*. London: Penguin

# 6
# Education, Culture and the Construction of Sexual Identity: an APPRAISAL Analysis of Lesbian Coming Out Narratives

*Helen Sauntson*

## Introduction

The primary purpose of this chapter is to explore the role culture plays in the coming out experiences of a group of young women identifying as lesbian. I argue that both context and culture play a crucial role in the discovery and construction of sexuality, with specific reference to female homosexuality. Researchers such as Morrish and Leap (this volume) are currently exploring relationships between sexual identity and geography, arguing that sexualities are always materially and geographically located. This geographical locating has an influence upon the shaping and experience of sexuality. In other words, geography has a material effect upon sexual experience and the social construction of sexual identity. In effect, gender and sexuality are to do with situated, negotiated and contested social and cultural constructions (Leap, 1995).

I aim to relate this argument to the notion of 'cultural locating', proposing that the women in question always locate their sexuality in specific and identifiable ways in particular cultural settings. In short, sexuality cannot be separated from its sociocultural context, and constructing sexual identity is as much a cultural process as it is an expression of sexual desire and articulation of object choice.

In the stories analysed, the opposition between compulsory and post-compulsory educational settings is striking and occurs in many of the narratives. This opposition has also been noted by O'Mara (1997) and Weston (1998). These two settings appear to be ascribed different sets of norms, values and attitudes by the narrators and, for this reason, it can be argued that they constitute different cultures. The main question addressed by this chapter then is 'how does this perceived cultural opposition between compulsory and post-compulsory education impact upon the experience of coming out and the construction of sexual identity?' Moreover, I aim to illustrate how a linguistic APPRAISAL (e.g. Martin, 2000; White, 2002, 2003) analysis can be useful in enabling us to move towards answering this question.[1]

The data analysed in this chapter comprise an electronic corpus of women's coming out narratives obtained from the US-based website www.comingoutstories.com. The website contains coming out stories from gay and bisexual men and women, transgendered and transsexual people and straight family and friends. While it would be interesting and fruitful to analyse stories from all of these categories, it would not be possible in the limited scope of this chapter. Therefore, I will focus on the stories produced by the women in the 15–25 age group identifying as lesbian because the educational environment is of particular importance to this age group, and therefore their stories are saturated with references to it.[2] Out of a total of 135 stories, 70 make at least one reference to education; 66 stories refer to compulsory education, while 31 make reference to post-compulsory education. Some refer to both. Of the stories, 34 present compulsory education using negative attitudinal markers; whereas only 10 stories use positive markers; 23 of the stories contain references to post-compulsory education that are evaluated positively, while only 4 stories describe post-compulsory education using negative attitudinal markers.

## Coming out narratives and cultural experience

As discussed in the Introduction to this collection, language and culture are inseparable. Cultural meanings are inscribed within the linguistic system and language itself both reflects and shapes cultural practice. As with all of the chapters in this collection, the research reported here centres around an analysis of situated linguistic practice rather focusing upon abstract theoretical notions of sexuality, culture and identity, although clearly this kind of linguistic analysis is closely linked to theory and is intended to provide a contribution to ongoing theoretical debates.

Before examining the data, it is perhaps useful to provide a working definition of 'coming out',[3] and to consider its role within narratives and the cultural contexts in which they are produced. While it is difficult to provide a central definition of 'coming out', Liang (1997: 291) offers the following as a useful starting point:

> The term for the act of naming and accepting one's same-sex emotions is coming out, the shortened form of coming out of the closet. It is a metaphor for both the recognition to oneself and the act of disclosing to another one's homosexuality.

Liang points out that coming out is a matter of degree rather than a binary opposition – some people are more 'out' than others and can be more or less out in different contexts. 'Coming out' is a sociocultural act and may perhaps be better understood as an ongoing process, rather than a single act.

A 'coming out narrative', then, is a text which reports, reflects and evaluates upon the ongoing process and experience of coming out. Because coming out narratives are a form of cultural practice, we can expect to find salient aspects of culture, including education, inscribed within the narrative. In all of the narratives examined, the narrators provide frequent evaluative descriptions of the levels of education in which they have experienced, and continue to experience, their coming out. These evaluative comments can give us an important insight into the ways in which sexualities interact with educational cultural practices in the US, and the ways in which education helps to shape sexual identities and experiences.

Perhaps the most crucial difference revealed by the analysis are the varying evaluative patterns surrounding compulsory and post-compulsory education. Weston (1998) has previously argued that the rural/urban opposition plays a part in constituting lesbian and gay subjects and that urbanisation is seen as central to the construction of lesbian and gay subcultures and communities. More specifically, Weston argues that this contrast is a symbolic one – it is the cultural values and norms associated with these different climates, rather than the geographical locations themselves, which are important to people's understandings and perceptions of sexual identity. Rural contexts are frequently associated with isolation and surveillance, whereas urban contexts are associated with a sense of belonging and group membership and freedom. In my data, I discovered that the opposition between compulsory schooling and non-compulsory higher education was very strong and played an important role in constituting the lesbian identities of the narrators. Many of the narrators in my data encoded references to the school in ways similar to the rural settings in Weston's data, and the university in ways similar to urban settings. The university campus and urban settings seem to share the same set of cultural norms and values for these narrators. Coming out stories frequently narrate the movement from one set of values, associated with a rural or compulsory schooling cultural climate, to another set of values associated with an urban or university campus cultural climate. In Weston's (1998: 40) words: 'The result is a sexual geography in which the city represents a beacon of tolerance and gay community, the country a locus of persecution and gay absence.'

Of course, this division is one which is constructed by the narrators themselves. But it is interesting to explore the semiotics which function to construct the narrators' lesbian identities through this kind of spatial and cultural contrast. I wish to develop Weston's work by examining the linguistic markers of attitude which accompany the descriptions of the school and university campus in the women's stories as a means of enhancing our understanding of the educational factors which affect these women's perceptions and constructions of their lesbian sexual identities.

The act of coming out and the act of producing a coming out narrative are both forms of sociocultural practice. Both are performative acts in the sense that producing them changes the social world of the narrator and those around them in some way. Coming out narratives share a common function – to report, reflect and evaluate interactions between desires, sexual identities and cultures. This common function is reflected in the linguistic forms and structures found within the narratives – APPRAISAL analysis may be one means of systematically identifying the kinds of evaluative patterns most commonly found throughout narratives of this type. More specifically, it can point to the particular ways in which education, as part of the broader culture, contributes to the individual's growing awareness and construction of their homosexuality. Coming out narratives provide a site where wider social discourses can interact with the individual's experience of sexual desire and identity. APPRAISAL analysis can illuminate some of the tensions between discourses and the effects that these have upon individual and social experience.

It is hoped that this preliminary research will contribute to our understanding of how the interaction between specific educational contexts and the individual shapes the individual's experience and construction of their sexual identity. The linguistic analysis is intended to be applied to reveal how lesbian identity can be constructed as positive or negative, depending on the attitudinal experiences of the narrator. In a society where the construction of a negative sexual identity is accompanied by affectual feelings of extreme negative self-worth, which are often manifested as a range of emotional and mental problems, this understanding of the factors influencing positive or negative identity construction is of crucial importance.

## APPRAISAL: **analysing linguistic evaluations of culture**

APPRAISAL is a means of analysing and describing evaluative language which is situated within a broad systemic functional framework (e.g. Halliday, 1994). The APPRAISAL system categorises the ways that social relationships and experiences are encoded in and enacted through language. Martin (2000: 145) defines APPRAISAL as: 'The semantic resources used to negotiate emotions, judgements, and valuations, alongside resources for amplifying and engaging with these evaluations.'

APPRAISAL consists of the systems of attitude, graduation and engagement. It is the system of attitude which is of most interest in this chapter. Martin identifies three broad subsystems of attitudinal positioning within the APPRAISAL system: AFFECT, which refers to the linguistic resources deployed for construing the individual's emotional responses; JUDGEMENT – the linguistic resources deployed for construing moral or social evaluations of behaviour; and APPRECIATION – the linguistic resources deployed for construing the 'aesthetic' qualities of processes and natural phenomena.

| | |
|---|---|
| AFFECT (*positive*): | I am gay and damn <u>happy</u> to be gay. |
| AFFECT (*negative*): | I carried this <u>feeling of loneliness</u> for years. |
| JUDGEMENT (*positive*): | I met a lot of <u>wonderful</u> professors, mentors and friends. |
| JUDGEMENT (*negative*): | I always had to pretend that I wasn't [gay] cos it [being gay] <u>wasn't something that was accepted</u> in my school. |
| APPRECIATION (*positive*): | I saw this movie 'The Truth about Jane', and I thought it was <u>pretty cool.</u> |
| APPRECIATION (*negative*): | I was queer in high school but was deathly afraid of coming out in such an <u>oppressive</u> environment. |

The examples show that each of these categories can have a positive or negative value. Positive and negative evaluations work on a sliding scale of AMPLIFICATION, where evaluations may be intensified (augment), played down (mitigate) and where comparisons may be drawn for amplifying effect (enrich). These three types of AMPLIFICATION resources are illustrated in the examples below.

| | |
|---|---|
| AMPLIFICATION: AUGMENT: | It hurt me <u>a lot</u>, and it made me <u>extremely</u> afraid to come out to anyone. |
| AMPLIFICATION: MITIGATE: | . . . on campus I am <u>just a number</u>. |
| AMPLIFICATION: ENRICH: | I became <u>more</u> secluded there. |

The categories of APPRAISAL are mainly distinguished semantically, and are realised primarily through the lexico-grammar of a text. Further degrees of delicacy are addressed by Martin and others. These are summarised in Figure 6.1 which provides an overview of the whole system of attitude. Figure 6.1 also illustrates how AMPLIFICATION choices can combine with attitudinal positioning choices.

At a general level, the three categories of attitude do overlap as they all encode feeling. An attitudinal marker may not necessarily directly express the feelings of the speaker (or another character in the narrative). The marker may, instead, construe someone's behaviour in positive or negative terms (JUDGEMENT) or it may evaluate a text, product or process (APPRECIATION). But direct markers of JUDGEMENT and APPRECIATION can imply an individual's affectual evaluations as well. In the example below, the narrator positively evaluates the behaviour of college professors using JUDGEMENT. However, the sentence simultaneously functions to indicate positive AFFECT – we deduce that because the professors are described as an inspiration (an evaluation of their behaviour), the narrator *feels* inspired by them. Therefore, the sentence can be 'double-coded' as both JUDGEMENT and AFFECT.

There are even <u>openly gay</u> and lesbian professors [Veracity – positive], who are a <u>big</u> [Amp. Augment] inspiration [Capacity – positive judgement of professors. Affect – positive].

These examples involve 'feelings' but the feelings are recast either as judgements of human behaviour or as qualities attributed to particular objects or entities. Martin (2000) refers to this concept as 'the institutionalisation of feeling' and it is illustrated in Figure 6.2.

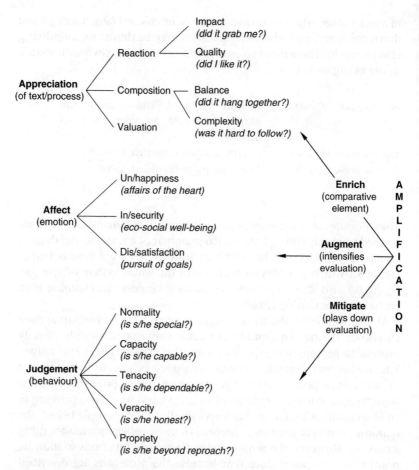

*Figure 6.1*  Options available within attitudinal APPRAISAL (adapted from Martin, 2000)

This concept relates to what Martin terms 'inscribed' (direct) or 'evoked' (implied) APPRAISAL. Martin (2000: 155) claims that APPRAISAL markers may be 'directly construed in the text, or implicated through the selection of ideational meanings which rebound with affectual meaning'. By this he means that an evaluation may represent a meaning which is not overtly marked as attitudinal, but which implies an attitudinal colouring. The interpretation of this implied evaluation often depends on the reader's social, cultural or ideological position (White, 2002, 2003).

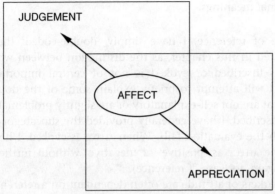

Ethics/morality (rules and regulations)
Feeling institutionalised as proposals

JUDGEMENT

AFFECT

APPRECIATION

Feeling institutionalised as propositions
Aesthetics/value (criteria and assessment)

*Figure 6.2* JUDGEMENT and APPRECIATION as institutionalised AFFECT (based on Martin, 2000; White, 2002)

*Inscribed affect* – I was <u>scared</u> of being harassed.
*Evoked appreciation ('token' of affect)* – At school I have had a lot of problems.

*At school I have had a lot of problems* functions as a negative evaluation of the school which is an entity, so it is coded as negative APPRECIATION. But we can also read a negative affectual response in the narrator in their presentation of their school environment as problematic. This example can, therefore, be read as a 'token' of negative AFFECT with the word *problems* (a word which is saturated with negativity) evoking our interpretation of the situation as embodying a negative affectual response in the narrator.

The identification of evoked APPRAISAL does depend somewhat on the subjective interpretation of the analyst, and where they are culturally situated. As mentioned in the introduction, many cultural meanings are encoded in the linguistic system – it is often necessary to be fully integrated into the culture in order to attach meanings to the attitudinal markers of evaluation. Eggins and Slade (1997: 126) point out that:

The interpretation of the meaning of lexical items is not only dependent on the co-text but also on the sociocultural background and positioning of the interactants. Appraisal analysis must therefore be sensitive to the potential for different readings or 'hearings' of attitudinal meanings.

For ease of reference, I have simply 'double-coded' the relevant extracts cited in this chapter, as the distinction between whether the APPRAISAL is inscribed or evoked is not of central importance here. However, I will attempt to briefly explain some of the double-coded extracts that are not self-explanatory or are slightly problematic. Where AFFECT is inscribed, I have generally provided the subcategory of AFFECT into which the evaluation falls. When AFFECT is evoked, I have simply labelled the AFFECT as 'positive' or 'negative' without further detailed analysis (again, for ease of reference).

Some markers of attitude are often dependent on a referent which is situated elsewhere in the co-text, i.e. not cited in the extracts included here due to lack of space. Where possible, I will attempt to justify the analysis if it is not immediately evident in the extract cited.

## JUDGEMENT

JUDGEMENT is the attitudinal system which is of particular interest in this chapter. Markers of JUDGEMENT occur frequently in the narratives analysed, particularly in reference to education. JUDGEMENT enables a speaker/writer to evaluate someone's behaviour as conforming or not conforming to a particular set of social/cultural norms. This is the aspect that deals with social evaluations of behaviour and social practice, and it is these aspects of evaluative language that position the individual within a broader social and cultural system. More specifically, the JUDGEMENT markers give us information about how, exactly, the narrators' sexuality is perceived by, positioned and experienced within that cultural context. We must remember that coming out is a social and cultural act – it changes the world in some way. Therefore, a linguistic reflection on this act in the form of a coming out narrative is an evaluative reflection upon a process of social and cultural change. As JUDGEMENT is central to exploring such issues, it is worth explaining this subsystem in a little more detail.

Like all appraisal categories, JUDGEMENT works on a sliding scale of positive and negative dimensions and can be subdivided into two broad areas:

- *Social esteem* – Assesses people in terms of their normality (how usual/unusual someone is), capability (how capable they are) and tenacity (how determined or resolute they are). Social esteem markers provide evaluations of how a person's behaviour conforms or does not conform to socially desirable standards in any given culture.

- *Social sanction* – Assesses people in terms of veracity (how truthful someone is) and propriety (how ethical someone is) and provides evaluative markers which indicate whether the behaviour of a person is seen as right or wrong in any given culture.

Figure 6.3 summarises the JUDGEMENT system. Examples from the stories are also provided below.

Analysing the JUDGEMENT markers in the narratives enables us to see how coming out is experienced as a sociocultural process, as well as a personal, emotional one. It enables us to see how certain aspects of the narrators' behaviour (and the behaviour of other characters in the stories) is either congruous or incongruous with social and cultural

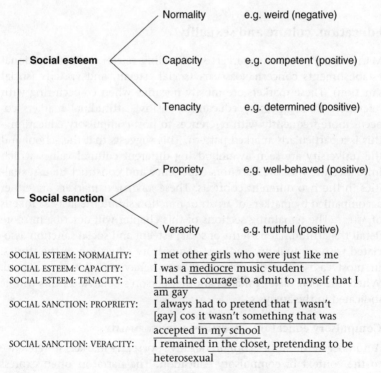

| | | |
|---|---|---|
| | Normality | e.g. weird (negative) |
| **Social esteem** | Capacity | e.g. competent (positive) |
| | Tenacity | e.g. determined (positive) |
| | Propriety | e.g. well-behaved (positive) |
| **Social sanction** | Veracity | e.g. truthful (positive) |

| | |
|---|---|
| SOCIAL ESTEEM: NORMALITY: | I met other girls who were just like me |
| SOCIAL ESTEEM: CAPACITY: | I was a mediocre music student |
| SOCIAL ESTEEM: TENACITY: | I had the courage to admit to myself that I am gay |
| SOCIAL SANCTION: PROPRIETY: | I always had to pretend that I wasn't [gay] cos it wasn't something that was accepted in my school |
| SOCIAL SANCTION: VERACITY: | I remained in the closet, pretending to be heterosexual |

*Figure 6.3* JUDGEMENT categories (based on Martin, 2000)

expectations of behaviour, and if there are any specific patterns of in/congruity throughout the narratives.

It is worth providing a brief note here on the narrative elements which explicitly refer to the narrator coming out or choosing not to come out. Such elements would include words and phrases referring to the state of being in or out (of the closet) such as *openly gay*. I argue that staying in and coming out are forms of human behaviour, which means that linguistic evaluations of being in or out generally fall into the attitudinal subsystem of JUDGEMENT. More specifically, the act of coming out, or deciding not to, seems to involve behaving in an honest or dishonest fashion respectively. This honesty/dishonesty distinction in relation to coming out is often explicitly mentioned by the narrators. In the context of these stories, a phrase such as 'I came out' is semantically equivalent to 'I was honest about my sexuality'. For this reason, it seems evident that references to coming out or not coming out should be coded as (evoked) positive or negative VERACITY within the system of JUDGEMENT.

## Education, culture and sexuality

Many of the JUDGEMENT markers surrounding references to educational establishments concern NORMALITY (social esteem) and VERACITY (social sanction). These markers are mostly negative when co-occurring with references to compulsory education. Positive attitudinal markers co-occur more frequently with references to post-compulsory education – this is a particularly marked pattern. This suggests that the school and the university are seen as embodying different cultural values which influence the way the narrators experience and construct their sexualities in the two different contexts. These JUDGEMENT markers are either accompanied by markers of AFFECT or function simultaneously as tokens of AFFECT. The remaining sections of this chapter will describe in more detail the attitudinal patterns of social esteem and social sanction associated with compulsory and post-compulsory education in the stories. In most cases, it is the narrators' own behaviour that is evaluated. Where the JUDGEMENT evaluates another person's behaviour, this will be indicated in the analysis.

### Compulsory education – social esteem (NORMALITY)

A number of the stories contain negative NORMALITY markers in reference to the context of compulsory education. The narrators often express feelings of being positioned as different, abnormal and as an outsider by the cultural value system operating in this context. The frequency of NORMALITY markers in these stories suggests that the boundaries of normality are strictly policed in the compulsory education context – there are punitive consequences for anyone who attempts to step outside or challenge these boundaries, as illustrated in Extracts 6.1 and 6.2. Isolation and alienation from the school community are common feelings expressed by the narrators throughout the stories, so it would appear that NORMALITY is an important cultural value in the context of compulsory schooling.

*Extract 6.1*

I then went to highschool. I became more [Amp. Enrich] secluded there [Normality – Negative. Affect – negative in that the narrator felt secluded] and did not know why. I decided that people just [Amp. Mitigate] didn't like me [Affect: Unhappiness – Negative. In this case, the affect is ascribed to 'people', not to the narrator] so I concentrated on school work.

*Extract 6.2*

Anyone who was thought of as being gay was teased and alienated [Propriety – Negative. Affect: Unhappiness: Antipathy (the narrator felt alienated, but the 'fellow peers' were doing the alienating, which would count as behaviour and, therefore, be another example of Propriety – Negative in the same way that *teased* is)] from the school community [Normality – Negative] by their fellow peers.

Extract 6.3 shows the construction of the narrator as abnormal by the rest of her school community as a result of her being a 'tomboy'.

*Extract 6.3*

Then when I was 11 and I was just starting secondary school I started to get the idea that girl who likes girls=lesbian lesbian-strange strange-unpopular [Normality – Negative]. Of course I kept it to myself [Veracity – Negative], but I was considered a tomboy [Normality – generally carries a negative cultural meaning] which people like down primary school [Affect – Positive] but not [Affect – Negative] in the new fresh 'grown up' world of secondary school. I did make friends and there was lots of people from my old school [Affect – Positive] but still 'the popular' people [Normality – Positive] (boys who act boyish and girls who act girly and with the exception of about 2 people had to be thin and fairly good looking) didn't want to know me [Affect – Negative, sourced to *the popular people*].

It is interesting to note the use of *of course* before the negative VERACITY marker – this implies that it is the cultural norm in this context to conceal homosexuality. It is assumed the audience shares this perspective and understands what the consequences would be of flouting this cultural value. Moreover, the narrator in Extract 6.3 discusses how the primary school setting enabled her to be a 'tomboy' and to transgress gender/sexuality expectations imposed by society. However, this was not permitted when she went to secondary school, because it was not considered to be 'grown up'. This suggests that different cultural values operate between different educational settings, even within the same compulsory context. The mature sexuality expected to materialise when the narrator reaches secondary school is heterosexuality. Non-conformity to heterosexual norms and values indicates sexual immaturity and is, thus, acceptable at primary school, but not in the adolescent world of secondary school.

Extracts 6.1–6.3 highlight the school as a site where culturally dominant modes of signification are promoted and perpetuated. 'Difference' is not a culturally acceptable value. Indeed, difference is a culturally constructed concept imbued with negative values. At school, the narrators seem to perceive 'normality' as, in part, defined as heterosexuality and difference is defined as non-heterosexual. School is a place where young people are encouraged to 'learn' how to be heterosexual. If this learning process is incongruous with the individual's sense of sexual desire and identity, negative NORMALITY markers emerge in their narratives along with negative AFFECT as a result. According to evaluative statements such as the ones above, the school context appears to do little to challenge hegemonic notions of compulsory heterosexuality.[4] The result is that the narrators themselves do not openly challenge heterosexuality by coming out – in this sense, the school itself becomes a kind of closet. The frequent markers of negative VERACITY surrounding the school indicate it as a place of habitual identity concealment, as discussed in the following section.

### Compulsory education – social sanction (PROPRIETY and VERACITY)

In the context of compulsory education, the culturally dominant values of social esteem (particularly NORMALITY) and social sanction (particularly PROPRIETY and VERACITY) seem to conflict. This is a key characteristic of the stories that is revealed by APPRAISAL analysis. To many of the narrators, school is not a place where they can be both normal and honest in terms of their sexuality. As both NORMALITY and VERACITY are seen as important cultural values, the dilemma the narrators face is which value to uphold and which to reject, when they really do not want to reject either. This tension between adhering to the cultural values of social sanction and social esteem is one which is seen to be resolved in the context of post-compulsory education, as will be discussed later. In terms of social sanction, Extracts 6.4–6.6 show how the markers of negative PROPRIETY attributed to compulsory education illustrate how homosexuality is constructed as wrong and immoral in the school environment. Negative PROPRIETY markers in the stories function mainly to indicate the oppressive climate of compulsory education.

### Extract 6.4
However, I never asked her out or anything because of the following reasons: (1) I went to a religious school and from past experience I knew that the Catholic take on the subject of homosexuality was not a positive one [Propriety – Negative].

### Extract 6.5
I wondered about it [being gay] in high school, definitely, but I wasn't in an environment where it was okay to be out [Propriety – Negative. The narrator's behaviour of 'being out' is evaluated as 'not okay'].

### Extract 6.6
I always had to pretend that I wasn't [gay] [Veracity – Negative] cos it wasn't something that was accepted in my school [Propriety – Negative] and my parents would have flipped [Affect: Insecurity: Disquiet – Negative, sourced to *my parents* rather than the narrator].

The negative affectual responses of the narrators are clear in most cases and negative PROPRIETY is also frequently linked to negative VERACITY, as in Extract 6.6, where PROPRIETY is presented as a justification for the narrator's perceived dishonesty. In Extracts 6.4–6.6, because homosexuality is constructed as immoral, or at least as a kind of behaviour that is improper and unacceptable, the narrator usually makes a decision to conceal what they believe is their true identity. In trying to adhere to the cultural values of NORMALITY and PROPRIETY in this context, the narrators perceive themselves as being forced to abandon the cultural values of VERACITY. These markers can refer to the narrators' overt pretence of heterosexuality, as well as simply their refusal to come out. A range of affectual responses (mostly negative) which are linked to negative VERACITY are also displayed in the following set of extracts.

*Extract 6.7*
I was pretty sure [Affect: Security: Confidence – Positive] I was queer in high school but was deathly [Amp. Augment] afraid [Affect: Disinclination: Fear – Negative] of coming out in such [Amp. Augment] an oppressive [Appreciation – Negative] environment [Veracity – Negative].

*Extract 6.8*
I made new friends at my school in a few months, though I remained in the closet, pretending to be heterosexual [Veracity – Negative].

*Extract 6.9*
But in high school, little by little, I began to acknowledge [Veracity – Positive] that when I stared at a girl, it wasn't just [Amp. Mitigate] simple admiration [Affect: Happiness: Affection – Positive]. I wanted to be with her. [Affect: Inclination: Desire] But I kept these feelings secret, thinking that if I could hide them, I wasn't really gay [Veracity – Negative].

*Extract 6.10*
There were other things on my mind – my school, my sports, music, friends – to have to worry about a boyfriend. I then found myself trying to like certain guys, just so I could say that I liked a guy [Veracity (evoked) – Negative].

*Extract 6.11*
I was so close to telling Alexis that I was bisexual before the harassment [Propriety – Negative (judgement of people doing the harassing – the 'people' who harass the narrator are mentioned elsewhere in the narrative). Affect: Unhappiness: Antipathy] started, I was scared of being harassed [Affect: Disinclination: Fear – Negative] so I didn't [tell] [Veracity – Negative].

*Extract 6.12*
I recall my participation in the seventh grade 'hot boys' discussion consisting of a forced giggle and a false heterosexual crush [Veracity – Negative].

*Extract 6.13*
So here I am now. Im 15, a sophomore in highschool. No girlfriend. Not out [Veracity – Negative] yet. Im <u>too</u> [Amp. Augment] <u>afraid</u> to come out [Affect: Disinclination: Fear – Negative].

The negative AFFECT markers which can be seen to accompany the negative VERACITY markers illustrate clearly how concealment and dishonesty have a negative emotional effect upon the narrators. In particular, the dislike and unhappiness created by pretending to be heterosexual is encoded in the negative AFFECT markers. The most common AFFECT subcategory co-occurring with negative VERACITY markers is DISINCLINATION expressing fear – the extent of the narrators' fear of coming out or of being found out is often emphasised through AMPLIFICATION resources as in Extracts 6.7, 6.11 and 6.13. This suggests that fear is an emotion the narrators wish to emphasise in their stories. Fear is thus construed attitudinally as having a strong impact upon the narrators' perception and construction of their sexual identities in the compulsory educational context. Unhappiness is also an AFFECT subcategory commonly associated with negative VERACITY markers.

In a small number of stories, some positive attitudinal markers are used when the narrators recount their experiences of compulsory education. These seem to occur where the narrator discovers and integrates with other gay and/or bisexual people at school. The narrator's immersion into these subgroups or 'cliques' means that they can adhere to the cultural values of both NORMALITY and VERACITY, even if only within the context of that subgroup. This seems to be enough to make the negative affectual responses to the school culture disappear, thus the emotional effects of the positive JUDGEMENT markers are significant.

*Extract 6.14*
I participated in the 2002 National Day of Silence. It was <u>really</u> [Amp. Augment] <u>cool</u> [Appreciation – Positive] to see the number of <u>supportive</u> people in my school [Propriety – Positive. Affect – Positive].

*Extract 6.15*
Highschool was a <u>great</u> time [Appreciation – Positive. Affect – Positive] for me because I met other girls who were <u>just</u> [Amp. Augment] like me [Normality – Positive. Affect: Happiness: Cheer – Positive]. There was the girl Jo that was gay and we were friends <u>well, sorta</u> [Amp. Mitigate]. I liked her [Affect: Happiness: Affection – Positive] and

I didn't know if my feelings were okay at the time [Affect: Insecurity – Negative] so I wanted to keep my distance. At the end of my freshman year I admitted to myself and my cousin that yes in fact [Amplification – augment] I was a lesbian [Veracity – Positive].

*Extract 6.16*
Once I finally put my finger on what made me so different [Normality – Negative] with the girls I had actually started to fit in with a group of people [Normality – Positive].

In these instances, the narrator's discovery of gay subcultures at school is the predominant means by which they are able to evaluate the compulsory school experience positively in any way.

**Post-compulsory education – social esteem (NORMALITY and VERACITY)**

While the cultural context of compulsory schooling is evaluated in negative JUDGEMENT and AFFECT terms, post-compulsory education at college and university appears to provide a more positive sociocultural experience for these young women. Differing APPRAISAL patterns suggest that a different value system operates in post-compulsory education, thus creating a contrasting cultural environment in which the narrator can engage and potentially renegotiate their sexual identity. The expression of different feelings and judgements in relation to this environment may, of course, partly be a result of the narrators' maturation and emotional development, but the clustering of JUDGEMENT markers in reference to post-compulsory education suggests that immersion into a different cultural environment does play a large part in the narrators' perceived shift from negative to positive affectual experience. It is interesting to note that some of the younger narrators are aware of this before they embark upon post-compulsory education. In Extracts 6.17 and 6.18, positive JUDGEMENT and AFFECT markers relate to future expectations. This suggests that the different cultural value systems associated with compulsory and post-compulsory education are widely disseminated and understood within the broader cultural context.

*Extract 6.17*
I cannot wait [Affect: Inclination: Desire – Positive] to go off to college and experience not feeling so alone [Normality – Positive. Affect – Positive (through use of the negative *not feeling so alone*)].[5]

*Extract 6.18*
[ . . . ] and was pretty much resigned to the fact that I wouldn't tell
my parents [Veracity – Negative] until I was off at college and at a
safe distance.

University seems to be a place where homosexuality is redefined
as normal, and is ascribed a more positive cultural value than in the
compulsory secondary school setting. So the NORMALITY markers found
co-occurring with references to university tend to be more positive as in
Extract 6.19.

*Extract 6.19*
And then I went to college, and I was introduced to the gay
community, and I felt like I had finally found my niche [ . . . ]
[Normality – Positive. Affect: Happiness: Cheer – Positive] I had
always [Amp. Augment] felt somehow alienated, [Affect: Unhappi-
ness: Antipathy – Negative] instead of fearing relationships [Affect:
Disinclination: Fear – Negative], I was wanting one [ . . . ] [Affect:
Inclination: Desire – Positive] with a woman.

The use of the word *finally* (which occurs in many extracts in this
section), indicates that the narrators' ability to evaluate themselves
positively in terms of normality is the result of a long and difficult
process. The use of the conjunction *instead* in Extract 6.19 marks a
contrast between two sets of experiences – the contrastive experiences
of being at school and being at college, and the different cultural
values that accompany these situations, are inscribed in the grammar
(e.g. through conjunctions), as well as the lexis.

The markers of VERACITY, similarly, tend to be positive in reference
to university where they were negative in reference to school. In
Extract 6.20, the interplay between positive and negative VERACITY is
particularly marked. The narrator clearly associates university as a place
where she can be out, and anywhere that is not the university campus
as sites where she must revert to concealing her lesbian identity. Her
outness is thus restricted to one particular location. In fact, there is
a strong polarity constructed between the university campus and the
narrators' home background in many of the stories. The two settings
are ascribed different cultural values in relation to sexuality, with the
narrators' home environment frequently experienced as isolating, lonely
and discriminatory, in the same way that they experience compulsory
schooling. The university campus setting is contrastingly experienced

as safe, accepting and welcoming the narrator as part of a recognisable community based on shared sociocultural values. The movement between these locations and their associated cultural values is very clearly marked through the use of attitudinal markers. Notice, again, the AMPLIFICATION resources (AUGMENT) used to emphasise the negative affectual experience of being in the closet.

*Extract 6.20*
Anyway – I move back home for summer and went WAY [Amp. Augment] back into the very back of that closet that I had been hiding in for so long [Amp. Augment] [Veracity – Negative].

It was pretty damn [Amp. Augment] dark in there [Appreciation – Negative]. [...] I got really [Amp. Augment] depressed to the point where I didn't get out of my bed for a while [Amp. Augment] [...] [Affect: Unhappiness: Misery – Negative] still I couldn't tell anyone ... else ... [Veracity – Negative]

When I returned to school in the fall – I came out again [...] [Veracity – Positive] this time got some counselling and got involved with some gay and lesbian groups ... things were starting to look better ... [Appreciation – Positive. Affect – Positive]

Extracts 6.21–6.24 illustrate how the narrators feel they can be out at university (positive VERACITY) and how their sexual identity is, or will be, a shared and social one – they become members of a community at college, whereas that is often not possible at school. The positive AFFECT markers which accompany the positive JUDGEMENT markers of NORMALITY and VERACITY often centre around feelings such as self-confidence, liberation and being welcomed rather than being lonely. The most common AFFECT subcategory linked to positive judgements markers is HAPPINESS.

*Extract 6.21*
Then came college. What a different place! [Appreciation – Positive, because school had previously been negatively evaluated in the text] I was completely [Amp. Augment] out, to my roommate, to all my friends [Veracity – Positive] (most of whom are queer as well) and such.

*Extract 6.22*
When I came to college this past September, it was one of the most liberating experiences of my life [Amp. Enrich] [Appreciation – Positive. Affect: Happiness: Cheer – Positive].

*Extract 6.23*
Throughout that time in college I allowed myself to let those innate feelings come out instead of shoving them back inside [Veracity – Positive].

*Extract 6.24*
Finally during my freshmen year of college I had had enough of hurting her and playing with guy's emotions. <u>I had the courage</u> [Tenacity – Positive] to <u>admit to myself that I am gay</u> [Veracity – Positive] and <u>damn</u> [Amp. Augment] happy to be gay [Affect: Happiness: Cheer – Positive].

It is interesting to note that in these extracts the narrators do not specify exactly what it is about the college environment that creates a different set of sociocultural values and, as a result, a different set of affectual responses for the narrator. It is often simply indicated as the place where they finally felt they could come out and therefore begin to judge their behaviour in positive terms of VERACITY.

In the following extracts, the narrators discuss how being at university enabled them to come out to their parents, and this is quite a common occurrence in the corpus of stories and has also been noted by Weston (1998). The shift in identity constructed in the college cultural context enables the narrators to subsequently renegotiate a different relationship with their family and friends from 'home'. The university is often constructed as providing a 'safe distance' for the narrator to come out to her family as in Extracts 6.25–6.28.

*Extract 6.25*
I carried this feeling of loneliness <u>for years</u> [Amp. Augment] [Affect: Insecurity: Disquiet – Negative] then I went away to school. My years at school, I started feeling <u>more</u> [Amp. Enrich] confident about myself, and my sexuality [Affect: Security: Confidence – Positive]. On my first Christmas vacation home <u>I decide to come out</u> to my uncle who's gay [Veracity – Positive] (but never came out to anyone) [Veracity – Negative judgement of uncle's level of honesty].

*Extract 6.26*
And so I left for college. [ . . . ] <u>I have come out</u> to most of my friends back home, [Veracity – Positive] losing a few, but <u>growing closer</u> to more of them [Affect: Happiness: Affection – Positive].

*Extract 6.27*
Finally, in 2001 – Four Months after I began college in the States –
I decided that I was going to come out to my best friend and to my
mother on my trip of Europe in the summer [Veracity – Positive].

*Extract 6.28*
She [narrator's mother] was surprised, [Affect: Insecurity: Surprise –
Negative, sourced to the narrator's mother] both about me being gay
and about how I'm 100% [Amp. Augment] <u>out</u> at Northwestern, my
college [Veracity – Positive].

Weston (1998) has argued that it is not necessarily the university environment that creates these opportunities for renegotiating and reconfig-
uring identities, but simply being 'at a distance' from family, although
these stories suggest that the university environment and its cultural
value system ensure that even if the narrator is rejected by their family
when they come out to them, they will still 'belong' at university. The
APPRAISAL patterns in these stories suggest that family and school construe
one cultural context, while university construes a different one. It is
only when the narrator becomes integrated into the post-compulsory
education culture that they can reconstruct their sexual identity at home
with their family.

In addition to the frequent JUDGEMENT markers, some of the stories
contain positive markers of APPRECIATION co-occurring with references to
post-compulsory education. These APPRECIATION resources do give some
indication of the specific processes and practices associated with post-
compulsory education that create a different social value (JUDGEMENT)
system that enables the narrator to come out and experience their
lesbian sexual identity more positively.

*Extract 6.29*
Luckily, I went to college several years ago and left many of those
voices behind. I am still in Oklahoma, but my large, public university
has many places – <u>progressive</u> [Appreciation – Positive] clubs, departments, and events – where members of sexual minorities can find
refuge. I didn't really seek these things out, but they came to me,
thankfully. I met a lot of <u>wonderful</u> [Capacity – Positive] professors,
mentors and friends that present an alternative to the <u>self-deprecating</u>
[Appreciation – Negative] life I'd known.

The key APPRECIATION marker in Extract 6.29 (which is also found in some other stories) centres around the progressive departments which are evaluated positively by the narrator. This creates a different value system which is congruous with the desired value system of the narrator, thus enabling them to come out. Coming out is then accompanied by positive affectual responses because all of the cultural values (NORMALITY, VERACITY, PROPRIETY) can be adhered to within the same context.

Some of the extracts already included contain references to specific lesbian and gay subcultures encountered by the narrators when they enter post-compulsory education. Participation in the groups enables the narrators to experience and express more positive judgements of NORMALITY, PROPRIETY and VERACITY. References to these kinds of groups are also commonly accompanied by positive markers of APPRECIATION. Extracts 6.30–6.32 highlight this. Again, it is interesting to note the use of the word *finally* in Extract 6.30 which suggests that the narrator's search for a place where they can be both normal and honest has been long and arduous, and the cultural values encountered in post-compulsory education have been desired for a long time.

*Extract 6.30*
I joined the campus LesBiGay Network. I'm <u>really</u> [Amp. Augment] <u>excited</u> [Affect: Satisfaction: Interest – Positive], and I've met some <u>really</u> [Amp. Augment] <u>awesome</u> [Capacity – Positive] people. I've <u>finally</u> found somewhere that <u>I feel I belong</u> [Normality – Positive. Affect – Positive].

*Extract 6.31*
Came out [Veracity – Positive] to my friends on campus, all of whom accepted me and TALK about it with me [Propriety – Positive sourced to *my friends on campus* with the narrator as the target of the evaluation]. My friends at LesBiGay are <u>really</u> [Amp. Augment] <u>cool</u> [Capacity – Positive]. They've <u>really</u> [Amp. Augment] helped me come to terms with myself and accept myself for who I am [Veracity – Positive. Affect – Positive].

*Extract 6.32*
I have been going to gay clubs and <u>enjoying myself</u> [Affect: Happiness: Cheer – Positive]; it's <u>such a</u> [Amp. Augment] <u>great thing</u> [Appreciation – Positive] to be accepted! [Affect – Positive, as the narrator feels good as a result of feeling accepted]

Coming out involves the simultaneous declaration and construction of an identity. The coming out that the narrators describe and reflect on in these final extracts seems to entail them becoming actors in the world, rather than being acted upon, as is often the case in the narrators' experience of school. In her study of processes of gay identity assumption among university students, O'Mara (1997) observes how the students encounter a gay community and a level of political engagement at university which enable them to actively produce their own lesbian and gay subjectivities. Extracts 6.30–6.32 illustrate this relationship between the narrators' immersion into a gay community on campus and the self-actualisations construed through the speech act of coming out which is evaluated positively. It seems that not coming out allows others to act upon the narrator, constructing their identity for them as either falsely heterosexual or as abnormal or immoral. Remaining in the closet, then, means that the narrators position themselves as complicit in maintaining heterosexuality as the dominant sociocultural norm. But coming out is a more active performance which, although resistant to culturally dominant norms and ideologies, is evaluated positively by the narrators.

## Conclusion

This chapter illustrated how APPRAISAL analysis of a group of young women's coming out narratives can help to reveal how their attitudes towards their sexual identities are often influenced by specific norms and values as they are mediated through the cultural institutions of compulsory and post-compulsory education. Thus, educational influences can be seen to have a notable impact upon the emerging sexual identities of these young women.

It is hoped that using APPRAISAL analysis to explore the specific impact of particular cultural domains, and the values they embody and endorse, upon the individual's emerging sexuality is useful for enhancing our understanding of how young lesbian women construct their sexual identities in specific educational settings. What is clear from the analysis presented here is that the narrators use coming out stories to reflect on how they act differently in different educational situations, and how they negotiate their way through the value systems typically associated with each situation to construct different sexual identities for themselves. Interestingly, sexual desire plays a limited role in many of the stories in the corpus. Instead, the narrators focus more upon their struggle to construct a coherent sexual identity for themselves within differing sets of sociocultural valuations and resources.

The main findings produced here suggest that, in the compulsory schooling context, the dominant cultural values of social esteem (particularly NORMALITY) and social sanction (particularly VERACITY and PROPRIETY), as they are perceived by the narrators, function to position homosexuality as outside what is culturally acceptable. There is often a perceived incongruity between social esteem and social sanction which causes predominantly negative affectual responses in the narrators. On the other hand, post-compulsory university education is a domain which permits and embodies a different set of sociocultural values, or it at least provides a safe space, where dominant cultural norms can be challenged and renegotiated. In this context, the attitudinal categories of social esteem and social sanction are experienced differently and the narrators find that their emerging sexual identities are compatible with the cultural values associated with these post-compulsory educational contexts. The positive JUDGEMENT markers of NORMALITY, VERACITY and PROPRIETY are all found to frequently co-occur with markers of positive AFFECT with reference to post-compulsory education.

The research presented in this chapter is preliminary and is intended to provide an introduction to exploring the construction of sexual identity in narratives using the tools of applied linguistics. It is important to point out that compulsory and post-compulsory education are not the only cultural institutions referred to by the narrators in their stories and it would be interesting to conduct APPRAISAL analysis in relation to a range of sociocultural settings, such as home and family, religion and the media.

The narratives examined in this chapter are produced mostly by speakers inhabiting a Western North American or north-west European culture. This is largely due to the restricted nature of the data. The website used is an English language US-based website. Exploring similar data from other cultures would be another important way to take this research forward. It might also be useful to apply similar analytical methods to the stories produced by gay men and bisexual women and men.

The APPRAISAL analysis reveals that all of the narratives examined in this chapter are produced in a broad culture of oppression where some sexualities are validated and celebrated while others are denigrated and suppressed. What is clear from the data is that educational environments are highly significant in the stories and are important arenas for the production of cultural values and social subjects. This makes them worthy of particular close investigation. The analytical framework of APPRAISAL offers new possibilities for illuminating these processes.

## Notes

1. All category labels used in the APPRAISAL system are indicated in the text by using SMALL CAPS, except in the examples, extracts and diagrams.
2. Apart from age, sexual orientation and location, no other demographic information about the narrators is included on the website.
3. 'Coming out' is an abbreviation of 'coming out of the closet', a metaphor for acknowledging and/or revealing one's homosexuality or bisexuality to oneself or to others.
4. The term 'compulsory heterosexuality' is attributed to Adrienne Rich (1980).
5. The evaluation here is what Martin (2000) calls *irrealis* which means that it is directed at some external agency or, as is the case in Extracts 6.17 and 6.18, projected into the future.

## References

Eggins, E. and Slade, D. 1997. *Analysing Casual Conversation*. London: Cassell

Halliday, M.A.K. 1994. *An Introduction to Functional Grammar* (2nd edn). London: Edward Arnold

Leap, W. (ed.) 1995. *Beyond the Lavender Lexicon: Authenticity, Imagination, and Appropriation in Lesbian and Gay Languages*. Newark, NJ: Gordon and Breach Publishers

Liang, A.C. 1997. The creation of coherence in coming-out stories. In Livia, A. and Hall, K. (eds) *Queerly Phrased: Language, Gender, and Sexuality*. Oxford: Oxford University Press, pp. 287–309

Martin, J. 2000. Beyond exchange. APPRAISAL systems in English. In Hunston, S. and Thompson, G. (eds) *Evaluation in Text: Authorial Stance and the Construction of Discourse*. Oxford: Oxford University Press, pp. 142–75

O'Mara, K. 1997. Historicising outsiders on campus: the re/production of lesbian and gay insiders. *Journal of Gender Studies* 6 (1): 17–31

Rich, A. 1980. Compulsory heterosexuality and lesbian existence. In Rich, A. 1986. *Blood, Bread and Poetry*. New York: Norton

Weston, K. 1998. *Long Slow Burn: Sexuality and Social Science*. London: Routledge

White, P. 2002. *Appraisal – the Language of Evaluation and Intersubjective Stance*. http://www.grammatics.com/appraisal (visited on 13.3.2003)

White, P. 2003. Beyond modality and hedging: a dialogic view of the language of intersubjective stance. *Text* 23 (2): 259–84

# 7

# The Transformed Gay Self: the Male Body and its Scenic Presence as Sites of Gay Self-Enunciation[1]

*Stephan A. Grosse*

## Introduction

> Our hearts hurt in a thousand ways in equal and opposite
> universes, spinning in polar rotations around the axis of desire.
>
> Nimmons (2002: 203)

The human body has always functioned as one of the key material mediations for individuals to resort to in conveying their subjectivities. Yet until recently, as Holstein and Gubrium (2000: 197) observe, it has operated as a form of 'absence presence' in that, despite its ubiquitous nature, it rarely used to be discussed as a subject of analysis in interpretive sociology. With the proliferation of complex institutionalised ways to apprehend the human body, however, attention has increasingly turned to the material body as a signifying surface for identity construction. We are today, it is fair to say, more obsessed than ever with our bodies in terms of physical beauty, health and well-being. The rising number of day spas, medical facilities specialising in plastic surgery and the ever-increasing number of personal gyms all attest to this significant obsession with the human body as a sign for who and what we are.

Yet what role does the physical self and its variegated performative aspects play in the narrative construction of gay male identities? How do gay men negotiate and enact their sexual identities by virtue of their daily narrative practices? What can be identified as the language resources and sociocultural processes underlying their self-enunciation? And to what extent is it possible to trace common narrative themes, such as longing, ageism, risk and pleasure, across variegated sites of gay discursive practice?

These are questions that I intend to address as part of the present ethnographic inquiry whereby gay physical selves along with their performative and contextual aspects are seen as key narrative resources governing the discursive construction of gay male sexualities and identities. In this context, a few key terms and phrases may merit brief definitions. Those include the use of embodiment as an abstract conception of the gay physical self, its scenic presence as its performative and contextual manifestations, and the notion of a 'culture of longing' in gay circles alluding to the potentially significant role of desire in the enactment of gay male sexualities and identities. To this end, the role of *language* and *culture* must be stressed as crucial to the present chapter, given that the narrative resources analysed in this study may be seen as indicative of particular sociocultural experiences and subjectivities of gay men in contemporary Western cultures.

In more general terms, it must be stressed that the present chapter may be seen as an unlikely marriage of sorts of various disciplinary currents, among them applied linguistics, interpretive sociology and the emerging field of languages and intercultural communication (LAIC), possibly giving new meaning to the interdisciplinary orientation of the entire book. These disciplinary currents, however, are all united in theoretical terms by their true dedication to qualitative and interpretive approaches to research. They are thus a far cry from traditional quantitative research paradigms dealing with similar social phenomena, such as in sociolinguistics, for instance. While interpretive sociology, ethnographic-type fieldwork from anthropology, an interest in language use in applied linguistics and the focus on identities and cultures in LAIC may seem like strange bedfellows at times with regard to their respective research foci, they are first and foremost united in the present chapter by way of the clearly delineated interest in instances of self-enunciation provided by gay men. Secondly, they are unmistakably united by their mutual recognition of similar qualitative and interpretive research methods to shed light on such instances of narrative identities, and thus their unequivocal rejection of traditional quantitative methodologies in reaching the same research goals.

In light of these views, the chapter initially takes a closer look at the qualitative analytic approach inspired by interpretive sociology and the emergent field of LAIC. It also discusses the use of self-narrative in the form of a personal diary or travel journal ('Tony's diaries') as the chosen data and introduces the methodological approach adopted in the study. It then proceeds to provide an ethnographic analysis of one diary as an example of gay self-enunciation by discussing the male body, its scenic aspects and how they are variably deployed in individual narrative. On the basis of this analysis, the chapter then outlines new transformative openings for the storying of gay male sexualities and identities across time and space.

## Theoretical underpinnings and analytic approach

This chapter on the gay body and its scenic aspects forms part of a broader ongoing inquiry into gay male sexual identities. This study is largely interdisciplinary in nature and draws on anthropology, applied linguistics and sociology among others both in its analytic approach and in the general research questions that inform it. My analytic design attaches great importance to the notions of subjective experience and critical reflexivity as envisioned by critical education theory (e.g. Barnett, 1997) and scholars in the emergent field of LAIC such as Phipps (1999). Both concepts constitute key features of ethnography and the backbone of the kind of critical, qualitative view that I seek to espouse in the present work.

### Foucault, interpretive practice and post-structuralism

The writings of Foucault are of vital importance to the present inquiry, as they constitute one of the most poignant attempts to conceptually grasp gay male sexuality and to outline ways in which gay culture may oppose itself to oppression by the heterosexual majority. In this context, Foucault builds his ideas of subversion on two complementary pillars of thought, i.e. creating innovative forms of friendships (Foucault, 1994a: 165), while at the same time intensifying feelings of sexual pleasure (Foucault, 1994b: 308).[2] On the latter, it must be stressed that Foucault's ideas on gay sexuality differ significantly from the sexual liberation movement of the 1970s, particularly from Hocquenghem (1972). Foucault sees the subversive force of gay male sexuality in its potential to create what he calls the 'economy of pleasures' (Foucault, 1994a: 125), i.e. new and publicly visible interpersonal pleasures based on innovative sexual relationships, rather than in more sexual activity with multiple partners per se.

In similar ways, the theories of Foucault help to inform the analytic approach in my study. It regards individuals' identities as closely related to their discursive practices and draws on Holstein and Gubrium's (2000: 94) sociological model of *interpretive practice*. The latter consists of an alternate focus on the *whats* of narrative identities, i.e. their underlying themes and resources, such as the body and its scenic presence in tune with Foucauldian genealogy, and the *hows*, i.e. the actual processes governing what I have referred to elsewhere as individuals' 'self-enunciation' (Grosse, 2001), i.e. how they convey their identities to others through narrative.

Finally, I must stress the post-structuralist underpinnings of Foucault's approach and their vital role in the present analysis. By attempting to grasp the nature of gay identities through an ethnographic inquiry into their sexual environments, I also acknowledge the belief that what we may refer to as gay identity is in constant need of being renegotiated and as such based on individual actions. 'Es la acción que genera la identidad' [*It is action that generates identity*], as Rodríguez Magda (1999: 244) puts it. Or echoing Eribon (2001: 165): '[ . . . ] en la medida en que esta identidad no viene dada sino que es creada, y siempre está por recrear [ . . . ]' ([ . . . ] *in the sense that this identity is not given but created and as such must always be recreated* [ . . . ][3]). In the light of these interpretations it is my contention that individuals' sexual identities are created and recreated through their discursive practices, as shall be explicated in the ensuing analysis.

### The emergent discourse of languages and intercultural communication (LAIC)

My theoretical perspectives are significantly informed by the annual conferences on LAIC first held at Leeds Metropolitan University (LMU) in 1996. Despite their focus on language learning and teaching, the LAIC conferences are truly interdisciplinary in orientation, as they unite scholars with research backgrounds as varied as anthropology (Phipps, 1999) and intercultural education (Tomic and Lengel, 1999). Rather than a mere exchange of ideas, however, the LAIC conferences aim to pave the way for the study of language and intercultural learning as an emerging area of study, a complex and often contradictory undertaking in the light of the project's interdisciplinary origins.

Scholars within LAIC have evoked numerous metaphors to account for their cross-cultural paradigm, many of which may also be appropriated for our present inquiry. Key metaphors include the 'third space of enunciation' as an alternative figurative space for narrative self-construction (Bhabha, 1995, in Tomic and Lengel, 1999: 149), 'creative

ways and provisional spaces' alluding to the continuous creative potential in cross-cultural awareness raising (Phipps, 1999: 26) and perhaps
most importantly 'encounter, engagement and exchange' seen here
as the vital role of interpersonal contact and involvement for self-
understanding and growth (Jack and Phipps, 2001). These metaphors
take on an almost ironic twist of meaning if applied to gay sexual environments. Most public cruising places,[4] for instance, are undoubtedly
provisional alternative spaces, in which gay selves are enunciated on
a daily basis. The forms of encounter, engagement and exchange
that occur in such environments are certainly not the kinds envisioned by Jack and Phipps in LAIC, in which intercultural, rather than
sexual selves, are enunciated, although a deeper confrontation with
the linguistic and cultural Other and, as a result, greater intercultural
empathy may also ensue in the process.

A comparative look at LAIC's emergent discourse and the present
ethnographic inquiry also reveals a parallel interest in the notions of
mobility, displacement and the search for alternative spaces. Scholars in
LAIC have used metaphors such as 'sojourning' (Byram, 1997: 1), 'provisional homes' and 'creative practices', and 'dwelling-in-travel' (Phipps,
1999: 25) to embrace their new spatial paradigm. In the discussion of
gay sexual identities, Eribon (2001: 21–2), by contrast, mentions what
he sees as a form of displacement to urban environments by gay minorities, such as San Francisco, Paris or Berlin, and calls for the creation
of: '[ . . . ] espacios, tanto prácticos como literarios o teóricos, de resist-
encia a la sujeción y de reformulación de uno mismo' ([ . . . ] *practical,
literary and theoretical spaces that allow for resistance to oppression and for
the reformulation of ourselves*).

The search for alternative spaces, as explicated above, is closely
related to the notion of transformation. In LAIC, Tomic and Lengel's
(1999) *transformation theory*, for instance, draws on critical pedagogy,
where culture is defined as 'a contested terrain, a site of struggle
and transformation' (Giroux, 1992: 165). In the present ethnography,
the notion of transformation is equally valid as a metaphor for gay
self-actualisation. Here Nimmons (2002: 213, emphasis added), for
instance, argues in favour of innovative transformational relations in
the gay community when he writes: 'We may channel a kind of
love into culture, a love beyond eros to agape, a radically *transformational* form of social communal relation.' It is precisely this interpretation of transformation that will be treated again in greater detail
in the concluding remarks of this chapter as a potential narrative
and linguistic opening for gay individuals to recast the story of

the gay body and its scenic presence in an effort to transcend what I have referred to as its 'culture of longing'.

## Study design

The research is centred primarily on an analysis of what I shall refer to as 'Tony's diaries', a series of travel journals recounting the experiences of Tony,[5] a young and attractive Latin artist, who for over five years travelled with a Colombian multimillionaire mostly around Latin America and Europe. For this research, Tony's diaries are regarded as an exemplary body of self-narrative for an ethnographic account of gay male self-enunciation in sexual environments. Tony's travels include many elements of ordinary tourism and 'sojourning' (cf. Byram, 1997), insights which may also be of relevance for an inquiry into the nature of intercultural selves. Most importantly, however, Tony's diaries are autobiographical tales of gay sexual relations and how they are sought and negotiated both in 'ordinary' gay environments and in the world of hustlers.

The research is also supported by my own ethnographic fieldwork carried out in gay sexual environments including cruising parks, saunas and centres of gay recreation worldwide. This fieldwork comprises my intentional ethnographic immersion into gay sexual environments unrelated to my own personal preferences, such as my ethnography of Spain's male prostitution scene, and combines it with a quasi-autobiographical account of my own personal experiences. Due to the central role attached to discursive practices in my conception of identity and how such narratives relate to individuals' actions and experiences, I have opted for this combination of ethnographic fieldwork and the analysis of Tony's journals as the backbone of the present interpretive study.

## Embodiment and its variegated realisation in gay narrative identity

If we agree that in contemporary Western society more importance than ever is placed on physical notions of fitness, beauty and personal well-being, then this development holds particularly true for gay circles, as illustrated by any look at gay publications, e.g. *Out* in Los Angeles or *Boyz* in London. Their numerous advertisements for liposuction or hair removal attest to the rampant narcissism and obsession with bodily perfection among gay men worldwide. As Rodríguez Magda (1999: 238) aptly points out:

[ . . . ] la gimnasio, la dieta, el culturismo, la estética publicitaria actúan como elementos que buscan transformar el cuerpo. El narcismo de la era postindustrial parece no tolerar que la anatomía frene la autosatisfacción del deseo y la propia imagen.

[ . . . ] *health clubs, dieting, body-building and the aesthetics of advertisement operate as elements that seek to transform the body. The narcissism of our post-industrial era no longer seems to respect the limits of our anatomies in seeking greater fulfilment of desires and our own personal images.*

It is interesting to observe that in gay circles the glorification of physical beauty and youth tends to perpetuate patterns of social marginalisation that most homosexuals are otherwise subjected to by the straight majority. Gay lifestyle magazines are thus highly *prescriptive* in the sense that they tend to impose the values supposed to be constitutive of our identities. On the latter, Eribon (2001: 191) remarks:

Es lo que ocurre sin duda en esos barrios donde se concentran los comercios gays, donde se exhiben a cada cual mejor el dominio de la moda, el culto de la juventud, de la belleza, de la virilidad, y donde se rehacen y vuelven a formularse las modalidades de la exclusión de todo lo que se sitúa fuera de esas normas.

*This is undoubtedly what happens in those sections with the highest concentration of gay businesses, where we can increasingly witness the prevalence of fashion and the glorification of youth, beauty and masculinity, and where the modalities of exclusion of anything outside those norms are once again reformulated.*

The use of bodily features as a resource of gay self-enunciation can also be traced throughout the writings of Tony. Particularly in tropical climes, the display of naked flesh and physical beauty often forms part of his discursive landscape. In this context, we can also observe a certain surrealism in Tony's account, whereby reality and fantasy become one and merge in the ultimate gay dream-come-true:

*Extract 7.1* Tony's diaries, Rio de Janeiro, December 1997
Por allí desfilan los más bellos especimenes de físicos fenomenales
[ . . . ] la belleza de muchos de ellos no tiene punto de comparación, la

moda es cuerpos rayados y bronceados y pantalonetas de baño [ ... ]
los cuerpos se ven como de postal o de película [ ... ] Ipanema es
como todo Río un sueño, pura fantasía y magia [ ... ]

*And there we witness the parading of the most outstanding specimens with
bodies to die for [ ... ] the beauty of most of them is beyond compare,
fashion there consists of radiant and tanned bodies and a bathing suit
[ ... ] their bodies seem to come right out of a postcard or movie [ ... ] Like
the rest of Rio, Ipanema is a dream, pure fantasy and magic [ ... ]*

As the passage above suggests, Tony feels overwhelmed by the excessive
beauty and abundance of new impressions during his first visit to Rio de
Janeiro. It marks the ultimate realisation of his sexual fantasies shared by
many other gay men worldwide – to break away from the often hostile
and homophobic environments in which they grew up and to immerse
themselves in alternative settings of exuberant narcissism, hedonism
and homo-erotic beauty in what Nimmons (2002: 160) calls with reference to activist Hakim Bey a 'temporary autonomous zone'. In this
context he argues:

They are places to try on the most deeply held dreams: a feeling of
freedom in a homosocial environment, easy availability of sex, ecstasies
of substances and of movement, safety in public, being proudly 'out'
[ ... ]. It is an oasis moment of social support, sexual adventure,
excitement and affirmation, a cherished chance to live out fantasies
involving a sought-for gay male tribalism. (Nimmons, 2002: 161)

The deep-rooted desire to immerse oneself in such tolerant and
supportive environments – to constantly 'live out that fantasy' – of
social acceptance and sexual fulfilment, may, therefore, be seen as one
constitutive feature of gay male identities as a 'culture of longing' and
will resurface again throughout the course of this chapter. It is this very
desire, particularly as it relates to sexual fulfilment and the narcissistic
longing for physical beauty, that drives many gay men to 'alternative
spaces', such as gay dance events, nudist beaches or saunas to enact,
discursively or otherwise, this formative aspect of their sexual identities.

### The gay male body between sexual self-expression and ageism

*Extract 7.2* Tony's diaries, Rio de Janeiro, December 1997
Vamos a Roger's [ ... ] y allí están los especimenes humanos
masculinos más perfectos del planeta entero y cualquier fantasía de
cualquier índole de toda clase de gays culmina allí [ ... ] rubios,

trigueños, morenos todos viriles y masculinos dispuestos a todo [ . . . ]
lo primero que ocurre allí es sentirse uno un poco fuera de este mundo
[ . . . ]

*We then go to Roger's* [ . . . ] *where we find the most perfect male human*
*specimens of the entire planet and fantasies of any kind for any type of gay*
*man culminate there* [ . . . ] *blond, medium dark, dark and all manly and*
*masculine and ready for anything* [ . . . ] *at first you tend to feel a bit like*
*out of this world* [ . . . ]

As Extract 7.2 illustrates, the gay male body is often enunciated
alongside the theme of sexual self-expression as its ultimate guiding
principle. In this respect, the conceptual boundaries between sexual self-
affirmation (something positive and worth striving for) and unbridled
casual sex (something compulsive and potentially self-destructive) are
often poorly defined. It is nonetheless illustrative that gay men perceive
themselves as quintessentially different from the majority culture by
virtue of their sexual activities. And many, but by far not all, may feel
an insatiable need to re-enact their gay physical selves by way of sexual
contacts as a symbolic action to assert their difference from mainstream
heterosexual culture. In a key passage, for instance, Tony's diaries refer
to this aspect of gay male sexuality:

*Extract 7.3*   Tony's diaries, Madrid, October 2000
[ . . . ] Alberto Ciñurriz con *El gran Salto* [retrata] con sutileza ambientes
y personajes conscientes de que el sexo es la mejor arma más subversiva
para dar el gran salto al triunfo donde la consigna es vencer, siempre
vencer, caiga quién caiga, sin perder la sonrisa, claro está, ni el empaque
y el abrazo oportuno, Detrás quedan cadáveres, pero es el precio que
hay que pagar para el reconocimiento económico y social.

[ . . . ] *Alberto Ciñurriz's book El gran Salto, 'The big jump', subtly describes*
*environments and characters aware of the fact that sex is the best tool*
*of subversion for the great battle for victory, where the goal is winning,*
*winning at all cost, whoever may fall in the process, and of course we*
*need to keep on smiling and playing our roles exquisitely, Casualties are*
*plentiful, but this is the price we need to pay for social and economic*
*recognition.*

This focus on sexual self-expression frequently coexists with a
deep-rooted desire on the part of many gay men to live life to the fullest
and to bask in complete hedonism as one way of making up for lost
time during earlier years of discrimination. As a positive and potentially

constructive theme, this 'living life to the max' philosophy may be indicative of a desire to live life consciously, yet responsibly. As a negative and possibly self-destructive force, however, it may be fuelled by a 'time is running out' anxiety and lead the gay body to reckless sexual behaviour. Again, it is often impossible to identify precisely which force may fuel this desire, as the positive/constructive and the negative/self-destructive may coexist in each individual or behavioural pattern. As Tony relates:

*Extract 7.4* Tony's diaries, Medellín, Colombia, Fall 2001
[ . . . ] sigo como en una carrera que va a finalizar y por eso siento la necesidad de aprovechar al máximo este tiempo que me queda en el que aún gusto y me puedo permitir rechazar contactos [ . . . ]

[ . . . ] *I feel like in a career that's almost over and for that reason I sense this need to enjoy to the max the little bit of remaining time in which I still attract guys and can afford to turn them down* [ . . . ]

As Tony's reflections illustrate, the themes of 'living life to the max' and 'time is running out' may be conceptually linked to *ageism*. The latter implies an extortionate celebration of youth and a marked discrimination against the gay body in old age, through which gay men recreate the same patterns of marginalisation that the outside world may impose upon them. As Eribon (2001: 191) observes:

El odio de los viejos, por ejemplo, parece ser uno de los esquemas que estructuran conversaciones dentro del medio gay en la medida en que la sexualización potencial de las relaciones entre los individuos induce a hablar en términos despectivos e insultantes de todos que ya carecen de valor en lo que es preciso dominar mercado sexual.

*Hate against older men, for instance, seems to be one of the constitutive schemes of conversations inside the gay world, whereby the potential sexualisation of individual relations may lead to the use of hateful and insulting terms for anyone of lesser value in what must be termed the sexual meat market.*

In this respect, Tony's writings equally reflect this obsession with beauty and youthfulness in gay circles when he comments on the fear of growing old as follows:

*Extract 7.5* Tony's diaries, Medellín, Colombia, Fall 2001
[...] el horror de pasar de los treinta, de envejecer y de no estar en forma con la belleza de un cuerpo suavemente cubierto de músculos [...]

[...] *the horrid fear of turning 30, of getting old and not being in shape anymore, of losing the beauty of a lean and muscular body* [...]

As the preceding extracts suggest, the gay male physical self may become enunciated alongside the discursive themes of sexual self-expression and the desire to live life to the fullest, while in many cases incurring possible risks, such as 'time is running out' anxiety or self-destructive behavioural patterns. We must remember, however, that individual selves may *variably* resort to these narrative resources for their own self-enunciation, thus allowing for considerable narrative play and, as I shall explicate further below, offering alternative accounts of the gay male self across time and space.

## Embodiment between the sexual Self and Other

The gay body not only functions as a signifying surface for who we are as physical beings at different points in our lives. It also operates in subtle and strategic ways as an instigator and perpetrator of potential personal and sexual relations, as careful observation in any gay sexual environment may confirm. The gay cruising ritual in contemporary Western cultures is heavily mediated by individuals' posture, eye contact, physical moves and proximity to each other, whereby reading subtle signs such as facial expressions and gestures may require extensive prior practice by those participating in it. On the latter, for instance, Tony comments:

*Extract 7.6* Tony's diaries, Havana, March 1998
Poco a poco el desfile de músculos y ropa ajustada se inicia, los ojos verdes, azules, miel, los rostros llenos de sensualidad, los mentones partidos, las cejas gruesas y las expresiones coquetas entre maldad y bondad [...] aquello merece un brindis y nada mejor que hacerlo con el ron de Cuba [...] me cuesta trabajo asimilar que estoy allí de nuevo en ese cielo infernal de la rumba gay en la isla de la fanasía [...]

*Gradually the parade of muscles and tight clothes gets under way, green, blue or honey-coloured eyes, faces oozing sensuality, divided chins, thick eyebrows and flirtatious gestures somewhere between good and evil* [...] *this deserves a toast and nothing better than to do it with Cuban rum*

[ ... ] *I find it hard to get used to the idea that I am here once again in this heaven and hell of gay life on the island of fantasies* [ ... ]

This mentioned obsession with physical beauty and youth in gay circles also can lead to instances of self-reflexivity, whereby individuals figuratively 'step outside' their bodies and critically reflect on the gay beauty cult and its implications for their own lives. It is now no longer the individual body that operates as a marker of self-inscription, but the gay body as an abstract entity that becomes the subject of critical reflection and analysis:

*Extract 7.7*   Tony's diaries, Rio de Janeiro, February 2001
[ ... ] los cuerpos cuidados ya son algo cotidiano casi una obligación dentro de la cultura gay, una moda que en el año 2001 es más que una necesidad una obligación, una moda que además es cada vez más exigente con respeto a los músculos desarrollados [ ... ]

[ ... ] *being in shape is something quite ordinary and almost a must in the gay world, a fad that in the year 2001 is more than a necessity, rather a liability, a fad which is on top of that becoming ever more demanding with respect to bulging muscles* [ ... ]

The use of embodiment as a key resource of gay male self-enunciation almost always implies a psychological tension between Self and Other based on physical features. This tension revolves around the dualities of individual narcissism and self-consciousness, of physical attraction and issues of self-esteem. The gay man becomes dependent in his sense of well-being and confidence in the approval and attention of others, whereby beauty and failure, youth and old age, fitness and obesity are only separated by a smile or a greeting. At the juncture of these extremes, the gay physical self becomes enunciated in variegated ways through individual narratives:

*Extract 7.8*   Tony's diaries, Rio de Janeiro, February 2001
Como hago en cualquier lugar cuando me levanto, me miro en un espejo, con este ritual inicio del día, me veo suavemente cubierto de músculos, sin envejecer todavía. Quisiera tener un cuerpo más grande y fuerte, más aún viendo todas maravillas cariocas, pero me conformo. Sé que aún gusto y que además hay que aceptar que en la pasarela de la vida hay determinadas cosas para cada uno.

*Just as I do anywhere else when I get up, I take a close look into the mirror,*
*this first ritual of the day, I see myself softly covered with muscles, no signs*
*of aging yet. I would like to have a bigger and stronger body, even more so*
*after seeing all those gorgeous Cariocas, but I content myself with what I*
*have. I know I still attract guys and what's more, we need to accept that*
*in the course of life we all have our particular strengths and weaknesses.*

This last paragraph aptly illustrates the ways in which embodiment may
function as a material mediation for the discursive inscription of gay
identities. Tony first starts out by strongly identifying with the gay body
cult in his discourse, but then uses the same narrative resource as a way
to distance himself again from that very ideal by suggesting that each
of us may have his or her individual strengths and weaknesses that may
transcend our purely physical selves.

## The *Scenic Presence* of Gay Narrative Selves

A partir del momento en que entra en un bar, de que liga en un
parque o en un lugar de encuentro, de que frequenta los sitios
de sociabilidad gay, [ . . . ] un gay se vincula con todos aquellos
que realizan esos mismos gestos [ . . . ]

*As soon as a gay man enters a bar, cruises in a park or another*
*meeting place or frequents any gay gathering place, [ . . . ] he is linked*
*with all others that carry out those very same actions [ . . . ]*

Eribon (2001: 89)

As Eribon describes in the above quotation, gay social and sexual environments are conveyors of identity in that they bestow particular identity traits upon all those that choose to frequent them. In this wider
context, it is interesting to observe the complex dialectics of individual
and collective identity that manifests itself in such locations. Many men
that frequent such environments may not identify with gay culture, or
may in fact not even self-identify as gay. They might, for example, still
live in the 'closet' and lead a double life. And yet by virtue of their
actions, they are collectively linked to all others engaging in the same
activities. As Holstein and Gubrium (2000: 191) observe:

The scenes of everyday life are as much present in defining who and
what we are, as we ostensibly are in our own spoken rights. The
intensity, certainty, and verisimilitude of our conduct and of the

selves we take for granted can be virtually bound up in their scenic presence.

When talking about any of these environments, it is interesting to observe that there tends to be a markedly *playful* element governing gay cruising rituals. For that reason, we may refer to such locales as gay playgrounds, in which cat-and-mouse games through dimly lit passageways and to unknown corners may unfold on a daily and nightly basis. Tony's diaries provide ample proof of such playfulness in sexual environments. On the cruising area of Valencia in Spain, he comments:

*Extract 7.9*   Tony's diaries, Valencia, November 2001
Luego regresamos los tres a la zona entre el puente moderno y el antiguo, allí justo donde antes pasaba el río, ahora los árboles y la penumbra contribuían a realzar la magia de un entorno perfecto para el juego de miradas en busca de roces y contactos, algo completamente surrealista, las grandes arcadas, los tipos yendo y viniendo y los gatos negros [ . . . ]

*The three of us then return to the area between the modern and the old bridge, exactly in the old river bed where now trees and twilight contribute to the magic of a perfect setting for the game of glances searching for faces and encounters, something entirely surreal, great arcades and guys coming and going and black cats [ . . . ]*

It is also interesting to point out that many such locations may seem inconspicuous for the casual heterosexual observer, particularly in broad daylight. A perfectly ordinary recreational park facility for families in an urban setting may after dark turn into a sexual playground, where individual and social gay male identities are negotiated and enacted continuously by virtue of their sexual activities.

## Performative aspects of gay sexual selves

The examples above clearly illustrate that our physical selves never exist in a spatial vacuum, but are always contingent upon our particular *scenic presence*, i.e. the social cultural settings in which our contacts with others unfold. Scenic presence as a discursive resource, therefore, signifies an extension of our bodies to the physical contexts in which we negotiate who we are in relation to others. This view of identity inscription corresponds most closely to Goffman's (1959) theatrical conception

of self-construction, whereby our subjectivities are significantly mediated by the material features of our performance on the stage of life.
Bodies, their posture, furniture arrangements, lighting and mood may
all have a considerable impact on the enactment of individual selves.
In this context, Goffman (1959: 252) observes: '[The self] derives from
the whole scene of [its] action', which shows significant parallels with
the views of Butler (1990), who embraces performative and theatrical
notions of identity for gendered selves in ways quite similar to my study
on gay male sexualities. In addition, such principles are equally reflected
in Holstein and Gubrium's (2000: 191) interpretive sociology, when they
write: '[ . . . ] who we are is more bound to the scenic presence of our
everyday lives than we might otherwise imagine'.

On the latter, it must be stressed that, in their qualitative studies,
Holstein and Gubrium (2000: 193) focus primarily on scenic aspects
of troubled selves, as their account of teddy bears and tissue boxes in
a psychiatric institution illustrates. The same analysis, however, lends
itself to the manifold environments in which gay sexual selves are negotiated on a daily basis. In this context, it is particularly remarkable
how uniform environments such as gay saunas or cruising areas are in
terms of layout and mood. Twilight, white towels, steam rooms, red
bulbs, condoms and showers are all part of the discursive landscape
that mediate the enactment of gay sexual selves in sauna environments
worldwide, in what Holstein and Gubrium (2000: 192) refer to as 'situated representations of experience'. As Tony recounts from his travel
experiences:

*Extract 7.10*   Tony's diaries, Rio de Janeiro, December, 1997
Luego vamos a un sauna, Redentor 64, las toallas blancas, las chan-
clas y los tipos por todos los lados sedientos de sexo, los videos, el
baño turco y los cuartos oscuros, el escenario ideal para tener sexo
fugaz [ . . . ] sonrisas, alguna que otra charla, [ . . . ] la penumbra y un
bombillo rojo, ir y venir, un cuerpo fenomenal, el sudor, la piel bron-
ceada, el semen, los músculos, los quejidos, una sonrisa, los leves
contactos de labios y piel, cruzar algunas palabras y los números tele-
fónicos luego chao [ . . . ]

*We then head to a sauna, Redentor 64, the same white towels, flip-flops*
*and guys everywhere starving for sex, videos, the steam room and dark-*
*rooms, the ideal setting for fast and dirty sex [ . . . ] smiles, one or the other*
*conversation, [ . . . ] the twilight and a red bulb, the comings and goings, an*
*outstanding body, sweat, tanned skin, semen, muscles, moaning, a smile,*

> *the soft touch of lips and skin, the exchange of words and phone numbers and then good-byes* [ . . . ]

As this extract illustrates, Tony's account is considerably bound up in the scenic presence of the sauna environment, in which each visitor can make variegated use of the material landscape to stage his own performance of who he is in relation to the sexual Other. In my own observations of such sauna settings, for instance, some visitors actually do enjoy the facilities and make ample use of the dry sauna and jacuzzi while regarding sexual interactions as secondary. Others, by contrast, merely go to such sauna environments to engage in sexual activities and rarely make use of the facilities there. The same *scenic presence*, such as the layout and amenities of gay saunas, may, therefore, prompt individuals to enact and enunciate their gay selves in variegated ways depending on their mood, social interactions, individual preferences or other contextual contingencies. On another occasion, this time in Europe, Tony recounts:

*Extract 7.11*   Tony's diaries, Paris, September 2001
[ . . . ] En la penumbra de una pantalla que proyecta un video porno y la débil luz de bombillas rojas, todos participan del desfile en la ansiosa búsqueda de sexo [ . . . ] las miradas y el juego de movimientos han terminado envolviéndome con un chico de rasgos orientales, nos encerramos en una cabina forrada en espejos y luz roja, después de alcanzar el extasis cruzamos palabras en inglés, ambos sonreimos al mencionar a Tahiti y Colombia, entonces decidimos salir de allí [ . . . ]

*In the twilight created by the screen showing a porn video and the dim light of red bulbs everyone is standing in line and anxiously searching for sex* [ . . . ] *at the end of this game of glances and moves I wind up getting involved with a boy of oriental features, we lock ourselves into a booth covered with mirrors and red lights, after the climax we exchange a few words in English, and both of us smile as we mention Tahiti and Colombia, we then decide to leave that place* [ . . . ]

As before, the scenic presence of the gay sauna mediates the discursive environment in which Tony presents himself as a sexually active gay male, initially identifying with and later distancing himself from the narrative resources of that setting. In addition, this particular experience illustrates that it may in fact be possible to harness and transcend this type of *encounter, engagement and exchange* in order to reach deeper, more meaningful confrontations with the cultural and linguistic Other, although its sexual connotations here may seem far removed from the intercultural ideals postulated by Jack and Phipps (2001).

The preceding discussion suggests that embodiment and scenic presence may function as particular material mediations for the discursive inscription of gay male identities and sexualities. Individuals may then, however, choose to pick up and elaborate these resources in variegated ways by identifying or distancing themselves from them according to their own beliefs and situational contingencies while redefining their own narrative identities in the process.

## Conclusion: the transformational potential of gay male self-enunciation

> At this millennial moment in culture, gay men's truly radical act is no longer simply to claim our sexuality, but to reclaim our hearts within it.
>
> Nimmons (2002: 209)

The analysis of language and cultural practices in this chapter has suggested that individual selves in gay sexual environments are up against several serious challenges that may threaten to derail their long-term well-being by trying to turn them into 'shadows' of what otherwise could become a promising story of gay male sexual identities. Among many such threats, gay male selves tend to tread a dangerously thin line in their discourse and practice, for instance, between sexual self-expression and emotional burnout, between sex as a life-affirming spiritual act and a suicidal act of self-destruction. And very often these behavioural patterns may coexist within one and the same individual rendering sexual self-actualisation and narrative identity construction a profoundly unsettling undertaking. Many gay male identities, for instance, may fail to become viable as long-term guarantors of personal happiness, unless they become empowered to transcend discrimination by their social environments, including instances of homophobia by the heterosexual majority and narrative practices of ageism and obsession with physical attributes within their own circles.

Yet how may individuals' language and cultural practices become empowered to transcend these potential threats? It is my belief that the writings of Foucault may adumbrate possible ways of transformation in which gay sexual selves could become empowered to subvert social oppression and to reinvent themselves. At the core of what Foucault

(1994a: 125) terms the 'economy of pleasure' lies a proactive commit-ment to visibility in public, i.e. the open display of our sexual identities and personal ties without fear of social discrimination. On the latter, Foucault (1994a: 124) stresses that it is the visible rather than the hidden pleasure. It is Foucault's (1994a: 261) belief that we may use gay male sexuality as a point of departure to create 'innovative forms of pleasure, relationships, coexistence, personal ties, love and intense emotions' (cf. Eribon, 2001: 429). It is this new 'economy of pleasures' that we may regard as potential 'spaces of freedom' (Eribon, 2001: 175) for our diverse sexual identities and alternative spaces of self-enunciation, in which viable and empowered gay sexual selves may emerge both in their language and cultural practices. As Nimmons (2002: 131) aptly observes in this context, 'it is our choice as to which parts of our story we tell'.

What Foucault (1994a) sees as the 'economy of pleasure' and what Eribon (2001) calls 'spaces of freedom' must, therefore, be seen as part and parcel of the same mission of narrative and performative gay male self-actualisation. In discursive terms, this means that gay men may become empowered to recast the story of their sexual identities through 'alternative spaces of self-enunciation' by responsibly drawing on the plethora of themes and resources in gay sexual environments and create new transformative openings for their narrative selves.

Nimmons (2002: 138) observes that 'to name a thing is to bring it into being, socially, emotionally, even spiritually'. By telling and enacting their own gay male story of the sexual, cultural and linguistic Self and Other, gay men may not be able to totally silence social oppression or to fully overcome the pull of 'desire' and 'longing' underlying their sexu-alities. They may become empowered, however, to tell their side of the story, to act out their individual ideals and, by extension, to adumbrate innovative and alternative ways of being, loving and understanding themselves and each other.

## Notes

1. A modified version of this chapter has appeared in Spanish as 'El cuerpo y la presencia escénica como recursos narrativos para la enunciación de las identidades gay' in *Debats*, No. 79, Winter 2002–3, Valencia: Institució Alfons el Magnánim.
2. 'What we must work on', Foucault (in Nimmons, 2002: 180) writes, 'it seems to me, is not so much to liberate our desires, but to make ourselves infinitely more susceptible to pleasure.'

3. This project was originally written in Spanish. For that reason, most references, even those by French- or English-speaking authors are quoted first in Spanish. All subsequent renditions into English (in *italics*), including quoted references and excerpts from personal diaries, are courtesy translations provided by the author. Wherever possible, the original sources are consulted and their references amended as the project progresses. For further questions, please send an e-mail to Solano69@yahoo.com

4. In gay sexual environments, the term 'cruising' generally refers to a highly ritualised and active search for mostly sexual and mutually consensual interpersonal encounters.

5. The name 'Tony' is a pseudonym used in the present study to protect the young artist's privacy. A written permission was given by the author to present and analyse extracts of his diaries for research purposes. His writings have not been published otherwise, although plans exist to display parts of his diaries in art exhibitions as they are fine examples of collage techniques featuring old tickets, tourist brochures, photographs and other personal memorabilia from his journeys. Any further questions should be directed to Solano69@yahoo.com.

# References

Barnett, R. 1997. *Higher Education: a Critical Business.* Buckingham: OUP

Butler, J. 1990. *Gender Trouble: Feminism and the Subversion of Identity.* New York and London: Routledge

Byram, M. 1997. *Teaching and Assessing Intercultural Communicative Competence.* Clevedon: Multilingual Matters

Eribon, D. 2001. *Reflexiones sobre la cuestión gay.* Barcelona: Anagrama

Foucault, M. 1994a. De l'amitié comme mode de vie. In Foucault, M. *Dits et Écrits* (Vol. IV). Paris: Gallimard, pp. 163–4

Foucault, M. 1994b. Le triomphe social du plaisir sexuel. In Foucault, M. *Dits et Écrits* (Vol. IV). Paris: Gallimard, pp. 308–14

Giroux, H. 1992. *Border Crossings: Cultural Workers and the Politics of Education.* London: Routledge

Goffman, E. 1959. *The Presentation of Self in Everyday Life.* New York: Doubleday

Grosse, S. 2001. Second language (L2) learning and the social world: Towards a critical account of identity assertion and the dialectics of Self and Other. In Killick, D., Parry, M. and Phipps, A. (eds) *Proceedings of the 4th Annual Cross-Cultural Capability Conference, 1999: 'Mapping the Territory: the Poetics and Praxis of Languages and Intercultural Communication'.* University of Glasgow/Leeds Metropolitan University, pp. 93–111

Hocquenghem, G. 1972. *Le Désir Homosexuel.* Paris: Éditions universitaires

Holstein, J.A. and Gubrium, J.F. 2000. *The Self we Live by: Narrative Identity in a Postmodern World.* Oxford/New York: OUP

Jack, G. and Phipps, A. 2001. Exchange ethnography as a reflexive methodology for the empirical study of languages and Intercultural Communication. In Killick, D., Parry, M. and Phipps, A. (eds) *Proceedings of the 4th Annual Cross-Cultural Capability Conference, 1999: 'Mapping the Territory: the Poetics and Praxis of Languages and Intercultural Communication'.* University of Glasgow/Leeds Metropolitan University, pp. 221–35

Nimmons, D. 2002. *The Soul beneath the Skin*. New York City: St. Martin's Press
Phipps, A. 1999. Provisional homes and creative practice: languages, cultural studies and anthropology. In Killick, D. and Parry, M. (eds) *Proceedings of the 'Languages for Cross-Cultural Capability: Promoting the Discipline, Marking Boundaries and Crossing Borders' Conference*. Leeds Metropolitan University, pp. 19–30
Rodríguez Magda, R.M. 1999. *Foucault y la Genealogía de los Sexos*. Barcelona: Anthropos
Tomic, A. and Lengel, L. 1999. Negotiating a 'Third Space': pedagogy which encourages transformational Intercultural Communication Education. In Killick, D. and Parry, M. (eds) *Proceedings of the 'Languages for Cross-Cultural Capability: Promoting the Discipline, Marking Boundaries and Crossing Borders' Conference*. Leeds Metropolitan University, pp. 146–62

# 8
# The Subversive Effect of the Signals of Erotic Text Patterning

*Michael Hoey*

## Background

From one perspective, the present chapter might be thought to be a sequel to a chapter I wrote for a volume called *Language and Desire*, edited by Keith Harvey and Celia Shalom (Hoey, 1997). This chapter has a number of features in common with its predecessor, in that both chapters deal with sexually charged material from the point of view of its discourse construction and signalling, and both are concerned with the cultural implications of the analyses they provide. They are however different in that the first chapter was a fairly rigorous study of 100 erotic narratives anthologised in Nancy Friday's volumes. In order to ensure that the male/female data were as comparable as possible, I took 50 heterosexual narratives written by American men and 50 heterosexual narratives written by American women from two anthologies of amateur narratives collected by Nancy Friday (1980; 1991), one anthology exploring male sexual fantasies, the other exploring female sexual fantasies. So the claims made in that chapter hold for amateur American heterosexual narrators writing (very) short stories in English. In this study, there appeared to be a gender difference associated with the pattern of organisation chosen. The question then of course arises of how and whether the patterns that were found to account for these narratives apply to other types of erotic writing, in other genres and in other cultures. This current chapter, then, is a literary stylistic analysis of a couple of rather disparate narratives (one an extract from a professional fiction, the other a poem), which are written in different languages and come from different cultural contexts.

In this chapter, I take the patterns found to organise the narratives of the amateur American writers and the signals associated with them and apply them to two very different kinds of data. The first of these comprises the opening paragraphs of a Mills and Boon narrative, ostensibly written by a British woman and certainly written for a female readership.[1] The other consists of erotic Portuguese poetry written by a man apparently for an audience of both sexes. Both describe heterosexual desire (the addressee in the poem is referred to as *ansiosa*, which in Portuguese is marked for the feminine gender). Thus, sexuality is held constant, but we have variation from the original data in that both texts emanate from professional published writers (unlike the authors of the narratives collected by Nancy Friday), and we have variation between the writers in respect of genre (novel, poem), nationality (British, Brazilian) and language (English, Portuguese).

As noted above, no conclusions can be drawn from the analysis of a single extract from a single novel or from the analysis of a single poem from a collection of poetry. This chapter does not pretend, as did its predecessor, to be able to make statistical comparisons nor to generalise about the narrative strategies that might be adopted by writers in these two very different genres and different languages. It sets itself two rather different goals. In the first place, it seeks to explore in a preliminary and impressionistic fashion whether there is any evidence for believing that the narrative practices found in the Nancy Friday anthologies of American amateur writers in English might be generalised to professional writers writing in different cultures and for different audiences. In the second place, it seeks to provide a closer literary stylistic analysis of the texts examined than was possible in the earlier chapter, given its database of 100 narratives. In so doing, it seeks to discover whether the sexual stereotyping found in the amateur erotic writing pertains also to such, presumably more sophisticated, professional writing.

## Patterns of (erotic) narrative

In the earlier study (Hoey, 1997), I argued that the patterns of organisation characteristic of erotic narratives differed subtly but significantly from those traditionally associated with narratives in general. A great many traditional narratives of the non-erotic kind are organised around the Problem–Solution pattern (e.g. Meyer, 1975; Winter, 1977; Stein and Glenn, 1979; Hoey, 1983, 2001) or the Goal–Achievement pattern (e.g. Hoey, 2001). The essence of these patterns is that a Situation is provided within which a character has a Problem (an aspect of the

Situation requiring a Response) or a Goal (an aspect of the Situation which someone wishes to change). A Response is provided for the Problem or a Means of Achievement is provided for the Goal. If this is described as having been positively evaluated or having given rise to a positive result, the particular narrative thread for that character comes to a close. If, however, the evaluation or result is negative, then the pattern recycles, with further Responses or Means of Achievement being expected by the reader (unless the negative result was so negative as to preclude such a possibility, e.g. the death of the character). The property of a pattern recycling in the event of an unsuccessful Response or Means of Achieving a Goal gives rise to the possibility of highly extended narratives, such as characteristically found in narratives. Problem–Solution and Goal–Achievement patterns may also interlock, so that one character's successful Response may be another character's Problem. This too contributes to the possibility of novel-length patterns of organisation.

In Hoey (1997), I noted that the use of such patterns in erotic writing will typically produce selfish narratives, with one character solving a sexual problem or meeting a sexual need at the expense of another. So, for example, the narrator of the following fabricated stories is morally reprehensible, since he uses another person as a sexual object, as a means of solving a problem or achieving a goal:

*Example 8.1*
I needed to kiss someone [PROBLEM]. So I kissed Mary [RESPONSE].

*Example 8.2*
I really wanted to kiss someone [GOAL]. So I kissed Mary [MEANS OF ACHIEVEMENT].

Both the Problem–Solution patterns (I need a woman) and Goal–Achievement patterns (I intend to make you my lover) are essentially self-centred and, though such narratives did occur in my data, they were relatively infrequent. The majority of the erotic narratives that I analysed were instead organised around two patterns that had not, to my knowledge, been previously identified in the literature: the Opportunity–Taking pattern and what I have termed the Desire Arousal–Desire Fulfil-ment pattern. The Opportunity–Taking pattern (self-evidently) takes the form of a Situation in which an Opportunity arises for a character which s/he takes with good or bad results. Opportunity–Taking patterns quite often occur within a larger Goal–Achievement pattern, where a character has a Goal which an Opportunity makes it possible for him/her to achieve. The pattern seems to remove the 'sexual object' sting of the earlier narratives, even when it is combined with a Problem or Goal statement:

*Example 8.3*
Mary looked at me invitingly and pursed her lips [OPPORTUNITY]. So I kissed her [TAKING].

*Example 8.4*
I needed to kiss someone [PROBLEM]. Mary looked at me invitingly and pursed her lips [OPPORTUNITY]. So I kissed her [TAKING = RESPONSE].

*Example 8.5*
I really wanted to kiss someone [GOAL]. Mary looked at me invitingly and pursed her lips [OPPORTUNITY]. So I kissed her [TAKING = MEANS OF ACHIEVEMENT].

Close inspection, of course, shows that Mary is still being treated as a sexual object in all three of these narratives, only she is being presented as a *willing* sexual object. A classic non-erotic instance of the Opportunity–Taking pattern occurs in Lewis Carroll's *Alice in Wonderland*:

*Example 8.6*
Soon her eye fell on a little glass box that was lying under the table: she opened it, and found in it a very small cake, on which the words 'EAT ME' were beautifully marked in currants.

'Well, I'll eat it', said Alice . . . So she set to work, and very soon finished off the cake. (*The Adventures of Alice in Wonderland and Through the Looking Glass* by Lewis Carroll, Heirloom Library, p. 8)

One of the features of the well-described patterns of Problem–Solution and Goal–Achievement is that the onset of the pattern is often well signalled, so that the reader can quickly bring into play the generalised schema necessary for the text's interpretation. Thus, for example, Problem is signalled by nouns, such as *difficulty, dilemma, obstacle* and *danger*, adverbs, such as *unfortunately*, adjectives, such as *difficult*, and verbs, such as *do about* and *not able to* (see, in particular, Hoey, 1983). Signals may be of two kinds, following Martin (2000) (Hoey, 2001). They may be inscribed, in which case it is intrinsic to their meaning/function that they signal the pattern in question; all of the examples just listed are instances of inscribed signalling. Alternatively, they may be evoking, in which case they tap into a shared set of cultural values or perspectives. So *sick, traffic jam, killer* and *shaky* are all, strictly speaking, factually demonstrable descriptions, but they evoke Problem and consequently require a Response – a curing of the sickness, a clearing of the jam, a catching of the killer or a steadying of the shaky.

Opportunity–Taking and Desire Arousal–Desire Fulfilment patterns also have their characteristic signals, but particularly in the case of the latter pattern they tend to be evoking, rather than inscribed. Opportunities are characteristically marked by some lexical marker of perception or discovery. In Example 8.6 we have both, occasioned by there being two Opportunity–Taking patterns in close proximity. In the first, the Opportunity is marked by the collocation *eye fell on*, coupled with an Object with unambiguous use, here a box. Indeed, so powerful is the connection between perception and Opportunity that some non-literal idioms signalling Opportunity in general English are constructed out of the combination (e.g. *saw an opening*). In the second, the Opportunity is marked by *found*, the object of unambiguous use being on this occasion a cake, which rather redundantly advertises its purpose with the words *Eat me*.

Of course the implication of all this is that a woman, for the narrator who uses this pattern, is an object of unambiguous use, and certainly the male amateur narratives discussed in Hoey (1997) seemed to be told on that assumption.

The Desire Arousal–Desire Fulfilment pattern offers the arousal of desire as an excuse for the narrator's opportunistic behaviour. Within a Situation, an Object of Desire comes into view for a character. This Object of Desire gives rise to an Arousal of Desire in that character (a specialised kind of Problem, really, in that a need – an aspect of situation requiring a response (Hoey, 1983) – is created). The character then seeks a means of fulfilling his/her desire, with, as always, good or bad results.

*Example 8.7*
Mary was gorgeous [OBJECT OF DESIRE]. I really wanted to kiss her [DESIRE AROUSAL (= GOAL)]. So I kissed her [DESIRE FULFILMENT (=ACHIEVEMENT)].

As well as occurring in love stories and erotic writing, the pattern occurs non-erotically in advertisements with considerable frequency. An example, which however appears to draw directly on the language of erotica, is the following advertisement for Nescafé Mocamba coffee, which appeared a few years ago:

*Example 8.8*
Relax. Take it easy. Sip delicately. Exotic. Juicy. Light and dusky. To make the eyes close and the senses awaken. Gentle Mocamba, you make me dream of sunset over the rolling hills of Kenya. A cup of coffee that can only come from the heart of deepest Kenya. And the soul of Nescafé. For people who truly, madly, deeply love coffee.

Behind the text was the photograph of a beautiful woman. The advertisement sets up the coffee as an Object of Desire and alludes to Desire Arousal in the final sentence. Desire Fulfilment of course is achieved outside the text by buying and drinking the coffee. The Object of Desire is signalled by references to its evoking physical properties – *juicy, light, dusky, gentle* – and the Desire Arousal is signalled by the inscribed *truly, madly, deeply love* and by *exotic*, which is often confused with the inscribed *erotic*, as well as evoking Desire in its own right. Further examples of evoking signals in the advertisement are *dusky* and *exotic*, both of which are conventionally associated with attractive women. Desire Arousal–Desire Fulfilment patterns make heavy use of evoked evaluation, and it is partly in connection with their use that the subversive effect referred to in the title of this chapter arises, as we shall see later.

In the 1997 study, the male writers tended to favour the Opportunity–Taking pattern as a way of organising their erotic narratives, whereas the female writers tended to favour the Desire Arousal–Desire Fulfilment pattern (though both patterns were fairly frequent in the narratives of both sexes). I argued that these preferences could be related to culturally stereotypical gender positions, with the men treating women as opportunities for sex and the women describing themselves as losing control of their desires/feelings and, therefore, not responsible for what they did. The questions that now arise are: do these patterns also characterise professional writing from different cultures, how is the patterning of these texts signalled and what does this signalling tell us about the cultural suppositions that underpin the creation and processing of such texts?

# The texts

A note of explanation is necessary for what might seem an eccentric choice of data. The opening paragraphs of a Mills and Boon novel and a Brazilian poem hardly seem natural bedfellows. They were not, however, despite appearances, chosen at random, nor on the other hand were they chosen in order to support a case. They were in fact chosen because they contrasted with my original data set on a number of parameters. To begin with, as already noted, both texts were written by professionals and were intended as acts of entertainment and stimulation (both aesthetic and erotic). The Nancy Friday articles were by amateurs and were presented as acts of self-expression in the first place, though the desire to entertain and arouse was probably not absent in many cases. The Mills and Boon extract differs from the Nancy Friday narratives in being inexplicit in its description of sexual acts, despite the erotic effect of the writing. The Brazilian poem is highly explicit, but is not couched as narrative, and is of course written in Portuguese. Thus, between them, the two texts I have chosen contrast with the 100 narratives on a number of counts.

## The Brazilian poem: 'Na Alcova'

The poem I have chosen to analyse, 'Na Alcova' by Paulo Augusto de Lima (1997), is closer to the amateur erotic writing than the Mills and Boon extract in a number of respects. In the first place it is sexually highly explicit, as are the great majority of the narratives in the Friday collections, and will be found pornographic by some readers. It also expresses what the writer would like to do to the desired other, which is a common factor in the Friday texts. Where it differs from the latter is in being non-narrative, linguistically sophisticated and of course in Portuguese. The analysis that follows is, therefore, designed to explore whether the culturally popular patterns and the signals of those patterns found in the amateur narratives potentially may generalise to non-narrative text, other languages and other genres. Whatever it finds, it cannot offer any evidence as to the frequency or normality of occurrence of such patterns or signals.

The poem is 'Na Alcova' from a collection of poems by Paulo Augusto de Lima, entitled *Aracnídea Vulva e outros poemas*, published in 1997. In my translation I have numbered places where I need to comment on the text and I have inserted the relevant Portuguese line in italics. I would like to have given the poem in full in its original Portuguese, but unfortunately it proved impossible to make contact with the poet or his publisher to clear copyright permission. (The translation is my own.):

Text 8.1 'Na Alcova'
<u>In the Small Windowless Bedroom</u>
When we are quite alone in the small windowless bedroom,
bodies hot, glowing, naked,
I want to make love[1] to your[2] lovable[3] anus.
*Quero comer[1] teu[2] amável[3] ânus.*
Shamelessly put my tongue within it.

To be able to tell you:
turn over love, turn over,
and you, anxious and quivering,
nevertheless will of course turn over.

I want poetically to bugger you
to the sound of violins,
or of a mad rock 'n' roll
or in the total silence of the night
and even in the midday sun.

Oh my love,
my erect penis,
lubricated with saliva
and a pinch of sadism
in the divine pleasure
of glorious penetration.

In this bum which in addition seems
sculpted by Michelangelo
I want to make love to your kind[4] arsehole
*Quero comer teu gentil[4] cú*
comme il faut,[5]
*comme il faut,[5]*
with complete relish.[6]
*com todo sabor.[6]*

And you will moan,[7]
*E tu gemerás,[7]*
you will grunt,[8]
*tu grunhirás,[8]*
perhaps we might scream,[9]

*talvez gritemos,*[9]
orgasmically we will scream.
And there
in the hot and in the delicious[10]
*no quente e no gostoso*[10]
the fruition.[11]
*o gozo.*[11]

As you would expect from a poem, there are a number of places where translation is difficult, either because of the strangeness of the Portuguese or because of the multiplicity of senses that the author's lexical choices on occasion have. The ones I have singled out for comment are numbered in the translation:

1. *comer* in Portuguese has as its most common sense 'to eat' but is also a slang word for 'to make love to'. Here the prime sense would seem to be the latter, though the other sense is evoked in several places in the poem, most notably in the following line, but also in the use of *sabor* and *gostoso*.
2. The use of *teu* is both intimate and old-fashioned and could almost be translated as *thy*. There is, therefore, a collocational conflict in the combination of *teu* and *ânus*.
3. The word *amavel* is translatable in several ways and the way we translate it affects the discourse pattern and the signalling of the text. Taylor (1958) translates it as 'amiable, lovable; kind, gracious, friendly, pleasant, likeable; engaging, courteous'. Needless to say, these are not qualities normally assigned to the anus.
4. The word *gentil* has a very similar range of meanings. Taylor (1958) translates it as 'courteous; kind; thoughtful, gracious; genteel, refined; noble'. The word *cú* is a slang word for the anus and is even less likely to occur with any of these attributes than its more polite synonym.
5. I have made no attempt to translate the French borrowing.
6. The word *sabor* can be interpreted as picking up the *comer*-eat meaning ('taste, flavour'), as well as fitting in with the 'making love' sense ('relish').
7. As is true for the English translation 'you will moan', *gemerás* can refer either to sexual noises or to noises caused by suffering, such as sobbing and lamenting.
8. The verb *grunhirás* refers to the noise of a pig; it can also be used to describe grumbling.

9. The verb *gritemos* includes in its meanings 'we would shout/cry out/shriek' as well as 'scream'.
10. The adjective *gostoso* again references the eating meaning of *comer*.
11. The final word *gôzo* is significantly ambiguous. All of the following are possible translations, according to Taylor (1958): 'enjoyment, delight; possession, use, fruition; cause for laughter'.

In terms of patterning, the text is quite complex as can be seen in Figure 8.1. In the first place, there is a Desire Arousal–Desire Fulfilment pattern. We have the description of the woman's bum as worthy of having been sculpted by Michelangelo, an Object of Desire, in the immediate context of an expression of the Desire that is aroused by it. If we interpret *amavel*-loveable as incorporating 'lovely', then the anus, too, may be seen as Object of Desire. The subsequent Goal–Achievement pattern is embedded as Means of Fulfilling the Desire. If we interpret *amavel* as 'kind', then we also have an Opportunity–Taking pattern, itself embedded inside a Goal–Achievement pattern. The Goal is explicitly

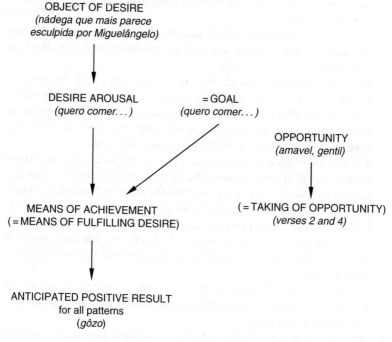

**OBJECT OF DESIRE**
*(nádega que mais parece
esculpida por Miguelângelo)*

**DESIRE AROUSAL**          = GOAL
*(quero comer...)*       *(quero comer...)*

                                    **OPPORTUNITY**
                                    *(amavel, gentil)*

**MEANS OF ACHIEVEMENT**          ( = TAKING OF OPPORTUNITY)
( = MEANS OF FULFILLING DESIRE)    *(verses 2 and 4)*

**ANTICIPATED POSITIVE RESULT**
for all patterns
*(gôzo)*

*Figure 8.1*  Patterns in 'Na Alcova'

signalled by *quero* (three times) and the means are described in the second and fourth verses, the means only being available because the *cú* is kind, the kindness providing the Opportunity; the positive outcome is *gôzo*, which can be seen as fulfilling the Desire (pleasure, fruition) and achieving the Goal (possession, use).

Thus far, we have cautious answers to our first two questions. The discourse patterns associated with the erotic narratives collected by Nancy Friday appear to be equally available to this poet and in this language and culture, though the evidence is less compelling for the Opportunity–Taking pattern. The patterning is signalled in similar ways to the texts previously considered in that we have inscribed signals – *quero, gostoso* – and evoking signals – *esculpida por Miguelângelo*. Our third question, concerning the cultural suppositions that underpin the creation and processing of the text, however, needs slightly more discussion. The first point to note is that the Object of Desire is a woman's bottom, not explicitly the woman herself. Secondly, her willingness to allow him to fulfil his Desire – her kindness – is ascribed to her anus. Taken literally, this means that both the Desire Arousal and its means of Fulfilment centre on a small and not noticeably distinctive part of the body. The woman is reduced to the orifice and its surrounds. This has also been found by Baker (2005), in his corpus analysis of gay and lesbian erotica.

## The Mills and Boon extract

In the previous section, we saw parallels in terms of patterning between the poem chosen for analysis and the amateur erotic narratives collected by Nancy Friday. The texts were also alike in many ways in being highly explicit and first-person oriented. Mills and Boon narratives are famed for their provision of romances for women and are carefully packaged as a product in which the publisher's name is a constant and the authors' names are apparently largely ignorable variants (though I have not interviewed habitual readers of Mills and Boon books to determine whether this is in fact the case). The books are, in my view, properly describable as erotic, but they are sexually inexplicit, in marked contrast both with the Nancy Friday narratives and the Brazilian poem. The passage I have chosen to analyse comprises the opening paragraphs of *The Dominant Male* by Sarah Holland, published in 1996. The plot of the novel is that an attractive young woman comes under the influence of a rich and handsome power broker who tries repeatedly to exert mastery over her. She is both attracted and repelled by the domination he tries to show over her, but resists all his crude attempts at seduction, since she has no intention of becoming a trophy mistress. Finally, he is nice to her and she succumbs, admitting to the guilty secret that she once had sex in bondage and quite enjoyed it. He in turn confesses that his attempts at dominating and humiliating her were ways of testing whether she was merely after his money. All ends happily ever after (if it can be called happiness for an independent young woman to end up married to a manipulative, overbearing control freak).

Many aspects of the larger narrative organisation will be apparent from the above brief summary of the storyline. Figure 8.2 represents a considerable simplification of the patterning of the novel.

Having given a bird's-eye view of the text's organisation, I want now to shift to a worm's-eye view in order to examine signalling and look at how the novel opens. After all, if the novel's organisation is to work and if the repeated attempts at sexual domination by the hero are not to be repellent, it is essential that the two main characters are clearly established as Objects of Desire for each other from the very beginning of the novel. The opening paragraphs read as below.

*Text 8.2*   The Dominant Male

Rhiannon attracted attention just by walking across the lawns. Dressed in scarlet and gold, as a wild, dark-haired gypsy, she was not only ravishing but rather out of place among the respectable and wealthy guests.

Kohl made her green eyes smoulder, her midriff was bare, and she wore gold bells in her ears, around her neck, on her wrists and around her slender, scented ankles.

She looked like an exotic, seductive slave. And suddenly she sensed a man watching her. Her green eyes flicked to him, a dark sidelong look from beneath her sooty lashes. A quiver of excitement and fear ran through her, as though she knew he would one day command her life, fill her senses and be the centre of her world.

Fanciful stuff . . . but he was gorgeous. Tall, very tall, with jet-black hair and steel-blue eyes which dazzled her with their life-force and inner power. *The Dominant Male* by Sarah Holland, Richmond: Harlequin Mills and Boon, p. 5

The narrative, as can be seen, plunges directly into a Desire Arousal–Desire Fulfilment pattern within two words of the beginning of the novel. The heroine is immediately set up as an Object of Desire and Desire Arousal is strongly suggested with the reference to her noticing

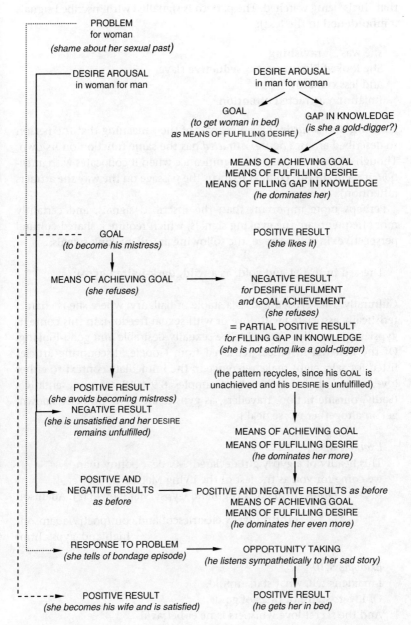

*Figure 8.2* The patterns that contribute to the organisation of *The Dominant Male*

that she is being watched. The pattern is signalled with inscribed signals (**emboldened** in the text):

> she was . . . **ravishing**
> She looked like an exotic, **seductive** slave
> and less certainly
> Rhiannon **attracted attention**

*Ravishing* and *seductive* have it as part of their meaning that the person so described arouses desire. *Attracted* has the same function on its own. Though it need not have this significance when it collocates with *attention*, it seems in this context to focus the passage on the way she attracts (attention).

Perhaps more important than the inscribed signals, and certainly more frequent, are the evoking signals, which require a shared cultural perspective. In this passage, the following are all evoking signals:

> Dressed in scarlet and gold, as a **wild, dark-haired gypsy**

Culturally, the 'gypsy maid' is a staple of balladry, where she is characteristically associated with love or with sexual freedom; in this context, gypsies are usually assumed to be sexually desirable and good-looking. Of the first ten instances retrieved from Google, discounting articles listed for sale, eight make reference in the immediate context to either love, sexual desire or beauty. Examples 8.9–8.12 are representative. (Sadly, outside fiction, travellers, as gypsies are more properly known, get an altogether worse deal.)

*Example 8.9*
This beauty of a gypsy girl declared 'My dear bonny man
we come for you as the last of the living MacIntosh clan . . . '
> From 'Dream of a Highland Gypsy Maid' by Ken J. Adamson

> > (http://www.electricscotland.com/poetry/adamson/
> > highland_gypsy.htm)

*Example 8.10*
I maidens tell, what stars unfold,
Of lovers sighs! of rings of gold;
And the secret love whispers is ne'er betray'd
By the merry young heart of the Gypsy maid.
Then list to me for sweet the spell,

The Gypsy knows to weave so well

From 'The Gypsy Maid' by Edward Fitzball

(http://www.pdmusic.org/1800s/50tgm.txt)

*Example 8.11*

... the film stars Jennifer Jones (Mrs. Selznick) as Hazel Woodus, a tempestuous Welsh gypsy maid who can't seem to stay out of trouble. Feeling more of a kinship with woodland animals than with human beings, Hazel enters into a loveless marriage with minister Edward Marston (Cyril Cusack). Believing she's been born under a curse which will punish her if she ever truly falls in love, Hazel does her best to suppress her carnal desires, but ...

From a film review on MSN Movies

(http://movies.msn.com/movies/movie.aspx?m=18016)

*Example 8.12*

Adventures of a man in the early 18th Century who puts aside luxury and sets off on the road with only his wits, soon falling in love with a gypsy maid who becomes to him like a goddess.

Synopsis of book by Jeffery Farnol

(http://www.violetbooks.com/CATALOGS/swashbucklerD.html)

The adjectives *wild* and *dark-haired* gain some of their value from their association with *gypsy*. Gypsies are conventionally assumed to be dark-haired and wild. A Google search for *dark-haired gypsy* retrieved 258 instances, *dark gypsy* retrieved 767 instances and *brunette gypsy* retrieved 21 instances (1046 in all). A search for *fair-haired gypsy* retrieved just three cases, while *fair gypsy* retrieved 389 and *blonde gypsy* recovered 170 (562 in all). Similarly, a search for *wild gypsy* produced 3950 hits, compared with four for *mild gypsy*, 18 for *calm gypsy* and none whatsoever for either *level-headed gypsy* or *sensible gypsy*. Even without conjunction with *gypsy*, *dark-haired*, like *blonde* or *red-haired*, is culturally considered to be attractive (as opposed to *brown-haired*, *mousey*, *grey-haired* or *ginger*, for example). Of 75 lines of *dark-haired* drawn from the Bloomsbury corpus of 50 million words, 12 also contain the words *beautiful*, *pretty* or some close synonym (*handsome*, *buxom*, etc.). Many more contain adjectives with connotations of good looks – *slender*, *slim*, *vibrant*, etc.

A similar point can be made about *green eyes*. The associations of *wild* are more ambiguous but include *wild sex, wild night, wild and free*, all of which might under some circumstances be thought to be attractive. Other evoking signals are *exotic* and *slave* in the following clause:

> She looked like an **exotic**, seductive **slave**.

We have already seen, in the Nescafé advertisement, how *exotic* is used to evoke desirability, and in conjunction with *seductive*, its rhyme association with *erotic* is foregrounded. In the Friday collection of male erotic fantasies, in a certain kind of dominant–submissive sexual fantasy, slave girls occur on several occasions. Given that the Mills and Boon book in question is mainly concerned with the attempt of the 'hero' to impose his will on the heroine, the use of *slave* here would appear to have this resonance.

Importantly, though, there are yet other evoking signals, and it is these I want to attend to especially. They are **emboldened** in the following passage:

> Dressed in **scarlet and gold**, as a wild, dark-haired gypsy, she was not only ravishing but rather out of place among the respectable and wealthy guests.

> Kohl made her green eyes smoulder, **her midriff was bare**, and she wore **gold bells in her ears, around her neck, on her wrists and around her slender, scented ankles**.

If you were required to provide a description of a woman, say for the police, consider how odd it would be to say that she had a bare midriff and slender scented ankles. Midriffs and ankles are not attended to in general/non-erotic social interaction. Their description therefore is designed to evoke her status as an Object of Desire. We are back to the poet's fixation with his lover's bottom. Furthermore, only someone in *very* close proximity could possible discern that someone's ankles were scented. But scent exists in the real world in order to make a man or woman desirable, and its mention here therefore, once again, evokes Object of Desire. A similar point might be made about *sooty lashes* and *smoulder[ing] eyes*. These do not belong in any non-sexual description. Apart from the darkness of her hair and the greenness of her eyes, we are not given any conventional details. We are not told whether Rhiannon is tall or short, slim or plump, swarthy or pale. Nor are we told her age or hairstyle, only that her lashes are sooty and her ankles scented. We are, however, given a fair amount of information about her apparel, things that in the real world would come off at night. So she is *dressed in scarlet and gold* and wears *gold bells*. Gold is much coveted, and by association this also makes her an Object of Desire. *Scarlet*, as a bright colour (unlike 'ochre', 'bistre' or 'beige', for example), is conventionally regarded as an attractive colour – and 'attractive' is, as we have seen, an inscribed signal of Object of Desire. *Scarlet* is of course associated with *woman*, a phrase that refers to a woman who indulges in sexual sins. The New Oxford Dictionary of English (1998) defines *scarlet woman* as 'a notoriously promiscuous or immoral woman'.

The setting up of Rhiannon as Object of Desire is not the only patterning move taken by the narrator. In the last sentences of the quoted passage, the 'hero' is also set up as Object of Desire. I have *italicised* the inscribed signals and **emboldened** the evoking signals in the representation of the relevant sentences below:

Her green eyes flicked to him, a dark sidelong look from beneath her sooty lashes. A quiver of *excitement* and fear ran through her, as though she knew he would one day command her life, fill her senses and be the centre of her world.

Fanciful stuff . . . but he was *gorgeous*. **Tall**, **very tall**, with **jet-black hair** and **steel-blue eyes** which *dazzled her* with their life-force and inner power.

We have not been privy to the Arousal of the 'hero'. The adjectives *ravishing* and *seductive* may represent the viewpoint of this character or may reflect a general (or the author's) opinion. Here, however, the viewpoint is undeniably that of Rhiannon. We have an instance of what has been termed Free Indirect Thought (Leech and Short, 1981; Semino and Short, 2004), and the lexis *excitement* and *dazzled* reveal Desire to have been Aroused. So does *gorgeous*, which functions in a very similar way to *ravishing*.

In addition to these inscribed signals of Desire Arousal, we have three evoking signals. Tallness conventionally evokes attractiveness, when applied to men, as does jet-black hair. *Steel-blue eyes* do the same as can be seen from a search on Google. Of the first 20 examples of the phrase retrieved, eight are used in a context where the person being described is unambiguously being described as attractive (of these, interestingly, three came from sites that described themselves as erotica or pornography), a further five were in contexts where the intention was ambiguous and seven were used without apparent intent to describe attractiveness.

Thus the passage utilises the same patterns as many of the Nancy Friday narratives and the Portuguese language poem, and both Objects of Desire are established through inscribed and evoking signals. Culturally, though, what is perhaps disturbing is that the poem's male-oriented, slightly sadistic sexual fantasy utilises a similar way of representing the Object of Desire as the Mills and Boon narrative's female-oriented, sexually inexplicit love story. The woman is reduced to her parts, whether it be her anus or her ankles. Of course the poem appears to paint a secure relationship within which its anticipated sexual act takes place and the novel goes on to describe its heroine's character in some detail. Nevertheless, when it comes to the Object of Desire pattern, the implications for these texts are that women are desired for their sexualised parts (neither the anus nor the ankle having an intrinsic sexuality). That it is not inherent in the pattern, but is a cultural variation on it, is indicated by the way the hero in the Mills and Boon passage is described as an Object of Desire. His description might allow one to recognise him: we are not invited to admire his eau-de-cologned wrists.

## Note

1. Mills and Boon is an English publishing house that specialises in romantic novels. The North American equivalent would be Harlequin.

## References

Baker, P. 2005. *Public Discourses of Gay Men*. London: Routledge
De Lima, P.A. 1997. *Aracnídea Vulva e Outros Poemas*. Ouro Preto: Tratos Culturais Produções
Friday, N. (ed.) 1980. *Men in Love: Their Secret Fantasies*. London: Hutchinson
Friday, N. (ed.) 1991. *Women on Top*. London: Hutchinson
Hoey, M. 1983. *On the Surface of Discourse*. London: George Allen and Unwin
Hoey, M. 1997. The organisation of narratives of desire. In Harvey, K. and Shalom, C. (eds) *Language and Desire: Encoding Sex, Romance and Intimacy*. London: Routledge, pp. 85–105
Hoey, M. 2001. *Textual Interaction*. London: Routledge
Holland, S. 1996. *The Dominant Male*. Richmond: Mills and Boon
Leech, G.N. and Short, M.H. 1981. *Style in Fiction: a Linguistic Introduction to English Fictional Prose*. London: Longman
Martin, J.R. 2000. Beyond exchange: APPRAISAL systems in English. In Hunston, S. and Thompson, G. (eds) *Evaluation in Text: Authorial Stance and the Construction of Discourse*. Oxford: OUP, pp. 142–75

Meyer, B.J.F. 1975. *The Organisation of Prose and its Effects on Memory*. Amsterdam: North-Holland

Semino, E. and Short, M. 2004. *Corpus Stylistics: Speech, Writing and Thought Presentation in a Corpus of English Writing*. London: Routledge

Stein, N.L. and Glenn, C.C. 1979. An analysis of story comprehension in elementary school children. In Freedle, R.O. (ed.) *New Directions in Discourse Processing* (Advances in Discourse Processes, 2). Norwood, NJ: Ablex, pp. 53–120

Taylor, J.L. 1958. *A Portuguese–English Dictionary*. Stanford: Stanford

Winter, E.O. 1977. A clause-relational approach to English texts. *Instructional Science* 6: 1–92

# 9
# Going 'Back to Basics': Moral Panics about Heterosexual Relationships
*Lia Litosseliti*

## Introduction and key issues

This chapter examines the increasingly heightened anxiety or 'moral panic' surrounding heterosexual relationships in Britain, in the context of women and men's shifting roles, identities and relations in a rapidly changing, so-called 'risk' society (Beck, 1992). It focuses on the discursive construction of deviance (Goode and Ben-Yehuda, 1994), of perceived threats to a 'moral'/'normal' heterosexual life, and to the social order itself (Thompson, 1998). Such threats typically include family breakdown (divorce, cohabitation, single parenthood), homosexuality, feminism going 'too far', and a 'crisis of masculinity'. Within the specific British sociocultural context, the chapter uses an example from written media as well as an extract of spoken interaction, to illustrate how dominant, resistant and alternative heterosexual identities are discursively constructed. The use of language (e.g. metaphors, exaggerated vocabulary, discourses of prediction, symbolisation and prescription) and culturally charged repertoires (e.g. about moral decline, and the individual and collective good – see Litosseliti, 2001, 2002a, b) construct particular representations, social identities and relations: for heterosexual men and women, for homosexuals, for married and cohabiting couples – and representations of the culture in general. A critical examination of these representations, identities and relations is crucial in order to avoid unproductive gender stereotyping and the stigmatising

204

of social 'outcasts' – and it is important that it happens in the particular social and cultural context that gives rise to them.

# Moral panics

Public debate around gender, and specifically about the perceived changes in gender roles and expectations within heterosexual relationships, has intensified in recent years. This is partly the result of structural changes, such as changes in the division of labour and the domestic division of labour, as well as cultural changes, including conflicts over identity, lifestyles and morals.

In addition, post-structuralism, the cross-disciplinary emphasis on discourse, and the large amount of constantly developing research on language and gender, have both put gender and sexuality issues in the centre of discussion and given rise to increasingly critical, nuanced and contextualised approaches to these issues. There has been a shift of focus from the idea of gender roles (as binary and fixed) to the social and linguistic (i.e. discursive) construction of a range of masculine and feminine identities (Hall and Bucholtz, 1995; Bergvall *et al.*, 1996; Cameron, 1998; Litosseliti and Sunderland, 2002). This shift means that instead of seeing men and women as producing different forms of language, it is the language that is seen as producing and sustaining gender. It also means that questions of interpretation, situated meanings, power and ideology have become more pertinent.

## Moral panics in the media

Public debate in the specific context of the British media, particularly newspapers, unmistakably suggests an increasing anxiety about issues facing men and women, and about their shifting roles, identities and relations in a society that is rapidly changing. While sometimes acknowledging the positive outcomes of such change, there is also anxiety which revolves around the arguably negative effects of the change on notions of femininity and masculinity and on the family. This focus inevitably involves the construction and perpetuation of gender discourses or 'ways of being' for women and men. These discourses are, unsurprisingly, dependent on normative assumptions about gender, that is, they concern heterosexual men and women, within what can be recognised as 'traditional' family relationships (see Coates, this volume, for an examination of the interaction between gender and sexuality).

They can be categorised in two broad and related areas presented in the following two sections.

### Anxiety over shifts in gender roles and the 'crisis of masculinity'

Within both popular and academic circles there is a widely held view that men are currently in a period of 'crisis'. Most accounts see this crisis as precipitated, firstly, by the shift from manufacturing-based economies to those organised around the service sector and computer-based technologies and, secondly, by the rising influence of the feminist movement (Porter, 1992; Edley and Wetherell, 1995).

The claim is that, consequently, the (post)modern man has lost a sense of his place in the social order. Long-term unemployment has disrupted his role as breadwinner and head of the family unit (Willott and Griffin, 1996); and changes in the composition of the modern household – with rising levels of divorce, single parenting and cohabitation – have had a destabilising effect on men's understanding of their role as fathers (Jagger and Wright, 1999).

There are a number of signs that men are in trouble, for example a sharp increase in male suicides (Frawley, 1998), an increase in the number of men reporting sexual problems such as infertility (Mason, 1993), and evidence of boys' underperformance right across the school curriculum (Bleach, 1998; Epstein *et al.*, 1998).

Parallel changes in women's roles – increasing visibility and participation in the public arena, consistently good school performance, greater international concern with women's rights – are also seen to be challenging traditional roles and gender divisions.

### Anxiety over family 'breakdown'

Modernisation, with the loosening of familiar communal bonds, and the arguable weakening of traditional beliefs about natural social hierarchies (including the familial hierarchy with a dominant father figure), has increased the sense of risk about family relationships and family breakdown. Anxiety over family 'breakdown' most often revolves around divorce and one-parent families, cohabitation, homosexuality, teenage pregnancy, the welfare state and gay parents.

The mass media typically create 'a signification spiral through moral discourses concerning episodes or trends that they portray as examples of immorality and violence due to family breakdown' (Thompson, 1998: 87). Media coverage in Britain of the murder of a toddler, James Bulger, by two teenage boys, as well as the Stephen Lawrence inquiry, illustrates this. Such discourses are urging for a return to traditional heterosexual moral values, particularly with regard to sex and marriage, and can result in the stigmatising of those constructed as social 'outcasts', for example cohabitants, homosexuals and single parents.

The above areas of anxiety often overlap, since changes in gender roles are likely to contribute to changes in the structure of the family, and vice versa. For instance, typical constructions of single parents (usually single mothers) in the British press often play up anxiety about gender roles, particularly the reality of children growing up without male role models. At the same time, they play up anxiety about morality, in that one-parent families are often represented as immoral, deviant and dependent on the state.

Heightened anxiety about such challenges facing men and women in contemporary, changing societies can be seen as a social/moral panic about gender in general, and heterosexual relationships in particular.

Sociological research on social/moral panics in Britain has focused on theories of deviance and examined panics over crime, 'sexual permissiveness' and British youth in the 1960s, drug abuse, illiteracy, sex and AIDS. In recent years, family breakdown, teenage sexuality, homosexuality and contagious disease have all been treated as threats to dominant perceptions of morality or as 'folk devils' (Cohen, 1972/80; Goode and Ben-Yehuda, 1994). In moral panics, a condition, episode, person or group of persons is depicted by the media as a threat to societal values and interests, and causes the concern (and often hostility) of the public and of authorities or opinion-makers. Socially accredited experts express such concern through diagnosis and the offering of solutions. The condition then disappears, submerges or deteriorates and becomes more visible (Cohen, 1972/80: 9). Importantly, the threat/panic is a moral one, because what is threatened is not something mundane, but 'the social order itself or an idealised (ideological) conception of some part of it' (Thompson, 1998: 8).

Moral panics are not new. What is new, however, is the current all-pervasive quality of the panics, that is, there is an increased frequency of moral panics which no longer tend to focus upon a single group. Another new element is the increasing rapidity in the succession of moral panics (Thompson, 1998). As morality combines intensely personal sentiments with impersonal standards for collective social living, moral concerns are characterised by a sense of urgency and controversy. This is perhaps especially so in modern Western societies, where moral boundaries may be less clear or sharp. For panics erupt when these boundaries are fuzzy, shifting and contested (Goode and Ben-Yehuda, 1994).

## The discursive construction of moral panics

It is currently appropriate to examine moral panics, as it is argued that they are likely to intensify, and particularly within modern 'risk societies' like Britain. According to Thompson (1998), moral panics tend to be particularly magnified in Britain, due to factors such as the loss of the authority of traditional elites, anxieties about national identity in the face of external influences and internal diversity, and the centralised character of the mass media.

There are also a number of reasons why it is important to examine and problematise the ways in which the changes described above are discursively constructed, and the heightened anxiety surrounding them.

Firstly, despite the increasing cross-disciplinary emphasis on the importance of discourse in producing and sustaining gender and sexual identities, the particular topic of gender change and its emerging tensions/anxieties have hardly been explored from a linguistic and discourse analytic perspective. In addition, despite research undertaken into the social context of panics and their impact, relatively little has been undertaken into their discursive construction within specific sites, such as newspaper texts. The limited linguistic work in this area has focused on moral panics *about* language (see particularly Cameron, 1995, on panics in Britain, in the late 1980s/early 1990s, about the so-called falling standards of spelling, punctuation and grammar usage), rather than the language of moral panics.

Secondly, we need to be aware that media treatment of events is stylised and follows conventional formats, in line with existing discourses 'reflecting an assumed or already constructed public opinion, which in reality may be nothing more than a figment of the media's own imaginative capacities or worldview' (Thompson, 1998: 100). Cohen (1972/80) confirms that what we often see in the press is the construction of 'pseudo-events' according to the dictates of an unwritten moral agenda which constitutes newsworthiness. Given all this, it becomes problematic to assume that newspaper writers and editors necessarily share a 'common lifeworld' (Habermas, 1990) with ordinary people. A critical and focused examination of gender and sexuality discourses in both newspapers and the everyday talk of women and men is necessary, in order to explore whether there are common threads between them. At the same time, we need to be wary that dismissing some newspaper discourses as expressions of panic may overlook important aspects of gender and sexuality that warrant concern.

And thirdly, public/media debate and panics about gender and sexuality need to be critically examined in the light of changes in the UK media overall, especially where such changes entail the development of some very specific and interesting linguistic phenomena. I am referring here to the rapidly changing face of the British media: increasing competition, globalisation, tabloidisation and centralisation (Thompson, 1998). According to Fairclough (1995), a tension in the media between information and entertainment ('infotainment') is behind their tendency to become increasingly conversationalised and 'marketised' in the direction of entertainment. 'Infotainment' is guiding a tendency in the newspapers to sensationalise, personalise and demonise in their eagerness to attract attention and stir up indignation (Thompson, 1998). This is evident in the use of prescriptive language and certain rhetorical, attention-grabbing features, such as melodramatic and exaggerated vocabulary, sensational headlines, metaphors, direct questions, personal narratives and dramatic stories (Tester, 1994; Litosseliti, 2002a).

## Methodological issues

I will be drawing on examples from two sets of data and analysis, both within a UK context. The specific methodological decisions behind the choice, gathering and analysis of both sets of data are discussed in Litosseliti (1999).

The first is a series of newspaper debates entitled *Head to Head*, published weekly in the broadsheet daily *Guardian* newspaper. *Head to Head* columns aim to include two opposing views on an issue of current affairs, represented in the form of a series of letters exchanged between two participants. Participants argue in male–female pairs, and are individuals broadly known and with access to positions of power within their respective fields. The debates represent written, public, constructed argumentation. I have focused on debates published in the second half of 1996, which concern explicitly 'moral topics' (i.e. those making claims about ideas and behaviours seen as morally 'right' and 'wrong'): the moral duties of business, euthanasia, marriage, vegetarianism and the politics of shopping. For my purposes in this chapter, I am concentrating on one of these debates, on the topic of marriage, which is fairly typical of the themes, as well as the linguistic resources employed in these columns.

The second data set is drawn from two mixed-sex focus group discussions, conducted in 1998, also on the topic of marriage. The discussions

represent spoken, more private, relatively spontaneous, interactive argumentation. Men and women participate in both groups, which consist
in one case of social scientists (in their late twenties or early thirties,
unmarried), and in the other case of various professionals (in their late
thirties/forties, either married or divorced). Participants come from the
north-west of England, with a variety of backgrounds, self-described as
heterosexual, and have no prior knowledge of other participants' views
on the topic of discussion. Again, due to limited space, only one representative spoken data extract is presented and analysed here.

Both the written and transcribed texts are analysed following a
discourse analytic approach, informed by a wider cultural and ideological reading of the context in which the texts occur (as, for example,
seen in van Dijk, 1985; Potter and Wetherell, 1987; Kress, 1989;
Fairclough, 1992). The analysis focuses on examining and problemat-
ising both the *text organisation*, i.e. the linguistic practices or conversational and rhetorical strategies used, and the *text content*, i.e. the
culturally charged repertoires and emerging or salient themes. While the
former involves looking at the ways arguers use linguistic resources to
achieve different aims and effects in their arguments, the second entails
identifying and exploring the attitudes and beliefs invoked in discourse
and understanding the consequences. The two are mutually constructed
and reinforced. As I have argued elsewhere (Litosseliti, 1999, 2002a),
moral evaluations are uniquely implicit, in the sense that they draw
on naturalised ideologies that appear to be common sense, and make
assumptions about values being known or shared (see also van Leeuwen,
2000). It is therefore important to maintain both text organisation and
text content orientations (with the assumptions made therein) in the
analysis of such discourse.

The analysis is not aiming to explore the sources of the salient themes
by asking questions about the groups whose actions may give rise to
and help sustain moral panics. There is considerable research in sociology and cultural studies aimed at addressing such questions as how to
define moral panics (indeed a contested issue), whose values are being
expressed by the panic, and how panics emerge. I refer the reader to
Goode and Ben-Yehuda (1994) and Cohen (1972/80) for their interpretation of interest groups, 'moral entrepreneurs' and the role of govern-
ments and the church; and to Thompson (1998) for a wider, critical
discussion of the social circumstances conducive to the amplification
and reception of moral panics. My interest here is to examine the
discursive process by which something is defined as a risk or threat to

society, and by which certain representations, identities and relations are constructed. This process involves examining a whole array of moral arguments, many of which are more appropriately discussed within the framework of moral panic theory.

## Analysis and discussion of key themes

Firstly, it is interesting that the newspaper text exhibits and exploits characteristics typically associated with moral panics, such as exaggeration and distortion. As I have argued elsewhere (Litosseliti, 2002b), the columns are good examples of the media shift towards 'infotainment' and conversationalisation. They aim to cover controversial issues and dilemmas, and to polarise two different positions on a topic. This becomes evident in the texts' layout, where participants' contributions are visibly separated, assigning one to 'YES' and the other to 'NO', and in the way pictures of them are opposed to one another. The headlines accentuate such polarisation, through adversarial descriptions of the debates ('spectacularly fail to agree', 'they clash') and provocative, often colloquial, statements and generalisations ('simply to make a profit', 'nonsense', 'oh, lighten up'). The use of sensationalist language and the mixture of professional and colloquial speech have a similar effect.

Let us look at these characteristics more closely, by focusing on one of the texts, on marriage. Appropriately, arguments about marriage raise questions about morality and the 'breakdown' of heterosexual family relationships, and at the same time about sexuality and gender representations, identities and roles. The particular text, entitled 'Only two can say', appeared (7/12/96) under the headline 'Marriage: who needs it? We all do, it's a moral strength, thinks sociologist David Marsland. Nonsense, retorts the unmarried journalist, Julia Langdon. If two people lack the will to stay together, you can't force them.'

The analytical comments in Extract 9.1 are an illustration of an analysis which aims to make evident the underlying links between the text content – salient themes or emerging repertoires, and within them representations, identities and social relations – and the text organisation, that is, how linguistic resources are used to different effect, and in relation to the Extract 9.1.

In terms of themes and emerging repertoires (evident in text underlined), we find a moralising discourse in favour of marriage or *Moral Decline Repertoire* (Litosseliti, 2002a), which contains elements of a moral panic: describing a society in crisis and moral decline, identifying

*Extract 9.1*   Only Two Can Say

| David Marsland's responses | Analytical comments |
| --- | --- |
| **(a)** The family is under pressure – from the impersonal forces of modernisation and its enemies among socialists, feminists, and gay liberationists. Marriage is the lynch-pin of the family. Remove it, and the whole institution collapses [ . . . ] The marriage contract is not just a scrap of paper. It is a covenant linking a man and a woman, their future children, the nation and its laws and customs, and not least God [ . . . ] So marriage is morally right and instrumentally useful. I'd venture to claim that marriage is one of our oldest habits and about the best. | **(a) Moral Decline Repertoire** War metaphor. Polarisation Threat/'folk devils' Prediction/threshholds Authorisation (legitimation by reference to the authority of laws, custom, God, age) **Individual vs Collective Repertoire** Value words ('morally right', 'best') Epistemic modality ('marriage is') |
| **(b)** Radical family reformers have argued like you for centuries that marriage is unnecessary. That individual commitment is sufficient. That all that really matters is 'love'. The evidence demonstrates the opposite [ . . . ] Love is of essence, of course, but it mostly needs the nourishment of symbols, family relationships, neighbourhood recognition, legitimacy and moral grounding if it is to survive and flourish. Only marriage provides all this [ . . . ] But why not change our laws, [ . . . ] and our decaying value system in order to preserve and strengthen marriage? Wouldn't this be more sensible than swinging over to untried alternatives? These may suit a 'sophisticated' few, but they are no good for most of us . . . Besides, we have too little ceremony in modern Britain, too much that is casual and merely personal . . . we need rituals, symbols, customs and beliefs which are older and bigger than ourselves. Freedom springs from moral and social obligation. | **(b)** Threat/'folk devils'. Polarisation. Authorisation (legitimation by reference to evidence, and the collective/ social structures) **Individual vs Collective Repertoire Moral Decline Repertoire** Illness metaphor ('decaying') Appeals to old and tried ways **Appeals to the authority of a majority**. Lamenting loss of custom, ceremony, collective/social structures Epistemic modality ('they are no good', 'we have too little') |

| | |
|---|---|
| (c) There is now widespread acknowledgement of the positive value of marriage and of the need to strengthen the family. The silent majority have been joined – late in the day – by our governing elites in rejecting the shallow, notions of the sixties [ . . . ] At last we can take permissive action on major social problems on the basis of national consensus [ . . . ] We *must* use [the law] to correct manifest faults in the legal, administrative and financial framework of the family. We should seek to prevent subversion of the family, to provide practical support for the institution of marriage: to re-moralise our concepts of sex and child-rearing. Mock the idea as you may, we have to go *back* to back to basics. | (c) Epistemic modality ('there is', 'have been joined', 'we can', 'we must', 'we should') Appeals to the authority and common sense of a majority Emotive language/exaggeration **Individual vs Collective Repertoire** Prescriptive language War metaphor ('subversion') Threshholds **Moral Decline Repertoire** Prescriptive language intensifies |

alleged threats to what is 'normal', 'natural', 'moral', making claims about 'right' and 'wrong' sexual behaviour, and proposing solutions. In this discourse, dominant sexual identities are constructed: the heterosexual married couple; and also resistant or alternative identities are constructed: those who do not see marriage as necessary, presumably cohabitants, also described as *radical family reformers, socialists, feminists* and *gay liberationists*. They are the 'folk devils', deviant and a threat to society. Groups of people with an interest in promoting family reform, a political agenda, women's and gay rights, are intensely portrayed as a dangerous minority. There is polarisation between those groups and a *silent majority*. As Thompson (1998: 8–9) states, we see in moral panics 'a high level of concern over the behaviour of a certain group of people and hostility towards that group'.

Furthermore, the threat extends from groups of people to broader attitudes, behaviours and cultural values. For the problem with the 'forces of modernisation', according to Marsland's lamenting argument, is individuals breaking with tradition and promoting alternative lifestyles that effectively undermine the collective good. This *Individual vs Collective Repertoire* attributes moral decline to increasingly individualistic and liberal attitudes, the loss of custom and the weakening of collective morality, i.e. the moral values espoused by a majority (Litosseliti, 2002b). The repertoire assumes that the 'crisis' can be resolved by reconnecting with collective sociocultural norms and structures, such as the institution of marriage, 'rituals', 'customs' and generally 'symbols, family relationships, neighbourhood recognition, legitimacy and moral grounding'. The writer authorises or legitimises his argument in favour of marriage by reference to such norms, rules and structures: these are well-established, old and tried, sensible, espoused by a majority – and, therefore, provide adequate evidence, guidance, prescription about where we *should* be going as a society.

In terms of text organisation, we see various discursive elements of moral panics being used here to carry these themes. A number of moral abstractions and value words (*morally right, best*), metaphors of war and illness (*forces, enemies, subversion, decaying value system*), and melodramatic or exaggerated vocabulary (*silent majority, shallow, permissive notions*) bring moral decline to the fore and construct it as an urgent matter. Exaggeration, according to Thompson (1998: 33), is about the 'deliberate heightening of those elements in a story considered as news' and seen through the frequent use of words and phrases such as 'riot', 'battle', 'attack', 'siege', etc. This sense of urgency and exaggeration may also suggest an element of *disproportionality*, common in moral panics (Thompson, 1998), where the threat is assumed to be more substantial than is warranted by a realistic appraisal – though I would argue that it is extremely difficult to make assessments and claims about that element in general and in the texts in particular.

In addition to the above, there are other elements in the discourse of moral panics which can be traced here. Apart from *exaggeration* and *distortion*, Cohen (1972/80) discusses the elements of *prediction* and *symbolisation*, as for example were seen in the media inventory of the Mods and Rockers events in 1960s Britain.

The first element is the prediction that the events were part of a pattern that would keep getting worse. Hall *et al.* (1978) talk about this as a spiral of amplification, which serves to make the perceived threat to the moral framework of society appear more and more serious. For example, this may happen through reference to *thresholds*, that is, where the limits of acceptable behaviour are being transgressed. This is illustrated in Extract 9.1 in talking about marriage as the *lynch-pin of the family – Remove it, and the whole institution collapses*, and in suggesting that we have already reached the point where *support for the institution of marriage*, remoralisation, and *going back to back to basics* is necessary. It is also evident in the use of epistemic modality, i.e. the degree of certainty involved in a proposition, such as in *The silent majority have been* joined..., *At last we* <u>*can*</u> *take action*..., and *'we* <u>*must*</u> *use...'* (see analytical comments attached to Extract 9.1 for additional examples of such modality).

Finally, symbolisation refers to the process where a word (e.g. Mod) becomes symbolic of a certain status (deviant) and objects such as clothing become symbolic of the status, and the emotions attached to the status (Cohen, 1972/80: 40). There is an element of that in the text above, in rooting the lack of support for marriage into the socialist, feminist and gay movements. These groups are seen here to epitomise the graphically described 'shallow, permissive notions of the sixties' and the 'subversion' of dominant positions on family, sex and child-rearing. This is not dissimilar to the symbolisation seen in moral panics about grammar in the UK (see Cameron, 1995). Symbolism there consisted of the associations made by the conservatives between grammar and order, tradition, hierarchy and rules: 'Grammar was made to symbolise various things for its conservative proponents: a commitment to traditional values as a basis for social order, to "standards" and "discipline" in the classroom, to moral certainties rather than moral relativism and to cultural homogeneity rather than pluralism' (Cameron, 1995: 95).

In sum, moral panics about heterosexual relationships are constructed in Extract 9.1 through a repertoire of moral decline, which is treated as given, and which is attributed to the prevalence of individualistic over collective moral values. Not surprisingly, such an argument turns those groups associated with family reform and with less established or alternative positions (women, gay people) into 'folk devils', while the heterosexual married couple comes to represent the dominant ideologies. The writer reinforces this point, and amplifies the alleged threat from these groups by using exaggerated vocabulary, value words, metaphors and other resources which create a sense of urgency and danger; and by drawing on concepts of prediction, thresholds and symbolisation.

Given the above, it is necessary to ask the question of how moral arguments and/or panics are consumed, negotiated and constructed outside the context of the mass media, and what kind of identities are thereby created. Let us look at some examples from spoken group interaction in focus groups on the topic of marriage (Litosseliti, 1999, 2001, 2002a). Pseudonyms are used in all of these extracts, which are taken from the group of professionals in their thirties and forties. A key to transcription symbols used can be found at the end of this chapter.

*Extract 9.2*   Relationships outside Marriage

Phil    There's so much hypocrisy in the tabloids / and people saying isn't this awful . and most people are DOING it ! / do we REALLY live like these moral standards are meant to make us to be ? / I do wonder . because I can't believe your Sun reader . to be frank . is exactly the moral paragon who the editor seem to expect them to be / I don't buy it / [ . . . ]

Anna    So what you're suggesting is that we've got a moral code which is our sort of public official story moral code /

Phil    I think we have yeah /

Anna    and it's not related to what we do / there's an official story of what we believe . and there is what we do /

Phil    I'm not sure how many seriously subscribe to it / [ . . . ] we like to be disgusted in great detail / *[Laughs]*

Simon   do you see any difference today? / it's interesting that people now are so more talking about relationships outside marriage . and yet I don't think . there's always been this thin veneer of morality / I don't think it's actually that different now / [ . . . ]

Phil    I'm sure if the same people were asked for public consumption whether they believe in sex outside marriage they'd say no / that's the whole point isn't / this sort of mythical moral code we're all meant to have though nobody goes along with it / the image is maintained / [ . . . ]

Anna    the point I was making earlier was about the traditional role of it / that when we had more solid formal set ups in society generally and marriage in particular. there was a code of licence in a way . an implicit licence about these things being allowed / it was absolutely explicitly **DENIED** and explicitly **NOT** allowed / but it was there [ . . . ] somehow the structures have fallen apart . because the FORM isn't really there in quite the same way /

Similarly to the media texts, the tension between a personal, private moral code and a collective or public morality has been a recurrent theme in the spoken data analysed (*Individual vs Collective Repertoire*). There is also an engagement with making sense of social change, of how structures and attitudes are shifting over time. While exploring these themes, the speakers also acknowledge the potential in the mass media to construct as well as confuse and constrict meaning; the accuracy of representations in the media is indeed contestable.

Contrary to the media texts, there are no clear or self-evident answers as to how these shifts come about, and rather than following the moralising and moral panic discourse so often found in the mass media, the spoken texts ironise and dissect it. While the *Individual vs Collective* and *Moral Decline* repertoires remain emerging and recurring themes, these conflicts and shifts are not attributed to particular groups or 'folk devils', but rather become part of subtle reflections on British society and culture. For example:

*Extract 9.3*　A Big Formal Occasion

George　I suppose there's FEW rituals in our society isn't there / there's not many times we can get dressed up and have ( . . . ) / when you talk about [the] mysteriousness [of the wedding] . is something quite special /

Phil　I think as a culture we have lost this formality and that's one of the few occasions when it comes back / [ . . . ] / I suppose a number of occasions where things are formally done in our culture have diminished substantially over the last two three decades since the sixties / so maybe the wedding is the last big one where you can say OK yeah this IS a big formal occasion . and after that there is nothing else /

These reflections, nevertheless, are drawing on some of the elements previously discussed, such as the idea of *threshholds* (*we have lost this formality*) and *symbolisation*, where a (heterosexual) wedding symbolises a culture where rituals and formality remain important. Perhaps more significantly, such comments by the focus group participants take us back to the point made earlier in this chapter about the relevance of culture. As suggested, moral panics erupt in sociocultural contexts where the moral boundaries are unclear, shifting, contested, where central norms and values are not strongly held by almost everyone – and are particularly common in British society. Thompson (1998) describes the dominant political discourse in 1990s Britain as a combination of neo-liberal individualism and a neo-conservative nostalgia for a moral golden age. This, in combination with debates about the role of traditional elites, anxieties about national identity, and the centralised character of the mass media, are aspects of the sociocultural landscape we have to take into account in understanding and interpreting the *Head to Head* data. The focus group participants also acknowledge these aspects in their discussions about 'hypocrisy in the tabloids' and the notion of a 'public official story moral code'. Their interaction can in a sense be seen as a critical commentary on the shift of social and moral boundaries in British culture, on the importance within that culture of maintaining a public image, and also on the hypocrisy of the media.

Finally, it is clear that this notion of a public official moral code also permeates the construction in the focus group of sexuality and gender identities, as seen in Extract 9.4:

*Extract 9.4*   The Safe Option

| | |
|---|---|
| George | gay couples want to get married / why? / yeah . what is it? / |
| Phil | it's a recognition isn't it? / it's not just between yourself and . it's official / other people have to acknowledge that it's REAL . what a piece of paper is saying ( . . . ) / [ . . . ] |
| Anna | I'm wondering what it is we WANT people to recognise / |
| Phil | I don't know *[Pause]* / it used to be that when you got married you'd got tax breaks / and that was a single major advantage / so the state recognised that you were different over someone who – |
| Irene | you were more likely to get promoted if you were married / *[Nods of agreement]* |
| Phil | oh yeah / a career move / it made sure you weren't gay for a start / you were SAFE / *[Nods of agreement]* [ . . . ] |
| Simon | as a MAN you're always regarded as being . you know the safe option if you were married / you know . if you're a young man unmarried then you will not ( . . . ) but if you're married . you have dependants . you have a stable relationship . you're a much safer bet / [ . . . ] |
| George | Matt Busby the famous Man-United manager always encouraged his players to get married / and he was always trying to find suitable wives for them / for that reason . cause he didn't want his players out all night – *[Laughs]* |

Unsurprisingly, and similarly to the newspaper texts analysed, the heterosexual married couple is constructed as dominant, though the use of the past tense (in Phil and Irene's contributions) signals a certain shift in attitudes in recent times. Unlike Extract 9.1, this extract treats marriage as only one part of the overarching theme, which is the importance of appearing to be following convention and acting in line with a set of public, collective moral rules; in this argument, individuals pretend to be acting in line with these rules, because they are aware of the benefits associated with doing so – a more pragmatic argument, compared to Marshland's moralising argument in *Head to Head*. Also, rather than undermining the social institution of marriage (as in Extract 9.1), homosexual couples are constructed here, not as 'other', but as also interested in conforming to the expectations of the institution and benefiting from its legitimacy (see opening lines). The moral vocabulary of exaggeration, prescription and prediction in the media debates is replaced in this extract by more subtle moral arguments. However, these arguments still rely on dominant, normative assumptions about sexuality, such as the concealment and stigmatisation of homosexuality (*it made sure you weren't gay for a start / you were SAFE*) and the desirability of heterosexuality. The arguments also rely on normative, stereotypical views about gender, such as the promiscuity of men, the role of the wife as controller of male activities, and the need to contain the social/ moral 'risks' involved in sexual relationships.

## Conclusion

Overall, we see certain similar themes in both sets of data, revolving around anxieties about shifts in values. These anxieties are sometimes expressed in blatant, urgent, exaggerated ways (moral panics about alleged moral decline), and other times as subtle moral arguments that have moral overtones and require implicit knowledge of the moral/cultural landscape within which they are expressed. Either way, we can identify in both the written and spoken examples an *Individual vs Collective Repertoire*, that is, a tension between a private moral code and a collective or public morality. In the newspaper debate examined, this tension is seen as contributing to the decline of moral standards, and therefore precipitating a moral panic about heterosexual relationships; the panic constructs the heterosexual couple as normative, and treats the 'other' (family reform advocates, women and homosexuals) as deviant and a threat. In the spoken group interaction examined, heterosexuality remains dominant, but the tension between individual and collective moral codes is seen in the context of making sense of social change, and of questioning the role of appearances when it comes to morality.

The focus group data also show that participants are clearly aware of a tendency within representations in the British mass media to mislead and to constrict meaning. In fact, the language used in the newspaper extracts analysed (e.g. war metaphors, exaggerated vocabulary, discourses of prediction, symbolisation and prescription) reinforces that view. Whether or not such types of media texts are misleading, their tendency to amplify alleged threats, polarise different positions and stereotype particular groups, is problematic. A critical examination of moral panics in the media is therefore necessary, and should involve an analysis of representations of people and groups (including the stigmatising of social outcasts), and the construction of identities, including sexuality and gender identities. Equally important is an examination of how moral arguments and/or panics are consumed, negotiated and constructed outside the context of the mass media, as well as across different cultures.

## Key to transcription symbols

| | |
|---|---|
| . | pause (a stopping fall in tone or break in rhythm) |
| *[pause]* | long, noticeable pause |
| / | utterance boundary indicated by intonation |
| - | interruption (by the utterance immediately following) |
| ( ... ) | inaudible, indecipherable speech |
| [ ... ] | omitted text |
| ? | utterance meant or understood as a question (rising intonation) |
| ! | exclamatory utterance (animated tone) |
| CAPS | spoken with emphasis |
| *[in italics]* | non-linguistic aspects (laughter, gestures, etc.) |

## References

Beck, U. 1992. *The Risk Society: Towards a New Modernity*. Cambridge: Polity Press

Bergvall, V., Bing, J. and Freed, A. (eds) 1996. *Rethinking Language and Gender Research: Theory and Practice*. London: Longman

Bleach, K. (ed.) 1998. *Raising Boys' Achievements in Schools*. Stoke-on-Trent: Trentham Books

Cameron, D. 1995. *Verbal Hygiene*. London: Routledge

Cameron, D. 1998. Gender, language and discourse: a review essay. *Signs* I: 945–73

Cohen, S. 1972/80. *Folk Devils and Moral Panics: the Creation of the Mods and Rockers*. London: MacGibbon and Kee

Edley, N. and Wetherell, M. 1995. *Men in Perspective: Practice Power and Identity*. London: Harvester Wheatsheaf/Prentice Hall

Epstein, D., Elwood, J., Hey, V. and Maw, J. (eds) 1998. *Failing Boys*. Buckingham: Open University Press

Fairclough, N. 1992. *Discourse and Social Change*. Cambridge: Polity Press

Fairclough, N. 1995. *Media Discourse*. London: Edward Arnold

Frawley, M. 1998. Suicide and depression in males of various ages: a rural perspective. Paper given at the National Forum on Men and Family Relationships, Canberra, 9–11 June

Goode, E. and Ben-Yehuda, N. 1994. *Moral Panics: the Social Construction of Deviance*. Oxford: Blackwell

Habermas, J. 1990. *Moral Consciousness and Communicative Action*. Cambridge: Polity

Hall, K. and Bucholtz, M. (eds) 1995. *Gender Articulated: Language and the Socially Constructed Self*. London: Routledge

Hall, S., Crichter, C., Jefferson, T., Clake, J. and Roberts, B. 1978. *Policing the Crisis: Mugging, the State and Law and Order*. London: Macmillan

Jagger, G. and Wright, C. (eds) 1999. *Changing Family Values*. London: Routledge

Kress, G. 1989. *Linguistic Processes in Sociocultural Practice* (2nd edn). Oxford: Oxford University Press

Litosseliti, L. 1999. Moral repertoires and gender voices in argumentation. Unpublished PhD thesis. Lancaster: Department of Linguistics and MEL, Lancaster University, UK

Litosseliti, L. 2001. Language, culture and gender identities: examining arguments about marriage. In Stroinska, M. (ed.) *Relative Points of View: Linguistic Representations of Culture*. London/New York: Berghahn, pp. 119–40

Litosseliti, L. 2002a. The discursive construction of morality and gender: investigating public and private arguments. In Benor, S., Rose, M., Sharma, D., Sweetland, J. and Zhang, Q. (eds) *Gendered Practices in Language*. Stanford: Center for the Study of Language and Information, Stanford University, pp. 45–63

Litosseliti, L. 2002b. Head to Head: the construction of morality and gender identity in newspaper arguments. In Litosseliti, L. and Sunderland, J. (eds) *Discourse Analysis and Gender Identity*. Amsterdam: Benjamins

Litosseliti, L. and Sunderland, J. (eds) 2002. *Discourse Analysis and Gender Identity*. Amsterdam: Benjamins

Mason, M-C. 1993. *Male Infertility: Men Talking*. London: Routledge

Porter, D. (ed.) 1992. *Between Men and Feminism*. London: Routledge

Potter, J. and Wetherell, M. 1987. *Discourse and Social Psychology: Beyond Attitudes and Behaviour*. London: Sage

Tester, K. 1994. *Media, Culture and Morality*. London: Routledge

Thompson, K. 1998. *Moral Panics*. London: Routledge

Van Dijk, T. (ed.) 1985. *Handbook of Discourse Analysis*. New York: Academic Press

Van Leeuwen, T. 2000. The construction of purpose in discourse. In Sarangi, S. and Coulthard, M. (eds) *Discourse and Social Life*. London, Longman, pp. 66–82

Willott, S. and Griffin, C. 1996. Men, masculinity and the challenge of long-term unemployment. In Mac an Ghaill, M. (ed.) *Understanding Masculinities: Social Relations and Cultural Arenas.* Buckingham: Open University Press, pp. 77–92

## Newspapers

*The Guardian* (7/12/96) *Head to Head*: 'Only Two Can Say'

# 10
# Women Like Us: Mediating and Contesting Identity in Lesbian Advice Literature

*Deborah A. Chirrey*

## Introduction

One of the key aims of this book is to explore how aspects of culture, sexuality and language can be brought together in order to investigate how people construct their sexual identities. A study of advice literature aimed at British lesbians is relevant to this, as it is a resource, albeit a marginal one, that is available to women who wish to change or alter aspects of their sexual identity, or to gain insight into how their sexual identities are constituted (Gauntlett, 2002: 2–3). Using aspects of critical discourse analysis, this chapter will explore how the discourse of self-help literature aimed at women who are coming to terms with their own lesbianism can provide insights into competing cultural constructions of lesbian identity that exist within British society.

Critical discourse analysis, contained in the work of, for example, Fairclough (1989, 1995) and Caldas-Coulthard and Coulthard (1996), examines language as discourse. For the most part, the object of investigation is written text, and the aim is to reveal the ideological forces that have shaped its production by means of close linguistic analysis. Underlying this process is the belief that texts can only be understood when the context in which they were produced is revealed. Thus, a text is produced in a particular social, historical and political context by a writer (or writers) holding a particular set of values, beliefs and objectives. The aim is to investigate links between these social and cultural elements and specific linguistic features of texts.

This chapter will explore how three advice pamphlets written by lesbians and aimed at nascent lesbians are used by their writers to critique various versions of lesbian sexual identity and to replace them with others. The pamphlets present existing heteronormative conceptualisations of lesbian sexual identity as problematic. In so doing, they give important insights into how lesbians themselves conceptualise and linguistically express their versions of lesbian sexual identity. In these respects, the pamphlets become the site of a vigorous contestation over what the reader should believe about lesbian identity. In mediating between these very different versions of lesbian identity, the pamphlets build bridges for their readers in order that they, the readers, can better manage the process of becoming and being lesbian.

The chapter begins by explaining the exclusive focus on lesbian advice pamphlets, rather than those aimed at both lesbians and gay men, and by describing in some detail the pamphlets that form the data for analysis. The discussion considers how the pamphlets can be regarded as texts of resistance to heteronormative ideology, as they contest lesbian invisibility, as well as the stereotypes, stigma and prejudice associated with and experienced by lesbians. The discussion considers features of discourse, such as topic choice and discourse structure, subversion and appropriation of text types and the use of collocation and lexical choice. It argues that the pamphlets' appearance and use can only be explained if they are read in the context of hegemonic heterosexism, lesbian feminism, and the relationship between lesbians and dominant discourses of heterosexuality.

## Lesbians only?

Although lesbians, gay men and other sexual minorities in contemporary British culture share a commonality of experience, for example around coming out (e.g. Chirrey, 2003), it can be argued that the experience is in fact a gendered one. Markowe (1992, 1996) highlights this in relation to coming out, stating that, '[i]n coming out, whether to self or to other, the lesbian must be seen as a woman, with all the implications that being a woman has in our society' (Markowe, 1992: 20). For example, the pay gap that exists between women and men in Britain also exists between lesbians and gay men. Consequently, lesbians will be generally poorer than gay men are. Lesbians are more likely than gay men to have been heterosexually married and, as divorce courts routinely award custody of children to mothers rather than to fathers, lesbians are more likely to be single parents than gay men, with all the social and economic consequences that entails. Lesbians, like straight women, may experience sexual discrimination and harassment. Women of all sexualities have less access to social space than men, whether straight or gay. Accordingly, in Britain, there are more magazines aimed at gay men than at lesbians, there are more bars and clubs owned, run and frequented by gay men than by lesbians. Thus the cultural, social and economic impact of coming out and of living a homosexual identity is different for a woman than for a man. Similarly, the typical model of, for example, sexual experience or the importance of romantic or emotional attachment to others, has been shown to be different for lesbians and gay men (e.g. De Monteflores and Schultz, 1978). Consequently, this chapter does not attempt to conflate the experiences of lesbians and gay men, but focuses primarily on lesbians, and the advice literature that is written by them and for them.

## The data

The data considered here consist of short pamphlets produced by various British organisations and held at the Lesbian Archive and Information Centre in Glasgow.[1] The archive holds around 20 self-help pamphlets on aspects of gay and lesbian life, published from the mid-1950s to the present day. Over half of them are aimed at both women and men. Some are written with a particular group of lesbians and/or gay men in mind, such as those produced by the Lesbian and Gay Christian movement, or a pamphlet that focuses on issues relevant to lesbian mothers and those who support them. For the purposes of this chapter, I have focused on three of these pamphlets, each of which fulfils certain criteria. Firstly, they are written by people who themselves identify as lesbians; they are aimed exclusively at women; they focus primarily on issues of sexual identity, rather than sexual health; and they are published in a paper format, rather than on the Internet.[2] For the purposes of comparison, I will occasionally refer to one other pamphlet, *Lesbian or Gay – Telling Your Parents* (1995), produced by the organisation Families and Friends of Lesbians and Gays (FFLAG). This pamphlet contrasts with the others, in that it is not written by lesbians or gay men, but by their heterosexual allies, nor is it aimed exclusively at lesbians.

The earliest pamphlet that I consider here, *Women Like Us*, was published in 1987 by London Lesbian Line. It is mainly text based, with a few cartoon strips. The pamphlet is divided into several sections, such as an introduction to and history of London Lesbian Line, a book list, and a contact list of lesbian organisations. The main body of the pamphlet is in two parts: a section entitled 'Some thoughts', structured around a question and answer format, and a section containing brief autobiographical accounts of women's experiences. The second pamphlet *I Think I Might Be a Lesbian . . . Now What Do I Do?* (1993) is a British adaptation of a pamphlet originally published in the United States. This pamphlet is specifically aimed at younger women and girls. It is entirely text based, and is organised solely around a question and answer format. The third leaflet is one published by London Lesbian Line in 1997. It is also entitled *Women Like Us*, but differs from the 1987 version. This later pamphlet is a multi-semiotic text, combining autobiography, cartoons and pictures, images, photographs and drawings.

### Advice, ideology and power

Advice texts aimed at lesbians have a certain amount of intertextuality with other forms of advice or self-help literature and, as a result, readers will have expectations about them. For example, they will expect to see their particular situation constituted as a problem which requires solutions. Indeed, the location of the 'problem' of lesbianism is one way of understanding the ideology of these pamphlets and others like them. The three pamphlets considered here are similar in that they each locate the problem within heteronormative society. For example, *Women Like Us* (1987) acknowledges that the practice of being lesbian is problematic because of a lack of reference points in society, so being a lesbian is made difficult as women have no accurate information freely available about what being lesbian means or entails:

> *Extract 10.1   Women Like Us* (1987: 9)
> Because there is little positive information on lesbian sexuality [ . . . ] contemplating a sexual relationship with another woman for the first time can be worrying and even frightening.

Concerns over the normality and naturalness of lesbianism are raised as a central problem for readers of *I Think I Might Be a Lesbian* (1993). In this case, the reader is instructed to downgrade and dismiss any negative evaluations of lesbianism, which she may have encountered in heteronormative culture, as a form of unthinking bigotry akin to racism or sexism, or as little more than a question of aesthetics:

> *Extract 10.2   I Think I Might Be a Lesbian* (1993: 2–3)
> We're told that it's sick or perverted, or sinful, or abnormal. But the people who tell us that are the same ones who say that women belong in the kitchen, and that Black people are inferior, and that handicapped people are useless. Who's to say what's normal? Some people think eating raw fish is normal, and other people think it's disgusting and abnormal.

In locating the problem within heteronormative society, the three pamphlets that I am focusing on differ ideologically from other advice pamphlets aimed at a lesbian or gay readership. For example, the self-help pamphlet *Lesbian or Gay – Telling Your Parents* (1995) describes coming out as involving 'news' that parents 'will find shocking' (3), and focuses on the problem of the child's sexuality and how that will be difficult for the parents, rather than the child, to cope with. This pamphlet makes it the young lesbian's (or young gay man's) business to take responsibility for minimising that shock and for mitigating its effects on parents:

*Extract 10.3 Lesbian or Gay – Telling Your Parents* (1995: 10)
If you are in a permanent relationship, try to gently introduce your partner into your family when you feel that they are most at ease with the idea of a same sex relationship. Remember, it can be difficult for some parents, especially fathers, to cope with physical displays of affection. Same sex partnerships often highlight the fact that there will not be grandchildren, and many parents will regret this.[3]

The motivation underpinning a reader's engagement with advice literature is that the writer is believed to be in possession of superior knowledge and experience which qualifies her to dispense advice. The linguistic expression of this power asymmetry varies from pamphlet to pamphlet. The authors of *I Think I Might Be a Lesbian* use covert means of exerting power over the reader. In making use of the question and answer format, the writer sets the agenda of the discourse, while all the time suggesting that the agenda is the reader's. In effect, the reader is having words put into her mouth. She is directed towards topics such as 'Am I normal?', 'Who should I tell?', 'How can I meet other lesbians?', 'Coming out' and 'What about sex?' By presupposing that these topics and concerns are on the reader's mind, the pamphlet naturalises them so that the reader begins to understand that they are allegedly central to becoming and being a lesbian. Here we begin to see the ideology invested in these pamphlets: lesbianism is not merely about being erotically and emotionally attracted to other women as the pamphlet told us on the first page, but actually involves engagement with a set of questions and answers. These questions and answers have inherent in them a new set of cultural values and practices, values and practices which the pamphlets present, rightly or wrongly, as consistently agreed by lesbians and fundamental to lesbian group membership.

An example of one of these new values and practices is the discourse in the pamphlets that surrounds coming out. All three of the pamphlets present coming out as one of the rituals that is central to lesbian culture. It is valorised as a difficult process that takes courage and bravery to go through:

Extract 10.4   *I Think I Might Be a Lesbian* (1993: 5)
It's hard to know who can handle the information and give you support. Some friends may accept you. Some may turn away from you or tell other people without your permission.
     Telling family/guardians can be very difficult.

It is a process that is presented as vital to the development, health and well-being of the young woman:

Extract 10.5   *I Think I Might Be a Lesbian* (1993: 6)
It's important to have someone to talk to because it's not normal or healthy for young people to have to keep secret such an important part of their lives.

Indeed, not to come out is to deny oneself a fulfilled and happy existence:

Extract 10.6   *Women Like Us* (1987: 6)
You may wonder why we do it. It seems most of us prefer to be honest about our chosen lifestyle, despite the difficulties, than to live a lie, remaining invisible and silent.

At this point in the pamphlet, the writer uses the exclusive 'we' pronoun, which sets the writer apart linguistically from the reader, who is referred to as 'you'. This device would seem to contribute to the assumption that, since the reader has not yet come out, she has not undergone the necessary ritual that allows her to be part of the in-group 'we'. It is almost to suggest that being a lesbian is constituted by undergoing a ritual by which one becomes a lesbian. Coming out to others is a necessary and vital part of this 'initiation'. In this respect, these pamphlets can be seen as a means by which lesbians transmit their counterculture to nascent lesbians. Readers are being instructed on the salient aspects of late twentieth-century British lesbian cultural values, as represented by these pamphlets.

From a grammatical viewpoint, the three pamphlets do not make use of overtly powerful language. For example, there is very little use of imperative sentences, with only three in *Women Like Us* (1987), and none in the remaining two pamphlets. Instead, the sentences are mainly declarative, with the occasional interrogative. Nevertheless, declarative sentences have a didactic quality that encourages the reader to collude with the opinions being expressed:

*Extract 10.7 Women Like Us* (1987: 6)
For some women the realisation that they are lesbians comes as a sort of revelation that what had been wrong with their lives up till then was that they had been trying to live as heterosexual.

*Extract 10.8 Women Like Us* (1997: 20)
In my experience the children of lesbians that I have met appear happy, strong individuals who are able to speak for themselves, and enjoy the quality of life we wish for all children.

In Extract 10.7, the reader is being given an essentialist explanation of her sexuality: retrospective examination of her life confirms that she was a lesbian all the time but had not noticed. Heterosexuality was therefore unnatural to her and consequently led to unhappiness. In Extract 10.8, the reader is being presented with a very positive version of the children of lesbians which disregards the negative experiences that many of them have as a result of heterosexism and prejudice, and the effects those experiences may have on them. These accounts may or may not be applicable to the reader, but the pamphlets assume the reader's agreement with and assent to what is being asserted.

*Women Like Us* (1997) is a collection of autobiographical writing, poetry, cartoons, photographs and drawings. The 16 autobiographical accounts are complex and diverse, with no unifying editorial text linking them or guiding their interpretation. It would appear that these stories are random and without intervention, but of course this is not the case. The accounts have been purposefully commissioned, selected and edited for inclusion in the pamphlet. The texts place individual women and their experiences at the centre of lesbianism. This format has its own power. Didactic text has been abandoned and in its place is auto-biography, which personalises the lesbian experience and appeals more to the emotions of the reader. This pamphlet seems to be trying to stress the diversity of lesbians, by letting us read the personal reflections of lesbian mothers, Black lesbians, married lesbians, young and old lesbians, working-class and middle-class lesbians. Nevertheless, it is possible to identify a strong formulaic element in the narrative structure. Most present lesbianism as more than sexual experiences and desires (the fourth story is the only one to refer to sexual experience). Instead lesbianism is represented as lifestyle choices, cultural norms and values, and common and predictable feelings and life experiences. All of the accounts share a core narrative structure, which displays certain expected characteristics of coming-out stories (e.g. Liang, 1997). They start with an unhappy beginning, during which the woman struggles internally with her sexuality, beset by fears and confusion resulting from misinformation from or misunderstanding by heteronormative notions of lesbianism. This is succeeded by a crisis point that is resolved through self-acceptance and through coming out either to self, to others or to both. In each case, there is a happy-ever-after outcome, inasmuch as the woman can now look back on her life with understanding and contemplate her present and future with self-acceptance and contentment (see also Sauntson, this volume).

## Mediating identity

Part of the process of becoming lesbian is identifying oneself with the existing sociocultural category of 'lesbian'. This can be problematic for a woman, as the existence of this category is often suppressed in heteronormative British society and its representation is often prejudicial. Coming out to oneself as a lesbian is partly a process of coming to terms with those prejudices (Liang, 1997: 290) and of reconciling them with one's own sense of self. One of the functions of this advice literature is to mediate in this process. The very existence of the pamphlets resists the suppression of lesbian identities. The pamphlets' presentation of those identities has to enable a woman to manage a way of successfully integrating lesbianism into the other facets of her identity without threatening her self-esteem. The three pamphlets considered here fulfil that need by presenting a model of lesbianism that the reader can use to achieve this aim.

In the following sections, three aspects of heteronormative lesbian identity that the pamphlets focus on are analysed: invisibility; stereotypes; and stigma and prejudice. The discussion will also consider the motivation behind their inclusion in the pamphlets.

### Lesbian invisibility

Heterosexuality is a highly visible and dominant discourse in British culture: it is enshrined in legislation, religious belief, educational policy and is represented in popular and elitist entertainment, art, literature and news media (see, for example, Dyer, 1997). By contrast, the existence of lesbianism is at best marginalised and at worst suppressed. The status of these pamphlets is symbolic of this situation, as they are not widely distributed and are difficult to come by. It is not easy for a reader to get her hands on these pamphlets. For example, she has to request them from relatively low-profile organisations (e.g. London Lesbian Line, or various Friend helplines), seek them out in particular venues, such as an alternative bookshop, or discover them during particular transient events, such as Mardi Gras or gay pride celebrations. They are peripheral and transient. Just as the pamphlets are marginalised, lesbian sexuality is also hidden away by heteronormative culture, and access to reliable information about it, written by lesbians for lesbians, is restricted. Lesbianism and the lesbian subject are rendered almost invisible. As Butler (1991: 20) argues, this is a subtle yet powerful form of oppression:

> Here it becomes important to recognise that oppression works not merely through acts of overt prohibition, but covertly, through the constitution of viable subjects and through the corollary constitution of unviable (un)subjects – *abjects* we might call them – who are neither named nor prohibited through the economy of the law. Here oppression works through the production of a domain of unthinkability and unnameability.

In a cultural context that renders lesbianism unthinkable and unnameable, these texts act as a means of countering this situation by asserting the existence of both.

The pamphlets highlight the invisibility of lesbians as a real and serious problem for women whose sexuality is not in line with heterosexuality. Invisibility makes it difficult for them to understand their own feelings and emotions. This in turn makes them feel isolated from heterosexual society. In addition, their understanding of what a lesbian is is based on a heteronormative value system:

*Extract 10.9 Women Like Us* (1997: 6)
There were no role models for lesbians then, Martina Navratilova wasn't even famous so life was a bit lonely. The only reference to a lesbian was a woman who lived in the town six miles away, and the L word was never used, girls were just warned to keep away from her.

The pamphlets attempt to build bridges for their readers by encouraging social contact with other lesbians. Two of them devote entire subsections to it. *I Think I Might Be a Lesbian* poses and answers the question 'How can I meet other lesbians?' (1993: 9). *Women Like Us* (1987: 6) has a section entitled 'Invisibility'. *Women Like Us* (1997) addresses the issue in many of the individual autobiographical stories, as in Extract 10.9 above. Each pamphlet also includes extensive contact lists of organisations and helplines. So, isolation is presupposed as a common problem for the reader, and becoming part of a lesbian community, whether virtual or real, is represented as a vital part of forming a resilient and robust lesbian identity:

> *Extract 10.10   Women Like Us* (1987: 5)
> Forming links and friendships with other lesbians and discovering lesbian culture and politics can strengthen our sense of identity and lessen the isolation we may feel from heterosexual society.

There is a further way in which these sections of the pamphlets initiate the reader into the value systems of British lesbians. From the 1970s, second-wave feminists had mounted a critique of sexism within British society. As Jagose (1996: 49–50) explains, at this time many lesbian feminists rejected what they perceived to be the masculinist agenda of the gay liberation movement, arguing that all men, regardless of their sexuality, oppress women. At the same time, lesbian feminism emphasised the connection between all women, no matter their sexuality. As a consequence, being part of a community of women or indeed being a separatist lesbian, was culturally important to lesbian feminists.[4] Here the pamphlets outline a salient cultural practice for the nascent lesbian to adopt.

## Lesbian stereotypes

The pamphlets represent the formation of new social links with other lesbians as important for another reason: they are a means by which the reader will gain access to the complexity of lesbian existence, rather than the stereotypes that she may have encountered previously. As Jenkins (1996: 122) notes, stereotyping is

> the labelling and classification of social collectives, albeit in a partial fashion, [which] simplifies information flows about complex situations [ . . . ] Although the word has come to attract wholly negative

connotations, stereotyping is a routine, everyday cognitive process upon which we all to some extent depend.

Thus, one social group will make sense of another social group by producing a stereotype of that second group that reduces its social complexity and makes it easier to understand. Heteronormative society constructs stereotypes of lesbians by selecting a few putative features that it imagines are shared by that group. For example, *Women Like Us* (1987: 6) refers to habitual portrayals of lesbians on television or in books as 'usually of a certain type – young, physically fit, white and single'. Although these stereotypes are not negative, they are restrictive. Prejudicial stereotypes are produced when one group wishes to enhance the solidarity of its members by producing an 'out-group'. From a psychological viewpoint, becoming a lesbian is a process of coming to terms with and going beyond these restricted or negative cultural stereotypes of lesbians, stereotypes which are as real to the nascent lesbian as to anyone else (Markowe, 1992: 97).

Research by Viss and Burn (1992) into lesbian stereotypes indicates that in Britain the perception of homosexuality as deviant behaviour persists among at least some heterosexuals. The subjects of their study who had a social distance from lesbians were shown to perceive them negatively as 'cowardly, sly, suspicious, shrewd, stupid, impulsive, ignorant'. Decreased social distance leads to more positive labels, such as 'individualistic', 'intelligent', 'honest', 'imaginative', 'neat' (Viss and Burn, 1992). However, knowing a lesbian did not significantly affect these subjects' views of lesbians. They either perceive that the lesbian/s known to them is an exception, or they categorise that person separately from other lesbians. Stereotypes are, therefore, resistant to change (Viss and Burn, 1992: 176). In her study of British attitudes to lesbians, Markowe (1992: 162) states that 'the lesbian stereotype is seen as abnormal, masculine, political/feminist and aggressive, while, in contrast, the heterosexual woman stereotype is seen mainly in terms of being normal and attractive'. If the woman who is becoming a lesbian is isolated from other lesbians, then her ideas of what it means to be a lesbian may be those of heterosexual society in which she lives. Markowe's study of the attitudes towards lesbians that lesbians themselves had held, prior to their coming out, reveals the nature of these beliefs:

Before coming out to others, 45% of the lesbian sample thought lesbians might be masculine or look like men. Over a third of the women suggested they had believed in or held a stereotype. More than 20% of them mentioned being frightened [ . . . ] fifteen percent [ . . . ] mentioned they were frightened of being attacked or seduced or out of control, or that they thought lesbians would be predatory or aggressive. (Markowe, 1992: 330)

It seems reasonable to deduce that coming to terms with being part of this particular out-group is a difficult undertaking.

The pamphlets address this issue in some depth. First of all they acknowledge the dilemma which nascent lesbians have to deal with:

*Extract 10.11   I Think I Might Be a Lesbian* (1993: 7)
It's hard for lesbian youth to feel good about ourselves because all around us are people who believe that we are sick, or perverted, or destined to live very unhappy lives.

*Extract 10.12   Women Like Us* (1987: 9)
Lesbian sexuality is usually portrayed as something dirty or perverted and women who have these feelings aren't meant to be normal.

*Extract 10.13   Women Like Us* (1997: 12)
I had heard of lesbians but they were PE teachers or women with beards and men's suits.

It is these stereotypes of heteronormative British culture that the pamphlets will take issue with. In doing so, as will be discussed below, they present an alternative version of lesbianism which is more palatable to the reader, seems more in keeping with the reader's view of herself, and is thus more helpful to the reader in constructing her sexual identity.

## Stigma and prejudice

Despite the tolerance and liberalism of minority sexual identities that we would like to ascribe to British society, research indicates a very different picture (e.g. Coia *et al.*, 2002; Trenchard and Warren, 1984). Coming out as a lesbian entails encountering homophobic prejudice, which may range from name-calling to threats of physical violence or actual physical violence. Coia *et al.* (2002: 45–6) list a wide range of settings where discrimination is experienced, noting that the most common loci for abuse and prejudice are in schools and in the street. This is not an issue that the pamphlets sidestep. Rather they portray lesbianism as an identity that will be subject to criticism and occasionally difficult to live out.

Extracts 10.14, 10.15 and 10.16 highlight the particular problems that lesbians will encounter just because they are young, and therefore lacking in social and economic autonomy and power:

*Extract 10.14   I Think I Might Be a Lesbian* (1993: 2)
Many adults will tell us that we are too young to call ourselves lesbian or that we are going through a phase or that we don't know what we are talking about.

*Extract 10.15   I Think I Might Be a Lesbian* (1993: 5)
But some lesbian youth [sic] have been kicked out of their home when their parents/guardians found out.

*Extract 10.16   I Think I Might Be a Lesbian* (1993: 5–6)
Some young lesbians live in children's homes and may have to deal with reactions not only from other young people in the home but also from social workers and care assistants.

Extracts 10.17 and 10.18 acknowledge that rejecting heterosexuality and taking on lesbian identity in adulthood has its own problems:

*Extract 10.17   Women Like Us* (1987: 2)
We are aware of the many pressures on women to become or continue to be heterosexual and the potential isolation, guilt and fear associated with acknowledging that you are a lesbian.

*Extract 10.18   Women Like Us* (1987: 6)
[ ... ] we have the added fear that if we do come out in public our children may be taken away from us by the courts as a lesbian is often not considered a 'fit mother'.

In addition, lesbianism may contribute to the prejudices that a woman already experiences on account of some other aspect of her identity:

*Extract 10.19   Women Like Us* (1987: 8)
Lesbians who aren't 'white British' suffer a double kind of oppression – that of being lesbian women and of being outsiders, foreigners, 'alien', other.

It may seem incongruous that the pamphlets draw attention to these unpleasant aspects of being a lesbian in Britain, as one might imagine that they would disturb the reader rather than reassure her. Nevertheless, because stereotypes, stigma and prejudice figure strongly in heteronormative discourses on lesbianism it is important that the pamphlets include them as major topic areas. As one might expect, however, the pamphlets aim to challenge these discourses and to present the reader with an alternative ideological viewpoint, as will now be explored.

## Contesting identities

The autobiographical writing contained in *Women Like Us* (1997) reveals some of the discomfort that women have experienced around naming lesbian sexuality:

> *Extract 10.20  Women Like Us* (1997: 6)
> The only reference to a lesbian was a woman who lived in the town six miles away, and the L word was never used . . .

> *Extract 10.21  Women Like Us* (1997: 16)
> 'Lesbian' was an insult in the junior school playground that made me not hold hands with another girl.

> *Extract 10.22  Women Like Us* (1997: 11)
> It took me a long time to call myself a lesbian.

These extracts indicate how the pamphlets highlight the negative aspects of beliefs surrounding lesbians and lesbian sexuality which are most damaging and which women will have to counter. The pamphlets contest these stereotypes in a number of ways. One method is simply to state that the stereotypes and prejudices are wrong:

> *Extract 10.23  Women Like Us* (1987: 5)
> Most lesbians don't fit the stereotypes in the least.

> *Extract 10.24  I Think I Might Be a Lesbian* (1993: 9)
> Remember: it's normal and natural to be a lesbian, just like it's normal and natural for some people to be heterosexual.

## Subversion

A more covert method is to appropriate and subvert heteronormative texts. *Women Like Us* (1997: 8) has a pastiche of a cartoon in the style of traditional British children's comics, such as *The Beano* or *The Dandy*. In the cartoon, two well-known characters, Minnie the Minx and Beryl the Peril, are pictured arm in arm, under the caption, 'It's love at last for Minnie and Beryl!' Below them, a second caption asks: 'but what of Tillie the Terror?', who is pictured with tears in her eyes, accompanied by a speech bubble asking: ' . . . Beryl. How COULD you?'

The choice of these characters is significant, as they are representations of girls who are not gender stereotypes. Thus, they have appealed to generations of British girls, no matter what sexuality, who enjoyed and perhaps identified with their transgressive behaviour. Furthermore, due to the cultural association that exists in Britain between gender nonconformity and lesbianism, Minnie and Beryl are potentially lesbian icons. However, it should be stressed that this association is merely a cultural one. Although a number of psychological studies have shown links between gender nonconformity and homosexuality, it would be foolhardy to suggest that the rejection of conventional femininity is a prerequisite or a cause of lesbianism in women (Markowe, 1996: 57).

The inclusion of the cartoon in this leaflet is destabilising in two ways: it questions the assumption that childhood is a time of sexual innocence and ignorance, and it juxtaposes childhood icons and lesbianism in such a way as to suggest that lesbian sexuality is normal and natural. The effect is made more powerful by the use of humour – laughing with the cartoon engenders feelings of solidarity.

## Collocation

A final way in which contestation is achieved is through collocation. Collocation is defined by Sinclair (1991: 170) as 'the occurrence of two or more words within a short space of each other in a text'. Word meaning does not remain fixed, and the processes by which it alters include the way in which words acquire new denotative and connotative meaning from the discourses in which they are used. I will focus on the contexts in which the word 'lesbian' appears in these pamphlets in order to examine how they imbue the term with new meanings for their readers.

In the pamphlets, the word *lesbian* is linked with various discourses in such a way that its meaning is either presented as a problem, is called into question, or redefinition is attempted. There are several examples of the word *lesbian* being constituted as a problem: 11 in *I Think I Might*

*Be a Lesbian* (1993), 15 in *Women Like Us* (1987) and 9 in *Women Like Us* (1997). Extracts 10.25–10.27 show four examples as, in each case, *lesbian* is linked with various discourses that have historically constructed the lesbian and her life in a negative and prejudicial fashion.

> Extract 10.25   *I Think I Might Be a Lesbian* (1993: 7)
> It's hard for <u>lesbian</u> youth to feel good about ourselves because all around us are people who believe that we are <u>sick</u>, or <u>perverted</u> or destined to live <u>very unhappy lives</u>.

In this extract, the words *sick* and *perverted* draw upon the discourses of physical, psychological and sexual health, in that they evoke physical disease, mental sickness and sexual abnormality. This long-standing and persistent discourse continues to be used by some to construct a version of the perceived reality of homosexuality. The reference to *unhappy lives* evokes and stands in contrast to dominant discourses surrounding heterosexual romance, in which men and women, united in hetero-sexual coupledom, live 'happily ever after'. The discourse of health is also drawn on in Extract 10.26 where lesbian sexuality is said to be *dirty* and *perverted*. Moreover, lesbians and their sexuality are linked in an antithetical relationship with *normal*:

> Extract 10.26   *Women Like Us* (1987: 9)
> <u>Lesbian</u> sexuality is usually portrayed as something <u>dirty</u> or <u>perverted</u> and women who have these feelings aren't meant to be <u>normal</u>.

*Normal* evokes discourses concerning all types of human beha-viour, including sexual behaviour, and denotes the unremarkable, the expected, the statistically common and culturally acceptable. The lesbian is then, by contrast, the maladjusted, freakish individual whose sexual development and behaviour have gone awry.

Extract 10.27 shows *lesbian* collocating with text that evokes discourses around gender role reversal, mannishness, and genetic or hormonal abnormality:

> Extract 10.27   *Women Like Us* (1997: 12)
> I had heard of <u>lesbians</u> but they were PE teachers or <u>women with beards and men's suits</u>.

Such discourses suggest that it is impossible for a woman to combine lesbianism with conventional femininity. The link between *PE teachers* and lesbians is not only a cliché, but taps into cultural discourses surrounding paedophilia, in which 'homosexuals' (men in particular) are commonly suspected to have a predatory sexual interest in children.

In contrast, Extract 10.28 presents the lesbian as a mother. The pamphlet immediately draws attention to and naturalises the seemingly counter-intuitive nature of this particular combination of identities. It further problematises lesbian mothers by embedding them in a discourse of legal conflict and by characterising the relationship of lesbian mothers with the courts as one of fear and persecution. Furthermore, lesbian mothers are represented as being a liability to their children due to their perceived inadequacy to fulfil their maternal role:

*Extract 10.28  Women Like Us* (1987: 6)
Women who [ . . . ] have children are assumed to be heterosexual – to many women the idea of a lesbian mother is an impossibility – but it is a reality for many women, although we have the added fear that if we do come out in public our children may be taken away from us by the courts as a lesbian is often not considered a 'fit' mother.

In this way, the pamphlets recall and reproduce the multiple discourses on lesbianism which construct lesbians as unhealthy, unhappy, unnatural women who are a danger to their own and other people's children. But this construction does not go unchallenged. For example, the meaning of lesbian is overtly interrogated through the use of wh-questions, such as:

*Extract 10.29   I Think I Might Be a Lesbian* (1993: 1)
How do I know if I am a lesbian?

*Extract 10.30   I Think I Might Be a Lesbian* (1993: 2)
What is it like to be young and lesbian?

*Extract 10.31   Women Like Us* (1987: 5)
What does it mean to call ourselves lesbians?

Here the reader is imagined as rejecting false and inadequate meanings of *lesbian* in pursuit of the 'real' meaning. The pamphlets are the source of that truth and redefine *lesbian* in numerous statements: *I Think I Might Be a Lesbian* (1993) has 27 redefinitions, *Women Like Us* (1987) has 29, and *Women Like Us* (1997) has 30.

*Extract 10.32   I Think I Might Be a Lesbian* (1993: 9)
Remember: it's <u>normal and natural</u> to be a <u>Lesbian</u>, just like it's <u>normal and natural</u> for some people to be straight.

As in Extract 10.26, *lesbian* is again linked with discourses surrounding normative development and behaviour, but this time the social approbation extends to lesbians. Extracts 10.33–10.35 illustrate how the link between lesbian and unhappy lives is contested by linking them with discourses of emotional fulfilment, social adequacy, integration and acceptance:

*Extract 10.33   I Think I Might Be a Lesbian* (1993: 9)
It helps to read good books about <u>lesbians</u> – books that have accurate information in them and that are written about <u>lesbians</u> who are leading <u>very fulfilled lives</u>.

*Extract 10.34   Women Like Us* (1997: 13)
Kate and Vic and Vic's lover made me realise that being a <u>lesbian</u> was <u>not something to be ashamed of</u>, in fact it could be <u>really amazing</u> [...] These gorgeous women took me to my first <u>lesbian</u> disco where for the first time in my life <u>I felt like I fitted in</u>.

*Extract 10.35   Women Like Us* (1997: 10)
It took me a long time before I was brave enough to go to either of these groups but it was excellent just hanging around chatting to older (30 year old!) <u>lesbians who were totally happy to be lesbians</u> and who made me want to be just like them.

Extracts 10.36–10.38 exemplify how *lesbian* is juxtaposed in the pamphlets with discourses of motherhood that are affirming and positive. These statements not only counteract the myth contained in Extract 10.28 that lesbians cannot be mothers, but also attest that lesbians can be competent mothers who are proud of their role as parents:

*Extract 10.36   Women Like Us* (1987: 6)
To many women the idea of a <u>lesbian mother</u> is an impossibility – but <u>it is a reality</u> for many women.

*Extract 10.37   Women Like Us* (1997: 5)
I had been married for over 30 years and raised a large family when
I finally phoned lesbian line.

*Extract 10.38   Women Like Us* (1997: 19)
I am a parent and feel so proud of this. The more lesbian parents
I meet with the prouder I am.

## Lexicalising lesbianism

Words such as *lesbian*, which reference minority sexual identity, are
problematic in both heteronormative and lesbian culture for a number
of reasons. They name that which Butler argues is the 'unnameable'
(1991: 20) and, in that sense, are taboo words. Also, as indicated above,
their uses and meanings are contentious. The three pamphlets that I
am considering make different choices concerning the lexicalisation of
lesbianism, and it is argued here that these choices are significant not
only for what they include, but for what they rule out.

Both *I Think I Might Be a Lesbian* (1993) and *Women Like Us* (1987)
make exclusive use of the term *lesbian*. *Women Like Us* (1997) differs,
in that it includes both *lesbian* and *dyke*, as well as attributive usage
of *gay* and, on one occasion, *queer*. As Fairclough notes, '[a]lternative
lexicalisations are generated for diverse ideological positions' (1995: 34).
Lexical choices are, therefore, important in aiding our understanding of
the presuppositions that writers bring to their texts. Cameron and Kulick
(2003: 24–9) provide an overview of the 'politics of naming' sexual
identities. They point out that names provide a means of 'satisfy[ing]
the desire of group members themselves for names and self-descriptions
they can readily identify with' (Cameron and Kulick, 2003: 25). There
are a number of presuppositions involved in the decision to use *lesbian*
and to exclude everything else. By presenting one term to the reader,
the pamphlets provide an identity label to which the reader can rally.
One label implies one category, one easily identifiable homogeneous
lesbian subject, and this subject is made more singular by her concern
with the predictable set of characteristic topics and questions which, as
was discussed earlier, the texts presuppose and naturalise.

The choice of one term over another is also significant, as it signals a
particular political position. *Lesbian* can be the term of choice for lesbian
feminists wishing to emphasise the importance of gender in issues of
sexuality (Cameron and Kulick, 2003: 27). *Gay*, therefore, is an unacceptable term, as it either obscures an individual's gender or implies male

gender (Zwicky, 1997: 23). *Dyke*, although having an exclusive female reference, is perhaps too taboo, in that it is identified with a more transgressive version of lesbian identity that is more challenging to heteronormative culture (Zwicky, 1997: 22). Furthermore, both *dyke* and *queer* have pejorative denotations, perhaps too pejorative for this context. In the late 1980s and early 1990s, when these pamphlets were published, the reclamation of *queer* had hardly begun and, although both *dyke* and *queer* have now been at least partially reclaimed by some speakers in some contexts, the process of amelioration is far from complete.

In this respect *Women Like Us* (1997) is different. In the autobiographical writings we find *lesbian* and *dyke*, as well as attributive uses of *gay* and *queer*. This wider range of terms presents the reader with a more diverse range of lesbian subjects. As has been pointed out, this pamphlet is multi-authored, with no guiding editorial voice. As a consequence we have a reflection of the naming practices of wider communities of lesbians. As a result, the monolithic lesbian identity presented in the other pamphlets is more fragmented. It is worth noting that this is the most recent pamphlet, and as such will reflect the ideological changes of its time: time and politics have moved on, and so have people's lexical choices.

There are two terms that are not used in any of the pamphlets: *homosexual* and *bisexual*. It is useful to consider this because, as Fairclough (1995: 5) reminds us, 'what is absent in a text is as important as what is present'. *Homosexual* would seem to be proscribed on two counts. Firstly, by virtue of the medical and psychiatric denotations that the word has, it is universally rejected on political grounds (Cameron and Kulick, 2003: 26). Moreover, because it is often regarded as a term that denotes sexual practice, rather than sexual identity, it may be regarded as inappropriate in this context (Zwicky, 1997: 22).

*Bisexual* is perhaps the more interesting case, as it reveals another instance of the interplay between ideology and labelling. It is quite possible that the reader is questioning her sexuality and, therefore, reading the pamphlets because she is attracted to both men and women, and is looking for guidance over how to articulate this and make sense of it. However, in these pamphlets bisexuality is not available as an option. Its exclusion as a subject position is one way in which these three pamphlets attempt to control the sexual identity that the reader may assume. The proscription of 'bisexual' as an identity label reveals the underlying ideology of the pamphlets, in which women's sexual identity is conceptualised as a binary choice between lesbian and heterosexual.[5]

## Conclusion

This chapter took as its focus advice literature written by lesbians about lesbians. Using aspects of critical discourse analysis, I have considered how such texts could enhance our understanding of the means by which British lesbian sexual identity is constituted both by lesbian and hetero-normative culture. I have argued that the topic choices of the pamphlets, their focus on lesbian invisibility, partial and negative stereotypes, prejudice and stigma, are only understandable if they are seen as a response to powerful cultural hegemonic discourses on lesbianism. The pamphlets challenge these discourses by appropriation and subversion and by collocation. In addition, lexical choices around naming lesbians are significant in that they reveal aspects of the cultural and ideological standpoint of the lesbians who wrote the individual pamphlets.

These pamphlets are only one of many ways of imparting aspects of lesbian identity and culture to women who are considering accepting it. Women have access to websites, helplines and organisations, as well as creative writing, magazines and films. Although the pamphlets may seem to be minor players in this, they are still an important resource to us as they record how British lesbians over a number of decades have recorded and communicated what they believe to be important issues in lesbian lives and identities.

## Notes

1. I would like to thank the women at the Lesbian Advice and Information Centre for their assistance in this research, and most especially the archivist, Marion Thom.
2. There are other discourses that a woman can use for this purpose, such as self-help books or works of fiction. There are also several websites available that deal with issues of sexual identity, e.g. www.comingoutstories.com.
3. It is worth noting how this pamphlet misleads its readers here by implying that being lesbian or gay prevents one from being a parent. The existence of advice texts (such as *Lesbian Mothers*) points to the fact that heterosexual identity is not a prerequisite for parenthood.
4. The authors of *Women Like Us* (1987: 3) note that 'all the women involved in London Lesbian Line are feminists'.
5. Other texts either ignore bisexuality or treat it differently. For example, *Telling Your Parents* (1995) addresses the reader as 'you' throughout the discussion of lesbians and gay issues. In the one paragraph devoted to bisexuality, bisexuals are referred to as 'they'. Thus bisexuality is presented as involving an entirely different group of people than those at whom the pamphlet is aimed, and are thus constituted as 'other'.

244    *Language, Sexualities and Desires*

# References

## Primary sources

Families and Friends of Lesbians and Gays. 1995. *Lesbian or Gay: Telling Your Parents*

Glasgow Women's Library. No date. *Lesbian Mothers: a Handbook for Lesbian Mothers and Those That Support Them*

Lesbian Information Service. 1993 (4th edn). *I Think I Might Be a Lesbian . . . Now What Do I Do?*

London Lesbian Line. 1987. *Women Like Us*
London Lesbian Line. 1997. *Women Like Us*

## Secondary sources

Butler, J. 1991. Imitation and gender insubordination. In Fuss, D. (ed.) *Inside/out: Lesbian Theories, Gay Theories*. New York and London: Routledge, pp. 13–31

Caldas-Coulthard, C.R. and Coulthard, R.M. (eds) 1996. *Texts and Practices: Readings in Critical Discourse Analysis*. London: Routledge

Cameron, D. and Kulick, D. 2003. *Language and Sexuality*. Cambridge: Cambridge University Press

Chirrey, D.A. 2003. 'I hereby come out': what sort of speech act is coming out? *Journal of Sociolinguistics* 7 (1): 24–37

Coia, N., John, S., Dobbie, F., Bruce, S., McGranachan, M. and Simons, L. 2002. Something to tell you: a health needs assessment of young gay, lesbian and bisexual people in Glasgow. Unpublished report funded by the Scottish Executive Health Improvement Fund

De Monteflores, C. and Schultz S.J. 1978. Coming out: similarities and differences for lesbians and gay men. *Journal of Social Issues* 34 (3): 59–72

Dyer, R. 1997. Heterosexuality. In Medhurst, A. and Munt, S. (eds) *Lesbian and Gay Studies*. London: Cassell, pp. 261–73

Fairclough, N. 1989. *Language and Power*. London: Longman

Fairclough, N. 1995. *Critical Discourse Analysis: the Critical Study of Language*. London and New York: Longman

Gauntlett, D. 2002. *Self-Help Books and the Pursuit of a Happy Identity*. http://www.theoryhead.com/gender (visited on 9.5.2003)

Jagose, A. 1996. *Queer Theory: an Introduction*. New York University Press

Jenkins, R. 1996. *Social Identity*. London and New York: Routledge

Liang, A.C. 1997. The creation of coherence in coming-out stories. In Livia, K. and Hall, K. (eds) *Queerly Phrased*. Oxford: Oxford University Press, pp. 287–309

Markowe, L.A. 1992. The coming out process for lesbians. Unpublished PhD thesis. London: University of London

Markowe, L.A. 1996. *Redefining the Self*. Cambridge: Polity Press

Sinclair, J. 1991. *Corpus, Concordance, Collocation*. Oxford: Oxford University Press

Trenchard, L. and Warren, H. 1984. *Something to Tell You: the Experiences and Needs of Young Lesbians and Gay Men in London*. London: London Gay Teenage Group

Viss, D.C. and Burn, S.M. 1992. Divergent perceptions of lesbians: a comparison of lesbian self-perceptions and heterosexual perceptions. *Journal of Social Psychology* 132 (2): 169–77

Zwicky, A.M. 1997. Two lavender issues for linguists. In Livia, K. and Hall, K. (eds) *Queerly Phrased*. Oxford: Oxford University Press, pp. 21–34

# Index